Wittgenstein

ANTHONY KENNY

Harvard University Press
Cambridge, Massachusetts
1973

Contents

Preface

So much of Wittgenstein's work has now been posthumously published that an overall study is bound to be selective, and so many volumes have been devoted to its elucidation that a new one may well appear superfluous. I have exercised selectivity by concentrating on Wittgenstein's philosophy of language and mind, and by almost ignoring the philosophy of mathematics to which he devoted nearly half his work; I have hoped to escape superfluity by emphasizing the continuity of Wittgenstein's thought and tracing its evolution through the recently published and little studied works of his middle years. The first and last chapters of the book trace the general continuity, the first in a simplified and biographical manner, the last in more technical summary. The second chapter attempts to provide sufficient philosophical and logical background to enable a reader to follow Wittgenstein's own writings. The intervening chapters are each centred on a single problem and a single work: thus chapter three deals with the early notebooks, chapters four and five with the *Tractatus*, chapter six with the conversations with Waismann, chapter seven with the *Bemerkungen*, chapter eight with the *Grammatik*, and so on. The abbreviations by which the works are referred to are given in a list on the following page.

I am indebted to many people but especially to Professor P. T. Geach, Professor G. E. M. Anscombe, Professor Norman Malcolm, Professor Ernst Tugendhat, Dr Anselm Müller, Dr Peter Hacker, Mr Brian McGuinness and Mr Haim Marantz for comments on portions of the text; to Messrs Macmillan for allowing the re-printing of material from my contribution to *The Private Language Argument*, ed. O. R. Jones; and to Messrs Routledge & Kegan Paul and Basil Blackwell for permission to quote from Wittgenstein's works. Passages from untranslated works I have translated myself; elsewhere I have commonly followed the Pears–McGuinness and Anscombe translations, occasionally preferring my own translation. I am grateful to Miss P. Lloyd for typing and other assistance in preparing the manuscript.

8 August 1971

Abbreviations in References to Works by Wittgenstein

NB   *Notebooks 1914–1916* Basil Blackwell, 1961. Followed by page number.

PTLP *Prototractatus* Routledge & Kegan Paul, 1971. Followed by sentence number.

TLP *Tractatus Logico-Philosophicus* Routledge & Kegan Paul, 1922 (Ogden and Richards translation); 1961 (Pears and McGuinness translation). Followed by sentence number.

RLF 'Remarks on Logical Form' in Copi and Beard, *Essays on Wittgenstein's Tractatus*, Routledge & Kegan Paul, 1966. Followed by page number.

LLW *Letters from Ludwig Wittgenstein*, with a memoir by P. Engelmann, Basil Blackwell, 1967. Followed by page number.

WWK *Ludwig Wittgenstein und der Wiener Kreis*, shorthand notes of F. Waismann, ed. McGuinness, Basil Blackwell, 1967. Followed by page number.

PB   *Philosophische Bemerkungen* Basil Blackwell, 1964. Followed by page number.

PG   *Philosophische Grammatik* Basil Blackwell, 1969. Followed by page number.

BB   *The Blue and Brown Books* Basil Blackwell, 1958. Followed by page number.

ML   G. E. Moore, 'Wittgenstein's Lectures in 1930–33', *Mind*, 63, 1954; 64, 1955.

PE   'Private Experience' ed. Rush Rhees, *Phil. Rev.*, LXXVII, 1968.

PI   *Philosophical Investigations* Basil Blackwell, 1953. Part I, followed by paragraph number; Part II, followed by page number.

RFM *Remarks on the Foundations of Mathematics* Basil Blackwell, 1956. Followed by section and paragraph numbers.

Z   *Zettel* Basil Blackwell, 1967. Followed by paragraph number.

OC   *On Certainty* Basil Blackwell, 1969. Followed by paragraph number.

ABBREVIATIONS

The abbreviation 'GB' stands for *Translations from the Philosophical Writings of Gottlob Frege*, ed. Peter Geach and Max Black, Basil Blackwell, 1960.

The titles of other works have been given in references in full.

CHAPTER I

Biographical Sketch of
Wittgenstein's Philosophy

'The philosopher' wrote Wittgenstein 'is not a citizen of any community of ideas. That is what makes him a philosopher.' Throughout his life Wittgenstein stood outside philosophical schools and despised contemporary fashions of thought; by his own work, whether he wished to or not, he created a new community of ideas. He published very little and avoided any kind of publicity; but the problems he discussed with a small group of pupils are now aired in universities throughout the world. 'Philosophers who never met him' Gilbert Ryle wrote at the time of his death in 1951 'can be heard talking philosophy in his tone of voice; and students who can barely spell his name now wrinkle up their noses at things which had a bad smell for him.'[1] In the two decades since 1951 nine posthumous volumes of writings have been published, and the bibliography of studies of them contains well over a thousand titles.

Though he taught in England and died a British citizen, Wittgenstein was born in Vienna in 1889 of an Austrian family of Jewish descent. The family was rich and artistic, the father holding a prominent position in the Austrian iron and steel industry, and the nine children sharing a variety of talents. Typical of the family was Ludwig's brother Paul, a concert pianist who resumed a distinguished international career after losing an arm in the First World War. Among the friends of the family was Johannes Brahms.

Until he was fourteen, Wittgenstein was educated at home. Then, after three years of school at Linz, he studied engineering in Berlin. In 1908 he registered as a research student at the University of Manchester, where he designed a jet-reaction

1. G. Ryle, *Collected Papers*, Hutchinson, 1971, Vol. I, p. 249.

engine for aircraft. While he was designing the propellor his interest shifted from engineering to mathematics, and later to the philosophical foundations of mathematics. As a youth he had read Schopenhauer's *The World as Will and Idea*, and had been impressed by the idealist philosophy of that work. Now he read Bertrand Russell's *Principles of Mathematics* and through it became acquainted with Gottlob Frege's realist philosophy of mathematics. Under this influence he gradually abandoned his early belief in philosophical idealism.

In 1911 Wittgenstein visited Frege at Jena and was advised by him to study under Russell at Cambridge. He followed this advice and spent five terms at Trinity College in 1912–13. When he arrived there Russell and A. N. Whitehead had recently published *Principia Mathematica*, a classic of the new discipline of symbolic logic. Russell has frequently described his early encounters with Wittgenstein.

At the end of his first term at Cambridge he came to me and said 'Will you please tell me whether I am a complete idiot or not?' I replied 'My dear fellow, I don't know. Why are you asking me?' He said, 'Because if I am a complete idiot, I shall become an aeronaut; but, if not, I shall become a philosopher.' I told him to write me something during the vacation on some philosophical subject and I would then tell him whether he was a complete idiot or not. At the beginning of the following term he brought me the fulfilment of this suggestion. After reading only one sentence, I said to him 'No, you must not become an aeronaut.'[1]

While in Cambridge, Wittgenstein made friends with the philosopher G. E. Moore and the economist J. M. Keynes. Besides his studies in mathematical logic, he made some experiments in the psychology laboratory concerning rhythm in music.

After five terms in Cambridge he went to live in Norway where he built himself a hut and lived in isolation until the outbreak of war in 1914. Notes and letters from this period survive and have been published posthumously: they show the

1. B. Russell, *Portraits from Memory*, Allen & Unwin, 1957, pp. 26–7.

germination of the philosophy which was to make him famous. In the preliminary remarks to some 'Notes on Logic' of 1913, he sketched an account of the nature of philosophy. It is not, he wrote, a deductive discipline; it cannot be placed side by side with the natural sciences. 'Philosophy gives no pictures of reality and can neither confirm nor confute scientific investigations.' Philosophy teaches us the logical form of propositions: that is its fundamental task (NB 93). This conception of philosophy he was to deepen and modify, but never to abandon.

When war broke out Wittgenstein enlisted as a volunteer in the Austrian artillery. He served on the Eastern Front, where he was repeatedly decorated for bravery, and in the southern Tyrol, where he was taken prisoner by the Italian army in November 1918. Some of his postcards and letters from the front survive and have been published by his friend Paul Engelmann. 'I am working reasonably hard (on philosophy)' he wrote in 1917 'and wish I were a better man and had a better mind. These things are really one and the same.' And later: 'Our life is like a dream. But in our better hours we wake up just enough to realize that we are dreaming. Most of the time, though, we are fast asleep' (LLW 5, 7).

During his military service Wittgenstein wrote his philosophical thoughts into notebooks which he carried in his rucksack. Most of these were destroyed by his orders in 1950, but three survived and have been published posthumously. Out of these notes grew the only philosophical book he published in his lifetime, the *Tractatus Logico-Philosophicus*. He composed it by selecting the best thoughts out of his notebooks and re-ordering and numbering them until he was satisfied with their sequence. One of his preliminary orderings has been recently rediscovered and published under the title *Prototractatus*.

The *Tractatus* was finished in August 1918 and carried by its author into captivity. From a prison camp at Monte Cassino a copy was sent to Russell through the good offices of Keynes. The two philosophers discussed the manuscript line by line in

Holland in 1919. It was published in German in 1921, and shortly afterwards in German and English with an introduction by Russell.

The twenty thousand words of the *Tractatus* can be read in an afternoon, but few would claim to understand them thoroughly even after years of study. The book is not divided into chapters in the normal way, but consists of a series of numbered paragraphs, often containing no more than a single sentence. The two most famous are the first ('The world is all that is the case') and the last ('Whereof one cannot speak, thereof one must be silent'). Some of them have proved easier to set to music, or to illustrate in sculpture, than to paraphrase. The style of the paragraphs is concise and economical, devoid of decoration, sparing in examples. By comparing the text with the *Notebooks* and the *Prototractatus* we can see how Wittgenstein refined and refined his thought to the essential elements. The result is austerely beautiful, but uncommonly difficult to comprehend.

The greater part of the book is concerned with the nature of language and its relation to the world, Wittgenstein's major philosophical concern throughout his life. The central doctrine it conveys is the famous picture theory of meaning. According to this theory, language consists of propositions which picture the world. Propositions are the perceptible expressions of thoughts, and thoughts are logical pictures of facts (TLP 3.5, 4, 4.001).

Propositions and thoughts, for Wittgenstein, are pictures in a literal, not just a metaphorical sense. An English sentence, such as 'Elephants never forget' or 'John is taller than he used to be' does not look much like a picture. But this, according to the *Tractatus*, is because language disguises thought beyond all recognition (TLP 4.002, 4.011).

However, even in ordinary language there is a perceptibly pictorial element. Take the sentence 'My fork is to the left of my knife.' This sentence says something quite different from another sentence containing exactly the same words, namely,

'My knife is to the left of my fork.' What makes the first sentence, but not the second, mean that the fork is to the left of the knife? It is the fact that *the words* 'my fork' occur to the left of *the words* 'my knife' in the context of the first sentence but not in that of the second. So here we have a spatial relationship between words symbolizing a spatial relationship between things. Such spatial representation of spatial relationships is pictorial in a quite straightforward way (TLP 4.012).

Few cases, however, are as simple as this. If the sentence 'My fork is to the left of my knife' were spoken instead of written, it would be the temporal relationship between the spoken words, instead of the spatial relationship between the written words, which would represent the spatial relationship between the physical objects. But this in turn is possible only because the temporal sequence of spoken words and the spatial array of written words have a certain abstract structure in common. It is in a similar manner that the score of a song, the notes sung by a singer, and the grooves of a record of the song have a structure in common (TLP 4.011).

According to the *Tractatus* there must be something which any picture, of whatever kind, must have in common with what it depicts, if it is to be able to depict it even incorrectly. This irreducible shared minimum is called by Wittgenstein 'logical form'. Propositions in general, unlike the untypical one chosen above, do not have spatial form in common with the situation they depict; but any proposition must have logical form in common with what it depicts. It is because of this shared form that propositions can truly be called pictures (TLP 2.18–2.182).

In ordinary language, as has been said, the logical form of thoughts is concealed. There are many reasons for this, Wittgenstein believed, one of which is that many of our words signify complex objects. For instance, my knife consists of a blade and a handle related in a certain way: so that if the sentence 'My fork is to the left of my knife' is to be true, the blade and the handle must be in a certain relationship. This

5

relationship is not pictorially represented in the expression 'my knife' in the way that the relationship between knife and fork is pictorially represented by the whole sentence. It would be possible, no doubt, to bring out this relationship by rewriting the sentence into a fuller account of the situation, thus: 'My fork is to the left of my knife-blade, and my fork is to the left of my knife-handle, and my knife-blade is attached to my knife handle.' But clearly, the fork, the knife-handle and the knife-blade are themselves complex objects consisting of parts in spatial relations. There appears to be no end to this further rewriting, or analysis, of the proposition, until we come to symbols which denote entirely non-complex objects. So, for Wittgenstein, a fully analysed proposition will consist of an enormously long combination of atomic propositions, each of which will contain names of simple objects, names related to each other in ways which will picture, truly or falsely, the relations between the objects they represent. Such full analysis of a proposition is no doubt humanly impossible to give; but the thought expressed by the proposition already has the complexity of the fully analysed proposition. The thought is related to its expression in ordinary language by extremely complicated rules. We operate these rules from moment to moment without knowing what they are, just as we speak without knowing the mechanisms by which we produce the particular sounds (TLP 3.2–3.24, 4.002).

Such, in crude outline, is the picture theory of meaning. The outline will be filled in later in the book. Meanwhile we may notice that according to the theory one very important connection between language and the world is made by the correlation between the ultimate elements of thoughts, and the simples or atoms which constitute the substance of the world. How the correlation between the thought-elements and the world-atoms is to be set up, we are not told. Indeed Wittgenstein confessed to Russell that he had no idea what the thought-elements were: it would, it seems, be a matter for psychology to discover (NB 129). One thing, however, seems likely: the correlation between names and what they name is something which each of us must make for himself; so that each of us is master of a language which is, in a sense, private to himself.

Much of the *Tractatus* is devoted to showing how, with the aid of various logical techniques, propositions of many different kinds are to be analysed into atomic pictures and their combinations. Would-be propositions which are incapable of such analysis reveal themselves as pseudo-propositions which yield no pictures of the world. Among these, it turns out, are the propositions of philosophy. Metaphysicians attempt to describe the logical form of the world; but this is an impossible task. A picture, Wittgenstein believed, must be independent of what it pictures: it must be capable of being a false picture, or it is no picture at all. It follows that there can be no pictures of the logical form of the world, for any proposition must itself share that logical form and cannot be independent of it. We cannot, so to speak, get far enough away from the logical form to take a picture of it (TLP 4.12–4.121).

What the metaphysician attempts to say cannot be said, but can only be shown. Philosophy, rightly understood, is not a set of theories, but an activity, the clarification of propositions. The propositions which philosophy clarifies are not themselves propositions of philosophy but non-philosophical propositions about the world. When these propositions have been clarified the logical form of the world will mirror itself in them: and thus philosophy will exhibit, in non-philosophical propositions, that which cannot be said by philosophical propositions (TLP 4.112, 4.121).

Above all, philosophy will not provide us with any answer to the problems of life. Propositions show how things are; but how things are in the world is of no importance in relation to anything sublime. 'God does not reveal himself *in* the world' Wittgenstein wrote. 'It is not how things are in the world that is mystical, but *that* it exists' (TLP 6.432, 6.44).

The real problems of life, indeed, cannot even be put into questions.

When the answer cannot be put into words, neither can the question be put into words. *The riddle* does not exist. If a question can be framed at all, it is also possible to answer it. Scepticism is *not* irrefutable, but obviously nonsensical, when it tries to raise doubts where no questions can be asked. For doubt can exist only where a question exists, a question only when an answer exists, and an answer only where something can be said. (TLP 6.5–6.51)

We feel that even when all possible scientific questions have been answered, the problems of life remain completely untouched. Of course there are then no questions left, and this itself is the answer. The solution of the problem of life is seen in the vanishing of the problem. (TLP 6.52–6.521)

Wittgenstein's condemnation of philosophical propositions as senseless applied, as he realized, to the propositions of the *Tractatus* itself. At the end of the book he compared it to a ladder which must be climbed and then kicked away if one was to enjoy a correct picture of the world. The *Tractatus*, like all metaphysics, was an attempt to say the unsayable. None the less, he believed, it contained all that was essential for the solution of the problems of philosophy (TLP, Preface).

With perfect consistency, once he had completed the book he gave up philosophy. On returning home from the war he gave away the large fortune he had inherited from his father in 1912. In 1919 he went to a teachers' training college in Vienna and from 1920 to 1926 worked as a teacher in remote Austrian villages. He was desperately unhappy during this period, and his letters to Engelmann reveal that he several times contemplated suicide. 'I know' he wrote 'that to kill oneself is always a dirty thing to do. Surely one *cannot* will one's own destruction, and anybody who has visualized what is in practice involved in the act of suicide knows that suicide is always a *rushing of one's own defences.*' Life as a schoolmaster was a torment to him, and he could not respect the people he worked with. 'I had a task,' he wrote 'did not do it, and now the failure is wrecking my life. I ought to have done something positive with my life, to have become a star in the sky. Instead of which I remained stuck on earth, and now I am gradually fading out.' 'The one good thing in my life just now' he wrote in 1920 'is that I sometimes read fairy-tales to the children at school' (LLW 29, 41).

At last, in 1926, he gave up schoolteaching to work for a while as a monastery gardener. For two years he assisted in designing a house for his sister in the Kundmanngasse in Vienna. During this period he was introduced to Moritz Schlick, Professor of Philosophy at the University and future founder of the Vienna Circle. With him, and with Rudolf Carnap, Friedrich Waismann and Herbert Feigl, he began once again to discuss philosophy. They read together the poems of Rabindranath Tagore and studied the *Foundations of Mathematics* of the Cambridge philosopher Frank Ramsey.

Wittgenstein had by now grown dissatisfied with some of the doctrines of the *Tractatus*, and in 1929 he returned to Cambridge to continue his philosophical work as a research student. He submitted the *Tractatus* – already internationally recognized as a classic – as a Ph.D. dissertation; and after a unique *viva voce* examination conducted by Russell and Moore he was awarded the degree. He became a research fellow of Trinity College and worked on a manuscript published posthumously as the *Philosophische Bemerkungen*.

During the vacations he returned to Vienna, where he found that the Vienna Circle had developed into a self-conscious philosophical movement with a manifesto and a programme. Its best-known slogan, the rallying-cry of logical positivism, was the verification principle: 'The meaning of a proposition is its method of verification.' The logical positivists admired the *Tractatus*, and at this time of his life Wittgenstein stood quite close to their doctrines. But then as always he fought shy of party philosophy, though he continued his friendship with Schlick and Waismann. The latter took notes of their conversations during the vacations of 1930–32, which were published posthumously in 1968 under the title *Ludwig Wittgenstein und der Wiener Kreis*.

The early thirties were the most prolific period of Wittgenstein's life. He wrote, but did not publish, two full-length books, *Philosophische Bemerkungen* and *Philosophische Grammatik*. In these works he recanted several of the characteristic doctrines of the *Tractatus*: he ceased to believe in logical atoms or to look for a logically articulate language cloaked in ordinary language. The centre of his interest shifted from the philosophy of logic to the philosophy of mathematics, and he wrote at length on the nature of mathematical proof and mathematical induction, on generality and infinity in mathematics.

Philosophers of mathematics sometimes debate whether new branches of mathematics are discovered or created by the mathematician. According to realist philosophers, the mathematician is a discover; according to constructivist philosophers, he is a creator. Wittgenstein now sided very definitely with the constructivists. 'History can be made or written' he said to Waismann; 'mathematics can only be made.' The realist Frege, he thought, had presented a mistaken alternative: either mathematics deals merely with marks on paper, or those marks stand for something. There is a third possibility, which Wittgenstein illustrated by considering the game of chess. The game is not about the wooden pieces, and yet the pieces stand for nothing; the significance of each piece is given by the rules for its movement.

'If you ask me' said Wittgenstein 'where lies the difference between chess and the syntax of a language, I reply: solely in their application. If there were men on Mars who made war like the chess pieces, then the generals would use the rules of chess for prediction' (WWK 104). The comparison between mathematics and a game was worked out in detail in the *Philosophische Grammatik*.

At the same time Wittgenstein grew more interested in the philosophy of mind. When he wrote the *Tractatus* he had thought that the study of such things as understanding, intention, desire and expectation was no special concern of philosophy (TLP 4.1121). Now he came to see that the study of such concepts was essential for the understanding of the nature of language and symbolism, and so belonged to philosophy and not just to empirical psychology. Consequently the *Bemerkungen* and the *Grammatik* contain detailed studies of mental concepts and the language used to express and report states of mind.

From 1930 onwards Wittgenstein gave lectures almost every year in Cambridge. Many of his pupils have given descriptions of them. They were held in his sparsely furnished rooms, where for a while the most conspicuous item of furniture was a fan installed to drown the noise of an undergraduate piano below. Wittgenstein sat in his deck-chair, in flannels, a leather jacket and an open-necked shirt. He used no manuscript or notes, but wrestled aloud with philosophical problems, interrupting his exposition with long silences and passionate questioning of his audience.

He was exhausted by these classes, and after them would relax in the cinema, munching a pork-pie in the front row of the stalls, utterly absorbed. His favourite films were Westerns, just as some of his favourite reading consisted in detective stories without intellectual pretensions. He once said that he wondered how anyone who could read detective magazines could face reading the philosophical journal *Mind* 'with all its impotence and bankruptcy'.

From the small classes in Cambridge the word went round that he was developing a radically new philosophy, different from that of the *Tractatus* and logical positivists. The class of 1933–4 had notes dictated to them about thought and meaning, about sensation and imagination, about realism, idealism and solipsism. These notes circulated in stencilled copies and became known as *The Blue Book*. Another, more carefully prepared manuscript dictated the following year was known as *The Brown Book*: it developed the comparison between language and games and investigated such psychological concepts as *recognition* and *voluntariness*. Unlike Wittgenstein's other works, these notes were composed in English. They were published posthumously and are the easiest to read and follow of all his writings.

In 1935 Wittgenstein visited the Soviet Union: had it not been for the growing tyranny of Stalin, it seems, he might have settled there. Instead he went once more to Norway, and lived for nearly a year in his hut. There he worked on the book to which, until his death, he devoted the best of his philosophical labour: the *Philosophical Investigations*.

He returned to Cambridge in 1937, and when Austria was annexed by Germany he became a British citizen. Notes of his classes in 1938 have been preserved by several of the students who attended them, and were published in 1966 as *Lectures and Conversations on Aesthetics, Psychology and Religious Belief*.

In 1939 he was appointed Professor of Philosophy at Cambridge in succession to G. E. Moore, but before he could take up his chair war broke out. He served as a medical orderly during the war, first at Guy's Hospital in London, and later in the Clinical Research Laboratory at the Royal Victoria Infirmary in Newcastle-upon-Tyne.

After the war he returned to his duties as professor, but as always he was unhappy in a formal academic routine. He thought university life led to hysterical artificiality. Writing to a pupil to congratulate him on his doctorate of philosophy, he said 'May you make good use of it! By that I mean: may you not cheat either yourself or your students. Because, unless I'm very much mistaken, *that's* what will be expected from you.' He described the life of a professor of philosophy as 'a living death' and after acting as a professor for only two years he resigned in 1947.

He left Cambridge and settled for a while in Ireland, first on an inland farm and later in a seaside hut in Galway, where the fishermen remarked on his ability to tame birds. In Dublin in 1948 he completed the *Philosophical Investigations*.

In 1949 he spent some time in America as the guest of his friend Norman Malcolm at Cornell. Malcolm has written a *Memoir* of Wittgenstein which gives a vivid picture of the philosopher's relationship to his friends and from which many details in this chapter are drawn. Wittgenstein once said 'Although I cannot *give* affection, I have a great *need* for it.' He made many friends, who were devoted to him in his lifetime and to his memory after his death. From Malcolm's narrative it is clear that he was a demanding friend with exacting standards: Malcolm recalls the sharp rebukes he received for expressing distaste of powdered eggs, for allowing a potted plant to die, for a rash generalization about 'the British national character'. 'What is the use of studying philosophy' Wittgenstein wrote to Malcolm 'if all that it does for you is to enable you to talk with some plausibility about some abstruse questions of logic, etc. and if it does not improve your thinking about the important questions of everyday life?'

Wittgenstein's health had now begun to deteriorate, and after his return to England in the autumn of 1949 it was discovered that he had an incurable cancer. He spent the last two years of his life with friends in Oxford and Cambridge, working at philosophy so far as his disease permitted until his death. Some of his notes from the last year and a half of his life were published in 1969 under the title *On Certainty*, and another volume concerning colour-concepts is being prepared for publication. He died in Cambridge, at the home of his doctor, on 29 April 1951.

The publication of the *Philosophical Investigations* in 1953 enabled the general philosophical public to acquaint itself at first hand with the philosophy that had developed out of the Cambridge classes and the privately circulated notes. Like the *Tractatus* the *Investigations* was composed by the repeated sifting and shuffling of paragraphs from notebooks, and since 1953 Wittgenstein's literary executors have published two other volumes of selections from the same notebooks, under the titles *Remarks on the Foundations of Mathematics* (1956) and *Zettel* (1967). Despite the similar method of composition, the *Investigations* contrasts astonishingly with the *Tractatus* in style and content. The carefully numbered aphorisms are replaced by a sequence of paragraphs in conversational tone. Where the earlier work was laconic and abstract, the later is diffuse and concrete, rich in vivid illustrations and colourful metaphor. But once again there are no chapters or chapter headings.

Like the *Tractatus*, the *Investigations* is largely devoted to discussion of the nature of language, but following the developments of the thirties the *Investigations* treats in great detail the relation of language to thoughts and states of mind. Consequently the *Investigations* is a classic not only of philosophy of language, but also of philosophy of mind.

As the *Tractatus* was dominated by the comparison between propositions and pictures, so the *Investigations* returns over and over again to the idea that in language we play games with words. Like the picture theory of meaning, the concept of language-game was much more than a metaphor. Words, Wittgenstein now insisted, cannot be understood outside the context of the non-linguistic human activities into which the use of the language is interwoven: the words plus their behavioural surroundings make up the language-game. Words are like tools: their functions differ from one another as much as those of a saw and a screwdriver. But their dissimilarities of function are hidden by their uniform appearance in sound and in print. (Similarly, a clutch-pedal is like a foot-brake to look at, but their mechanical functions are totally different.) The similarity between words of different kinds makes us assimilate them all to names, and tempts us to try to explain their meaning by pointing to objects for which they stand. But in fact the way to understand the meaning of a word is to study it in the language-game to which it belongs, to see how it contributes to the communal activity of a group of language-users. In general, the meaning of a word is not an object for which it stands, but rather its use as a language (PI I, 11–12, 24, 43).

The study of language-games shows that not all words are names; but even naming is not as simple as it appears. To name something it is not sufficient to confront it and utter a sound: the asking and giving of names is something which can be done only in the context of a language-game. This is so even in the relatively simple case of naming a material object: matters are much more complicated when we consider the names of mental events and states, such as sensations and thoughts (PI I, 28–32).

Wittgenstein considers at length the way in which a word such as 'pain' functions as the name of a sensation. We are tempted to think that for each person 'pain' acquires its meaning by being correlated by him with his own private, incommunicable sensation. This temptation must be resisted: Wittgenstein showed that no word could acquire meaning in this way. One of his arguments runs as follows.

Suppose that I wish to baptize a private sensation of mine with the name 'S'. I fix my attention on the sensation in order to correlate the name with it. What does this achieve? When next I want to use the name 'S', how will I know whether I am using it rightly? Since the sensation it is to name is supposed to be a private one, no one else can check up on my use of it. But neither can I do so for myself. Before I can check up on whether 'This is S' is true, I need to know what I mean by the sentence 'This is S', true or false. How then do I know that what I now mean by 'S' was what I meant when I christened the first sensation 'S'? Can I appeal to memory? No, for to do so I must call up the right memory: in order to summon the memory of S I must already know what 'S' means.[1] There is in the end no check on my use of 'S', no possibility of correcting any misuse. That means the talk of 'correctness' is out of place, and this shows that the private definition I have given myself is no real definition.

---

1. In philosophy it is important to be careful to employ quotation marks when using a word to refer to itself, instead of using it in the normal way. Obviously enough, Rome is a city, 'Rome' is a four-letter word. Less obviously, in the paragraph above 'S' is a dummy name, S is a would-be sensation. Carelessness about quotation – though great philosophers, including Wittgenstein, have been guilty of it – can lead to confusion of symbols with what they symbolize.

This argument is one strand of Wittgenstein's famous attack on private languages. The conclusion of the attack is that there cannot be a language whose words refer to what can only be known to the speaker of the language. The language-game with the English word 'pain' is not a private language, because whatever philosophers may say, other people can very often know when a person is in pain. It is not by any solitary definition that 'pain' becomes the name of a sensation: it is rather by forming part of a communal language-game. For instance, a baby's cry is a spontaneous, pre-linguistic expression of pain; gradually the child is trained by his parents to replace this with the conventional, learned expression of pain by language. Thus pain-language is grafted on to the natural expression of pain (PI I, 244).

What is the target of the attack on private language? Who is Wittgenstein arguing against? It is not as if there was in existence, when he wrote, an influential school of thought committed to the defence of private languages. Why is it important to show that they are not possible?

It seems likely that in this part of the *Investigations*, as in others, Wittgenstein is arguing against his own earlier views. In the *Tractatus* the connection between language and reality depended on the correlation between elements of thought and simple atoms of the world. In the *Investigations* Wittgenstein argues that the notion of atoms which are simple in some absolute sense is an incoherent notion, and that a private correlation between thought-elements and items of reality is impossible to make. The ultimate data in the *Tractatus* are the atoms which form the substance of the world; the ultimate data of the *Investigations* are the forms of life in which the language-games are embedded.

But the interest of the private-language argument is not merely internal to Wittgenstein's own philosophy. Philosophers as different from each other as Descartes and Hume have thought it possible for an individual mind to classify and recognize its own thoughts and experiences while holding in suspense the question of the existence of the external world and of other minds. Such a supposition seems to entail the possibility of a private language or of something very like one. If Wittgenstein is correct in thinking such a language impossible, then both the Cartesian and empiricist traditions in philosophy need radical overhaul.

Moreover, Wittgenstein's philosophy of mind had implications for empirical psychology. Philosophy of mind has often been a battleground between dualists and behaviourists. Dualists regard the human mind as independent of the body and separable from it; for them, the connection between the two is a contingent and not a necessary one. Behaviourists regard reports of mental acts and states as disguised reports of pieces of bodily behaviour, or at best of tendencies to behave bodily in certain ways. Wittgenstein rejected both dualism and behaviourism. He agreed with dualists that particular mental events could occur without accompanying bodily behaviour; he agreed with behaviourists that the possibility of describing mental events at all depends on their having, in general, an expression in behaviour. On his view, to ascribe a mental event or state to someone is not to ascribe to him any kind of bodily behaviour; but such ascription can only sensibly be made to beings which have at least the capability of behaviour of the appropriate kind. The *Philosophical Investigations* is full of painstaking investigations of psychological concepts such as sensation, thought, understanding, volition. Experimental psychology, Wittgenstein believed, was often vitiated by conceptual confusion on these and kindred matters (PI II, 232).

Despite the differences between the *Tractatus* and the *Investigations* there is continuity in Wittgenstein's conception of the nature of philosophy. He continued to regard philosophy as an activity rather than a theory, as the activity of clarifying propositions and preventing us from being led astray by the misleading appearances of ordinary language. But now the way to clarify propositions is not to analyse them to reveal their hidden structure, but to show how they are applied in language-games. Still, as in the *Tractatus*, Wittgenstein believes that the metaphysician must be shown that he has given no meaning to certain signs in his utterances; but the way to do this, in the *Investigations*, is to show that the signs have no part to play in a language-game. Wittgenstein still denies the possibility of philosophical theses; the aim of philosophy is a therapeutic one, to cure us from talking nonsense and being tormented by problems for which there is no solution. When philosophy achieves clarity, this is not by the solution of philosophical problems but by their disappearance. 'Why is philosophy so complicated?' Wittgenstein once asked himself. His answer sums up his conception of its nature.

Philosophy unties the knots in our thinking, which we have foolishly put there; but to do that it must make movements which are just as complicated as those knots. Although the *result* of philosophy is simple, its method cannot be if it is to arrive at that result.

The complexity of philosophy is not in its subject matter, but in our knotted understanding.[1]

1. PB 52; translated by Norman Malcolm, *The Philosophical Review*, Vol. LXXVI, p. 229.

CHAPTER 2

The Legacy of Frege and Russell

Wittgenstein's philosophy of language cannot be understood without some knowledge of the work of Frege and Russell and earlier logicians on which he built. This chapter will attempt to provide this background information.

The picture theory of meaning, which was sketched in the previous chapter, is a theory of the nature of the proposition. We must ask what Wittgenstein meant by this word 'proposition' (*Satz*) which he took over from a philosophical tradition. As a first approximation, 'proposition' means the same as 'sentence', and indeed Wittgenstein's German word can be translated by either English word, and was so translated by him when he was writing in English. Thus the sentences 'Caesar invaded Gaul', 'Thrushes' eggs are blue', 'Two and three make five', 'Either John will come tomorrow or he won't' would all be naturally said to be propositions. However, the command 'Polly, put the kettle on' and the wish 'O to be in England, now that April's there' and the question 'Who is Sylvia?', though perfectly good sentences, would not normally be called propositions. On the other hand, a sentence such as 'If Eclipse wins the Derby then I shall be rich' would be thought of by a philosopher as a proposition built up out of two other propositions 'Eclipse wins the Derby' and 'I shall be rich' by means of a connecting link 'if . . . then . . .'; whereas to the non-philosopher 'If Eclipse wins the Derby' would more naturally be described as a *clause*, a hypothetical clause, than as a sentence, or a sentence plus part of a connective. So it seems then that not all sentences are propositions, and not all propositions are sentences: summing up thus far, a proposition is an indicative sentence capable of standing on its own, whether or not it is actually doing so.

But there are further complications. 'Brutus killed Caesar'

and '*Brutus occidit Caesarem*' are two different sentences: one is an English sentence and the other is a Latin sentence. But because they mean the same in two different languages they would not be regarded as specimens of two different propositions. So in addition to the qualifications already made we must say that a proposition is a sentence considered with respect to its meaning and not (say) with respect to its sound when spoken or appearance when written.

Some philosophers have preferred to say, not that a proposition *is* a sentence (of a certain kind, considered in a certain way), but that a sentence *expresses* a proposition, which is thought of as a more abstract and less tangible entity. On this view, for example, the second law of thermodynamics is a proposition which may be expressed in many different forms and in many different languages; it always was a proposition long before there were any human beings to discover it, think of it, or talk about it.[1] Throughout his life Wittgenstein was opposed to such a conception of the proposition. The philosophy of language, he insisted in the *Philosophical Investigations*, deals with the spatial and temporal phenomenon of language, not with some fiction outside space and time. But the philosopher talks about words and sentences 'as we talk about the chess pieces when we are stating the rules of the game, not describing their physical properties' (PI I, 108). What he says here fits his usage also in his earlier writings.

When he wrote the *Tractatus*, though he did not speak of sentences as expressing propositions, he did speak of sentences, and propositions, as expressing *thoughts* (TLP 3.2). This was indeed one traditional function ascribed to propositions ever since Aristotle, in the *De interpretatione*, wrote that 'spoken sounds are symbols of affections in the soul' (16a3). The content of a man's thoughts or beliefs is capable of expression in sentences: for instance, if James believes that revolution is inevitable, then James's thoughts can be expressed by the

1. Cf. W. and M. Kneale, *The Development of Logic*, Oxford University Press, 1962, p. 361.

sentence 'revolution is inevitable.' Some people have believed that there are thoughts which are inexpressible in words. Whether this is so or not – and this is a point to which we will have to return – it is clear that the great majority of thoughts are expressible in language; and so a study of the nature of language will also throw light on the nature of thought. The philosopher of language studies both at the same time. Thus Wittgenstein sums up the aim of the *Tractatus*: 'The aim of the book is to set a limit to thought – or rather, not to thought, but to the expression of thoughts' (TLP Preface). The philosophy of the *Tractatus* aims to show what is thinkable by showing what is sayable, to mark the limits of thought by setting the limits of language.

Three features of propositions had interested logicians since the time of Plato and Aristotle: first, that they were composed of subject and predicate; secondly, that (unlike questions and commands) they were capable of being true or false; thirdly, that they stood in relationships to each other, so that from one proposition it was sometimes possible to infer or deduce other propositions. These interests were all present in the theory of syllogism, the study of a certain form of argument which was for centuries regarded as the main business of the logician. Consider, for instance, the following argument:

	All platypuses are web-footed creatures
And	All web-footed creatures can swim
So	All platypuses can swim.

Each one of these propositions has, on the face of it, a subject and a predicate (e.g. 'platypuses' or 'all platypuses' appears to be the subject of the first and third proposition, and 'can swim' appears to be the predicate of the second and third propositions). The third proposition, the conclusion of the argument, follows from, or can be inferred or deduced from, the first two propositions which constitute the premisses of the argument. What is meant by this is that if the premisses are true the conclusion must be true also, so that one can safely pass from asserting the premisses to asserting the conclusion without fear of passing from a true assertion to a false one. I do not myself know whether either of the premisses is true; but I do know that if the premisses are both true then the conclusion is also. What I am ignorant of is a pair of facts in elementary zoology; what I know is a matter of logic. For logic is, at least in part, the study of rules governing the safety (the validity, as it is called) of inferences between propositions.

In the three decades before Wittgenstein went to Cambridge the study of logic had been revolutionized by the work of Frege. Frege formalized the theory of inference in a way which was at once more rigorous and more general in its application than the traditional syllogistic. To do so he invented a symbolic system or 'concept-script' (*Begriffsschrift*), as he called it, to formalize ordinary language on the model of the language of arithmetic.

One feature in which this system differed from traditional logic was that it rejected the normal grammatical distinction between subject and predicate. The subject of 'Caesar conquered Gaul' is not the same as the subject of 'Gaul was conquered by Caesar'; yet whatever inferences can be drawn from the first proposition can be drawn from the second; so the difference between them is irrelevant to the theory of inference. In Frege's system the grammatical distinction between subject and predicate is replaced by a distinction between function and argument, a distinction drawn from the terminology of mathematics.

An algebraic expression such as '$x^2 + 1$' may be said to represent a function of x: the value of the number represented by the whole expression will vary in accordance with the numeral we substitute for the variable 'x' in the expression. Thus the value of the function $x^2 + 1$ for the argument 1 is 2, for the argument 2 is 5, since

$$1^2 + 1 = 1 + 1 = 2$$

and
$$2^2 + 1 = 4 + 1 = 5.$$

An expression such as '$x^2 + 1$' represents a function with a single argument. This is shown by the expression's containing only a single variable, 'x'. There are also functions of two or more arguments, such as the functions represented by '$x^2 + y$' and '$2xy + z^3$'. In each case the function will have a specific value only if all its argument places are completed, and the value will normally differ for different arguments.

Frege made two innovations: he extended the notion of function to equations as well as to expressions for numbers (e.g. to '$x^2 = 1$' as well as to '$x^2 + 1$') and he extended it to expressions in ordinary language as well as to expressions in mathematical notation. Thus he called 'the capital of x' the expression of a function, which takes London as its value if Britain is supplied as the argument. And a sentence such as 'Caesar conquered Gaul' he regarded as signifying the result either of completing the function

$$x \text{ conquered Gaul}$$

with the argument Caesar, or of completing the function

$$\text{Caesar conquered } x$$

with the argument Gaul, or of completing the function

$$x \text{ conquered } y$$

with the arguments Caesar and Gaul in the appropriate places (Frege GB 1–3, 21ff.). The incomplete expressions signifying the functions can now be called 'predicates' in a logical, as opposed to a grammatical, sense.

The value of the function $x^2 + 1$ for any given argument is a number; the value of the function signified by 'the capital of x' for any given argument of the appropriate kind is a city. What is the value of functions signified by e.g. '$x = 1$' and 'x conquered Gaul'? Frege's answer is ingenious.

Take the expression '$x^2 = 1$'. If we replace x successively by -1, 0, 1, 2, we get:

$$(-1)^2 = 1$$
$$0^2 = 1$$
$$1^2 = 1$$
$$2^2 = 1$$

Of these equations the first and third are true, the others false.

Frege called the truth or falsehood of an equation its 'truth-value' – and this truth-value, he suggested, should be regarded as the value of the function for the different arguments.

I now say: 'the value of our function is a truth-value' and distinguish between the truth-values of what is true and what is false. I call the first, for short, the True; and the second, the False. Consequently, e.g. '$2^2 = 4$' stands for the True, as say, '2^2' stands for 4. And '$2^2 = 1$' stands for the False (GB 'Function and Concept', 29).

Similarly, for Frege, 'Caesar conquered Gaul' stood for the True, and 'Pompey conquered Gaul' stood for the False; the values of the function *x conquered Gaul* for various arguments was always a truth-value.

The analogy which Frege drew between sentences and mathematical expressions has proved a fruitful one in logic; but few logicians or philosophers have been prepared to follow him in this step of regarding sentences as names for objects which can be designated as 'The True' and 'The False'. Wittgenstein, in particular, rejected this; but he followed Frege in replacing the traditional notion of subject and predicate with the concepts of function and argument (TLP 3.333, etc.), and in calling the truth or falsehood of each proposition its 'truth-value' (TLP 4.063, etc.).

In the traditional syllogistic the validity of inferences depended on making the appropriate substitutions in the subject and predicate places in certain permitted patterns of argument, for instance.

	No M is P
And	All S is M
So	No S is P.

Frege placed in the centre of logical theory types of inference that did not depend upon breaking up sentences into subject and predicate, or even into function and argument, but which treated them as whole units. The inference 'If birds can fly, then birds have wings; but birds can fly; therefore birds have wings' for instance is of the form

If p, then q; but p; therefore q.

Any inference of this form is clearly valid provided we substitute the same proposition for each 'p' and for each 'q' respectively; it does not matter what the propositions are about, or whether 'p' and 'q' have their subject or predicate in common.

The area of logic in which the internal complexity of propositions is thus ignored is known nowadays as the *propositional calculus*, in contrast to the *predicate calculus* or *functional calculus* which takes into account the manner in which propositions are constructed out of their parts. In the propositional calculus when set out formally two kinds of symbols appear: *variables* (e.g. 'p', 'q' and 'r') to mark places for propositions and *constants* to correspond to the conjunctions such as 'and', 'or', 'if . . . then' which build up complex propositions out of simpler ones, and to the sign of negation ('not' or 'it is not the case that . . .') which will form the contradictory of any proposition.

Though the propositional calculus is only a small part of logic, there are many arguments which can be formalized within it. For instance:

> Either the butler killed him or the parlourmaid killed him
> The parlourmaid did not kill him

Therefore   The butler killed him

is a valid argument, and its validity has nothing to do with butlers or parlourmaids or murders, but simply with the meaning of 'either', 'or' and 'not'. The argument is valid because it is a logical truth that if either p or q, and not q, then p. And indeed to every valid argument of the form 'A, B, therefore C' there corresponds a logical truth of the form 'If A and B, then C' in the manner just illustrated. Frege systematized propositional logic not by systematizing directly the arguments which occur in it, but by systematizing the logical truths which correspond to the valid inferences. He showed that all these logical truths could be set out in an axiomatic system like Euclidean geometry: that is to say, given a handful of such truths as postulates or axioms and the single pattern of inference 'From "A", and "If A then B" infer "B"' one could derive an unlimited number of other logical truths as theorems. Frege himself in his *Begriffsschrift* chose half-a-dozen axioms including 'If p, then not not p' and 'if, if p then q, then if not q, then not p'; none of the axioms contain any connectives except 'not' and 'if . . . then', and the others are defined in terms of these (e.g. 'either p or q' is defined as 'if not p then q'). Many other sets of axioms are possible and have been studied by later logicians; one of the most famous was a set used by Russell and Whitehead in *Principia Mathematica* in 1910 which used 'or' and 'not' as primitive constants instead of 'if' and 'not'.

By itself the propositional calculus is not rich enough to symbolize the obviously valid argument

> All men are mortal
> Socrates is a man
Therefore   Socrates is mortal.

This can of course be symbolized as 'p, q, therefore r', but this symbolism will not bring out the validity of the inference, since 'Grass is green, lavender is blue, so chalk is cheese' is of exactly the same form.

However, it had often been noticed that there was an analogy between the inference set out above and the following inference of a slightly different pattern

> If Socrates is a man, then Socrates is mortal
> Socrates is a man

Therefore   Socrates is mortal.

This second inference is a valid inference in the propositional calculus, of the familiar form 'If p then q; but p, therefore q.' But it does not yet seem to be quite a fair translation of the first inference, since it makes the first premiss look as if it states something about Socrates in particular, whereas if 'All men are mortal' is true then

> if x is a man, then x is mortal

will be true no matter whose name is substituted for the variable 'x'. Indeed it will not be false even if we substitute the name of a non-man for x, since in that case the antecedent 'if x is a man' will not be fulfilled. Using Frege's terminology of argument and function, we might say that the function signified by

> If x is a man, then x is mortal

is true for every argument, or more briefly, true for all x. Thus we can express the traditional subject–predicate proposition

> All men are mortal

in a more or less Fregean notation as a universal proposition in this way:

> For all x, if x is a man, x is mortal.

This means: 'Take anything you like: whatever thing you take, if it is a man, it is mortal.' The truth that if Socrates is a man then Socrates is mortal will then be an instance of this more general truth, and in a full formalization of the argument to prove his mortality would be set out as such.

Frege adopted for particular propositions (e.g. 'Some men are mortal') a device parallel to his treatment of universal propositions. If some men are mortal, then there will be some argument for which the function

x is a man and x is mortal

will take the truth-value *true*; so we may translate 'Some men are mortal'

For some x, x is a man and x is mortal.

The two expressions 'for some x' and 'for all x' are nowadays called *quantifiers*, and play an important part in logic.

In traditional logic it had long been observed that 'some' – understood as meaning 'at least one' – could be translated into 'all' and 'not': thus 'Some men are mortal' is equivalent to 'Not all men are not mortal.' Frege made use of this in his system, and took the universal quantifier 'for all x' as being primitive, and the particular quantifier 'for some x' as corresponding to the expression 'It is not the case that for all x it is not the case that . . .' Thus, by adding to his propositional calculus the universal quantifier, with rules for its use, Frege was able to develop a complete system of logic covering all, and much more than, the ground covered by the traditional syllogistic logic.

Frege introduced into logic from mathematics the sign of equality '$=$', and used it to mean 'is identical with'. In this connection he met with a philosophical problem. Consider one of Frege's examples, which has become a cliché.

(A) The Morning Star is identical with the Evening Star. If this is true, then it seems that what 'the Morning Star' means is the same as what 'the Evening Star' means. But if so, then it seems that in any sentence we can substitute one expression for the other without altering the meaning of the whole. Suppose we do this to the proposition set out above, we get:

(B) The Morning Star is identical with the Morning Star. But (B) does not seem to mean the same as (A) at all; for what

(A) enunciates was an astronomical discovery, while what (B) seems to say is an empty truism. Frege suggested, to solve this puzzle, a distinction between two sorts of meaning: sense (*Sinn*) and reference (*Bedeutung*). 'The Morning Star' means the same as 'the Evening Star' in that both expressions *refer to* the same thing, they both denote or stand for the planet Venus. But the two expressions mean different things in that they both have a different *sense*, e.g. they would be paraphrased in different ways. 'A = B' will be a truism if 'A' and 'B' have the same sense, but not necessarily so if they have the same reference. Frege seems to have believed that all expressions had both a sense and a reference: a proper name like 'Aristotle', for instance, though it might not have an agreed paraphrase like the common noun 'planet', would have a sense which might vary from user to user (e.g. for one man it might mean 'Plato's brightest pupil', for another 'Alexander's tutor').

Frege's logical work is constantly presupposed in Wittgenstein's writings. Like Frege, Wittgenstein allots a fundamental role in logic to the propositional connectives 'if ... then', 'not', 'and', 'or', and to the quantifiers. Along with the sign of identity, he called these 'the logical constants' (an expression reserved by other writers for the propositional connectives) and much of his early work could be summed up as an investigation into the functioning of the logical constants. If he could get clear about their meaning, he felt, the nature of logic, and with it the nature of language, would become clear. Like Frege, Wittgenstein made technical use of the terms 'sense' and 'reference', though he disagreed in several respects with Frege's theory of meaning. Admiration for Frege is mingled with criticism of his views in many places in the *Tractatus*.

Wittgenstein invented one formal device which passed, like so many of Frege's inventions, into the logical textbooks (TLP 4.31–4.45, 5.101). It is possible to define the propositional connectives by setting out in a table the truth-conditions of propositions containing them (TLP 4.31). Thus the table

p	q	p and q
T	T	T
F	T	F
T	F	F
F	F	F

represents that 'p and q' is true in the case in which 'p' and 'q' are both true, and false if (a) 'p' is false and 'q' is true (b) 'p' is true and 'q' is false (c) 'p' and 'q' are both false. The truth-value of 'p and q', as this table brings out, is determined unambiguously by the truth-values of the propositions 'p' and 'q' out of which it is compounded. Using once again the language of function, we can say that the truth-value of the compound proposition is a function of the truth-values of its constituents, or that the compound proposition is a *truth-function* of its constituents. Putting it the other way round, the possible combinations of the truth-values of the constituents are the *truth-conditions* of the truth and falsehood of the compound propositions (TLP 4.41).

Like 'p and q', a proposition of the form 'p or q' is a truth-function of its components; and this is so whether it is interpreted as an exclusive disjunction (i.e. as 'p or q but not both') or as an inclusive one (i.e. as 'p and/or q'). If it is interpreted in the latter way (as it was by Frege and Wittgenstein and most logicians) then it has the following truth-table.

p	q	p or q
T	T	T
F	T	T
T	F	T
F	F	F

Propositions of great length and complexity may be built up by repeated use of connectives such as 'and' and 'or'; but, however complex they are, their truth-value can always be determined from the truth-values of the simple propositions which make them up (TLP 5.31). This is done by repeated applications of the tables belonging to the particular connectives. Consider, for instance, the following propositional formula:

Either p and q, or p and not-q.

This is a truth-function of 'p' and 'q' as is shown in the following table.

p	q	Either	p	and	q,	or	p	and	not-	q
T	T		T	T	T	T	T	F	F	T
F	T		F	F	T	F	F	F	F	T
T	F		T	F	F	T	T	T	T	F
F	F		F	F	F	F	F	F	T	F

This table is constructed in the following manner. First the columns under the single propositional variables are filled in by copying out the values given in the two left-hand columns, which represent a conventional arrangement to ensure that all possible combinations of truth-values are covered (TLP 4.31). Then in the second column from the right the truth-value of 'not-q' is filled in under the connective 'not' by reversing the truth-value of 'q' on the principle that 'not-q' is false whenever 'q' is true, and true whenever 'q' is false. Then the columns under the 'ands' are filled in by deriving the truth-value of the conjunctions from the truth-value of the propositions the 'ands' connect in accordance with the first table given above. Finally the 'or' column is completed, the truth-values being derived from those of the two complex propositions which the 'or' connects by means of the table for 'or'. The 'or' column shows the value of the whole formula 'Either p and q, or p and not-q' for every possible combination of truth-values of 'p' and 'q'. It turns out, not surprisingly, to be true when 'p' and 'q' are both true, or when 'p' is true and 'q' is false, and to be false in the other possible cases. It is an expression with the same truth-value as 'p' in all cases. This result could have been foreseen by anyone who understood the first formula; but in the case of more complicated formulae it is often impossible to see the truth-conditions in this way without making a calculation by means of a table.

When we construct the truth-tables for complex propositions in this manner, we sometimes find that they take the same truth-value for every possible truth-value of their arguments. Thus the proposition 'p or not-p' is true whether 'p' is true or false, as we see thus:

p		p	or	not-	p
T		F	T	F	T
F		F	T	T	F

On the other hand, the proposition 'p and not-p' is false whatever 'p' may be:

p		p	and	not-	p
T		T	F	F	T
F		F	F	T	F

A proposition which is true for all truth-possibilities of its elementary prepositions is called a *tautology*, a proposition which is false for all truth-possibilities is called a *contradiction* (TLP 4.46). It can be seen that the negation of a contradiction (since it will turn all the 'F's of the contradiction into 'T's) will be a tautology. Thus 'Not both p and not-p', the negation of the contradiction 'Both p and not-p', is a tautology, as can be seen in this table.

p		Not both	p	and	not-	p
T		T	T	F	F	T
F		T	T	F	T	F

The study of tautologies proves to be of great importance in logic. The tautology 'Either p or not-p' corresponds to the traditional Law of Excluded Middle; the tautology 'Not both p and not-p' corresponds to the traditional Law of Contradiction; and these are two of the three traditional Laws of Thought. Wittgenstein believed, as we shall see, that *all* the propositions of logic were tautologies. If that is true, or even only an approximation to the truth, it is clearly of great advantage to have a mechanical method, such as Wittgenstein's truth-tables provide, of testing to see whether a proposition is a tautology.[1]

It can be shown that all formulae of the propositional calculus which are tautologous by Wittgenstein's test are either axioms or theorems of the system of Frege's *Begriffsschrift*; and conversely, that anything which can be proved from Frege's axioms by his rules will be tautologous by Wittgenstein's test. Wittgenstein's truth-table method, therefore, and Frege's axiomatic system may be regarded as two different formal methods of handling the same material, namely, the logical truths of the propositional calculus. However, there are important differences between the methods, and when he wrote the *Tractatus* Wittgenstein thought his method superior in several ways.

First, in Frege's system a number of formulae are given a privileged status as axioms; but the choice of axioms is to some extent arbitrary, as is shown by the possibility of alternative equally consistent and powerful axiom-sets, such as that used by Russell and Whitehead. The method of truth-table testing is applied to all formulae alike, so that all logical truths are seen to be of equal rank, with none essentially primitive and underivable (TLP 6.127).

Moreover, the primitive propositions are presented in Frege's system without justification as self-evident; Wittgenstein distrusted the appeal to self-evidence, and offered instead a method of calculation which was mechanical in the literal sense that it could be carried out by a machine (NB 3; TLP 6.1271).

Again, given a formula of the propositional calculus, we can always settle, by applying the truth-table method, whether or not it is a tautology. No similar method exists in Frege's system. By discovering a proof of the formula from Frege's axioms we can show it to be a theorem of his system; but if we

1. An alternative method is given by Wittgenstein at 6.1203.

fail to discover a proof this does not show that it is not a theorem of the system; it may simply be that we have not been ingenious enough to find a proof. Thus if we are given a formula of the propositional calculus and asked 'Is this a tautology or not?' Wittgenstein's method offers us a foolproof way of settling the question either way, while Frege's method offers a way of answering 'yes' with certainty, but no way of giving a certain answer 'no'. To sum up in the customary technical expression, Wittgenstein offers, while Frege does not, a *decision procedure* for propositional logic.

What is the relation between a formal script like Frege's and ordinary language? Frege himself compared it to the relationship between the microscope and the naked eye: by which he meant that it enabled one to discriminate between things which in ordinary language appear blurred and confused. Thus – to give a sample of Wittgenstein's choosing – the word 'is' in ordinary language signifies in three different ways, which correspond to three different variations of symbol in Frege's notation. Sometimes it appears as a copula linking subject and predicate – as in 'James is whistling' – in which case it will be absorbed, in Frege's notation, into the function-sign '. . . is whisling'. Sometimes it appears as the sign of identity, as in 'twice two is four', in which case it will be translated by the equals-sign, as in '$2 \times 2 = 4$'. Sometimes it is an expression for existence, as in 'There is a devil', in which case it will be translated by means of the particular quantifier, as 'For some x, x is a devil', where the 'is' is now simply part of the predicate '. . . is a devil' (TLP 3.323).

Failure to discriminate between such differences of significance can lead to confusion in our own minds about what we mean, and the drawing of false inferences. For the inferences which can be drawn from propositions of the form 'S is P' differ according to which 'is' comes in question. Can we, for instance, conclude from 'S is P' to 'P is S'? If the 'is' is the 'is' of identity, we can: four is indeed twice two. But if the 'is' is the copula we cannot: 'whistling is James' if not a poetic inversion is a piece of nonsense. This shows the importance of distinguishing the copula from the sign of identity; and confusion of the copula with the sign for existence can lead to an equally nonsensical conclusion. Thus a philosopher may be struck by the fact that whatever exists can be said to *be*; and taking this verb as a copula, or predicate-marker, he may seek to investigate the nature of the attribute corresponding to this predicate which is applicable to everything in the world. He may be struck by the mystery of this *be-ing* which is not *being red* or *being a man*, but just pure *be-ing*. He may even deify his muddle by defining God as Pure Being.

In order to avoid such errors, Wittgenstein thought when he wrote the *Tractatus*, we need a language which does not use the same sign with different modes of signification: a language whose grammar is governed by logic, a language with a logical syntax instead of the superficial syntax of ordinary language (TLP 3.325). Frege's conceptual notation, Wittgenstein said, was only a preliminary attempt at such a language, and it failed to exclude all mistakes.

One of the distinctions which Frege failed to make was a distinction between names and descriptions. In Frege's system 'Socrates' and 'the teacher of Plato' are treated as the same kind of symbol, as being a name with a sense and a reference. Before Wittgenstein, Russell had argued that this was a mistake: a name like 'Socrates', if it was a genuine proper name, had meaning solely by having a reference; and an expression like 'the teacher of Plato' should not be called a name at all, if only because unlike a genuine name it had parts which were significant symbols in their own right. Russell's positive account of such expressions is called his *theory of definite descriptions*: it was much admired by Wittgenstein and had a considerable influence on his thought.

In *Principia Mathematica* Russell introduced the topic as follows:

Suppose we say 'The round square does not exist.' It seems plain that this is a true proposition, yet we cannot regard it as denying the existence of a certain object called 'the round square'. For if there were such an object, it would exist: we cannot first assume that there is a certain object, and then proceed to deny that there is such an object. Whenever the grammatical subject of a proposition can be supposed not to exist without rendering the proposition meaningless, it is plain that the grammatical subject is not a proper name, i.e. not a name directly representing some object. Thus in all such cases the proposition must be capable of being so analysed that what was the grammatical subject shall have disappeared. Thus when we say 'The round square does not exist' we may, as a first attempt at such analysis, substitute 'It is false that there is an object *x* which is both round and square.' (*Principia Mathematica*, 2nd ed., p. 66)

So far Russell's theory is an application of Frege's method of treating existence, as outlined above. But when it comes to sentences which consist of a definite description and a predicate, like 'The author of *Hamlet* was a genius', Russell parts company with Frege. For Frege such a sentence is of the same form as 'Shakespeare was a genius'; for Russell it is of quite different form and has a hidden complexity. For the sentence to be true, it must be the case that one and only one individual wrote *Hamlet* (otherwise no one has the right to be described as '*the* author of *Hamlet*'). So Russell proposes as an analysis of the sentence the following:

> For some *x*, (1) *x* wrote *Hamlet*
> and (2) for all *y*, if *y* wrote *Hamlet*, *y* is identical with *x*
> and (3) *x* was a genius.

This formulation uses the first element to say that at least one individual wrote *Hamlet*, and the second to say that at most one individual wrote *Hamlet*; so between them the first two elements say that exactly one individual wrote *Hamlet*. The formulation uses the third element to go on to say that that unique individual was a genius. In the unanalysed sentence the expression 'the author of *Hamlet*' looks like a complex name (and would have been so treated by Frege); in the analysed sentence no such expression appears, and instead we have a combination of predicates and quantifiers.

What is the point of this complicated analysis? To see this we have to consider a sentence which, unlike 'The author of *Hamlet* was a genius' is not true. Consider

(A) The sovereign of Great Britain is male.
(B) The sovereign of the United States is male.

Neither of these sentences is true, but the reason differs in the two cases. The first sentence is clearly false because though there is a sovereign of Great Britain she is female; the second sentence is untrue because there is no such individual as the sovereign of the United States. The analysis brings out the two different ways in which such a sentence can be untrue. If (A) and (B) were analysed on the model of 'The author of *Hamlet* was a genius', then (A) would be untrue because of a falsehood affecting (3), whereas (B) would be untrue because of a falsehood affecting (1).

It will be seen that on Russell's view a sentence such as 'The sovereign of the United States is male' is not just untrue but positively false; and consequently 'It is not the case that the sovereign of the United States is male', which negates this falsehood, is true. (On the other hand 'The sovereign of the United States is not male', which asserts that there *is* a non-male individual who is sovereign of the United States, is, like 'The sovereign of the United States is male', positively false.) In this respect sentences containing vacuous definite descriptions differ sharply in Russell's system from sentences containing empty names, i.e. apparent names which name no objects. For Russell a would-be sentence such as 'Slawkenburgius was a genius' is not really a sentence at all, and therefore neither true nor false, since there was never anyone of whom 'Slawkenburgius' was the proper name.

Some philosophers have objected to Russell's treating a

sentence such as 'The sovereign of the United States is male' as being false. Surely, they say, if there is no sovereign of the United States such a sentence is not so much false as misleading; the question its of truth-value does not arise. When I affirm 'The author of *Hamlet* was a genius' I do not assert, but rather presuppose, that one and only one individual wrote *Hamlet*.

Something of the kind is often the natural thing to say about our use of such definite descriptions in ordinary language; but Russell, like Frege, was interested in constructing a language which would be in some ways a more precise and scientific instrument than ordinary language for purposes of logic and mathematics. Both Frege and Russell regarded it as essential that such a language should contain only expressions which had a definite sense, by which they meant that all sentences in which the expressions could occur should have a truth-value. Neither therefore was prepared to let a proposition such as 'The sovereign of the United States is male' count as truth-valueless. Frege proposed to avoid such truth-value gaps by arbitrarily stipulating a reference for vacuous definite descriptions and empty names – e.g. that 'the sovereign of X' shall refer to the sovereign of X if X is a monarchy and otherwise shall refer to the number '0'. Russell's analysis, according to which 'the sovereign of X' is not a referring expression at all, whether or not X is a monarchy, achieves the definiteness sought by Frege by far less artificial means.

Wittgenstein, when he wrote the *Tractatus*, accepted Frege's requirement of definiteness of sense (TLP 2.0211, 4.063, 5.4733) and Russell's method of securing this definiteness for propositions containing definite descriptions. He was interested in particular in applying and modifying Russell's theory to fit descriptions which described complex objects by enumerating their parts. 'Every statement about complexes' he wrote 'can be resolved into a statement about their constituents and into the propositions that describe the complexes completely' (TLP 2.0201). Consider, for instance, the sentence

Austria-Hungary is allied to Russia.

This sentence was untrue when Wittgenstein wrote the *Tractatus*, because Austria-Hungary was at war with Russia. It is untrue now for the quite different reason that the political unit called 'Austria-Hungary' does not exist. Clearly the two possibilities of falsehood here parallel those for 'The sovereign of X is male'; and 'Austria-Hungary' can be looked on as a definite description, roughly, 'the union of Austria and Hungary'. We can adapt Russell's theory to this as follows

> For some x and some y, $x =$ Austria
> and $y =$ Hungary
> and x is united to y
> and x is allied to Russia
> and y is allied to Russia.

Or more simply we can say that 'Austria-Hungary is allied to Russia' means: 'Austria is allied to Russia and Hungary is allied to Russia and Austria is united to Hungary' (NB 4; PI I, 39, 60). (Here the use of the identity predicate, or of the proper name, renders superfluous the use of the uniqueness-securing clause.) As we shall see, Wittgenstein in the *Tractatus* built a great deal of metaphysics on the possibility of analysis of this kind. 'Russell's merit' he wrote 'is to have shown that the apparent logical form of a proposition need not be its real form' (TLP 4.0031).

What drove Russell and Frege to devise a more rigorous language, however, was not initially an interest in metaphysics but a desire to place mathematics on a firm logical basis. Both of them were dedicated to proving that mathematics, and especially arithmetic, was in fact a branch or extension of logic involving no special subject-matter of its own and derivable from purely logical axioms. This task was the object of Frege's major work *Die Grundgesetze der Arithmetik* (1893 and 1903) and of Russell and Whitehead's *Principia Mathematica* (1910–13). Both works define numbers as classes of classes with the same number of members: thus the number two is the class of pairs and the number three the class of trios. If this definition is not to be circular, it must be possible to say what is meant by two classes having the same number of members without making use of the notion of number.

This is not as difficult as it might appear. Frege observes that a waiter may know that there are as many knives as there are plates on a table without knowing how many of each there are, if he observes that there is just one knife to the right of each plate. He knows, that is to say, that the class of knives on the table has as many members as the class of plates on the table, though he does not know the number of members in either class. Two classes have as many members as each other if each member of one class can be correlated with a different member of the other class leaving none over. Two such classes are called equivalent classes. We can thus revise the definition of number given above, and say that a number is a class of classes with as many members as a given class. Thus we could define four as the class of all classes which have as many members as the class of gospel-makers. But such a definition would clearly be useless for the purposes of reducing arithmetic to logic, since the fact that there were four gospel-makers is a contingent fact which is certainly no part of logic. If Frege's and Russell's programme is to succeed, they must find, for each number, a class not only of the right size, but a class whose size is guaranteed by logic.

What they did was to begin with the number zero, which they defined as the class of all classes with as many members as the class of objects which are not identical with themselves. Since there are no objects which are not identical with themselves, that class has no members; and since classes which have the same members are the same classes, there is in fact only one class which has no members. Zero is therefore the class whose only member is the class with no members, the null-class, as it is called. The fact that there is only one null-class is used in proceeding to the definition of the number one, which is defined as the class of classes with as many members as the class of null-classes, or (what comes to the same thing) the class of classes with as many members as the class whose sole member is the number zero. Two can then be defined as the class of classes with as many members as the class whose members are zero and one, three as the class of classes with as many members as the class whose members are zero and one and two, and so on *ad infinitum*.

This is a very ingenious way of building up the series of natural numbers out of the merely logical notions of identity, class, class-membership, and class-equivalence. It contains, however, as Russell discovered, a fatal flaw. If we are to proceed in this way we must be able without restriction to form classes of classes, and classes of classes of classes, and so on; in other words, classes must be treated as classifiable, they must be capable of being members of other classes. Now can a class be a member of itself? Most classes are not (e.g. the class of men is not a man) but some apparently are (e.g. the class of classes is a class). It seems therefore that classes divide into two: the class of classes that are members of themselves, and the class of classes that are not members of themselves.

Consider now this second class: is it a member of itself or not? If it is a member of itself, then since it is precisely the class of classes that are *not* members of themselves, it must be not a member of itself. But, if it is not a member of itself, then it qualifies for membership of the class of classes that are not members of themselves, and therefore it is a member of itself. It seems that it must either be a member of itself or not; but whichever alternative we choose we get into trouble. This frustrating discovery is known as Russell's paradox, and it showed that something must be wrong with the permissive procedure of forming classes of classes *ad lib*.

Russell's remedy for the trouble is known as the theory of types. The root error, he thought, lay in treating classes as randomly classifiable objects. Classes and individuals, he now thought, were of different logical types, and what can be true or false of one cannot be significantly asserted of the other.

'The class of men is a man' should be regarded, not as false, but as meaningless. What can meaningfully be said of individuals cannot meaningfully be said of classes, and what can meaningfully be said of classes cannot meaningfully be said of classes of classes, and so on through the hierarchy of logical types. If the difference of type between the different levels of the hierarchy is observed, the paradox cannot be meaningfully formulated.

But now another difficulty met Russell. Once there were prohibitions on forming classes of classes, how was he to define the series of natural numbers? He retained the definition of zero as the class whose only member is the null-class, but he now treated one as the class of all classes similar to the class whose members are (a) the members of the null-class, plus (b) any object not a member of that class. Two was treated in turn as the class of all classes similar to the class whose members are (a) the members of the class used to define one, plus (b) any object not a member of that defining class. In this way the numbers can be defined one after the other, and each number is a class of classes of individuals. But the natural-number series can be continued thus *ad infinitum* only if there is an infinite number of objects in the universe; for if there are only n individuals, then there will be no classes with $n + 1$ members, and so no cardinal number $n + 1$. Russell accepted this and therefore added to his axioms an axiom of infinity, i.e. the hypothesis that the number of objects in the universe is not finite. This hypothesis may be, as Russell thought it was, highly probable; but on the face of it it is far from being a logical truth; and the need to postulate it is therefore a sullying of the purity of the original programme of deriving arithmetic from logic alone.

Wittgenstein was profoundly dissatisfied with the theory of types and the axiom of infinity, and a great part of his early work on logic, reflected in his *Notebooks*, arose from this dissatisfaction.

CHAPTER 3

The Criticism of *Principia*

'All theories of types' Wittgenstein wrote to Russell in 1913 'must be done away with by a theory of symbolism showing that what seem to be *different kinds of things* are symbolized by different kinds of symbols which *cannot* possibly be substituted in one another's places' (NB 121). During 1913 and 1914 Wittgenstein was working out such a theory of symbolism, and his earliest attempts can be seen in the 'Notes on Logic' (September 1913), the notes dictated to G. E. Moore in Norway (April 1914) and the notebook dating from the second half of 1914.

Wittgenstein came to think that what was wrong with the theory of types was that it was an attempt to say something which was unsayable. The theory of types says that certain types of symbols cannot sensibly be combined: e.g. 'The class of men is a man' is a piece of nonsense. But this itself is a piece of nonsense; or rather, it does not achieve what it tries to. For what is meant by the subject of the sentence below?

(A) 'The class of men is a man' is a piece of nonsense.

If what is in quotation marks is meant to be just the sounds, or marks on the paper, then the whole sentence states at best a trivial empirical fact about arbitrary linguistic conventions, for there is nothing in that set of sounds which disqualifies it from being given a meaning. Surely there could be a language which was exactly like English, except that the sign 'class' was used as English uses the sign 'tallest'. In that case the set of signs in the quotation marks would have perfectly good sense and express a truth.

All this, however, is clearly irrelevant to Russell's purpose. What (A) is meant to be about is not the sounds, but their meaning. So shall we say rather the following:

(B) 'The class of men is a man', when that expression has the meaning it has in English, is a piece of nonsense.

It seems that *that* won't do, for if the expression is a piece of nonsense then it doesn't *have* any meaning in English. So it seems that we are brought back again to consider the sentence as being about meaningless marks (cf. NB 2; TLP 5.473).

Shall we say that the symbols 'the class of men' and '. . . is a man' cannot be combined to make a sensible sentence? This seems to offer us a way out, but does not. For if the expressions in quotes refer to the sounds then again we are just expressing a trivial empirical truth. On the other hand, if it refers to the sounds with their meaning, to the symbols with their logical properties, what can we mean by 'combination' when we say that they cannot be combined in a certain way? The most plausible account is: 'the class of men', meaning what it does in English, cannot be the subject of a sentence whose predicate is '. . . is a man', meaning what *that* does in English. We may doubt whether this in turn is meaningful, but even if it is, it may well only postpone the evil day. For can we account for the meaning of the fragmentary expressions without giving an account of the sentences in which they can occur? If not, all our earlier problems will meet us again.

Wittgenstein's way out of this difficulty is to lay down that the rules of logic must be entirely syntactical rules, i.e. rules about the manipulation of symbols. We cannot formulate semantical rules, rules about the meaning of symbols, nor can we give a justification of syntactical rules based on the meaning of the symbols (e.g. we cannot say: any symbol for such and such an object must have such and such rules) (NB 116; TLP 3.33–3.331). In order to say what the logical properties of language are, we should need a language without these properties (for otherwise we should be taking for granted what we are supposed to be explaining). But a language lacking these properties, an illogical language, is impossible (TLP 3.031, 5.4731).

The theme of much of Wittgenstein's writing in 1914, taken up again in the *Tractatus* (TLP 5.473), is that logic must take care of itself. By this Wittgenstein was rejecting the possibility of a philosophy of logic as Frege and Russell had conceived it. In *Principia Mathematica*, in addition to the symbolic expressions, there occur passages in English prose containing words like 'property', 'relation', 'logical constant'. This, Wittgenstein came to think, was illegitimate and superfluous. Logic did not need a philosophical theory to justify it, nor could philosophy set limits to its application. 'Everything which is possible in logic is also permitted' (TLP 5.473).

The only propositions which really belong in logic books are the tautologies whose nature is shown by the truth-tables. Being tautologies, they say nothing about the world, because they are true in every possible state of affairs and consequently cannot pick out one state of affairs rather than another. They are propositions of a unique sort, because their truth can be discovered by a mere study of the symbols which express them. They say nothing about the world, but they reveal the structure of the symbols which make them up. Thus 'It is raining or it is not raining' tells me nothing about the weather; but the fact that it is a tautology shows that 'It is raining' and 'It is not raining' contradict each other (TLP 6.1–6.201).

The would-be propositions of philosophical logic, Wittgenstein thought, were attempts to *say* what was *shown* by the tautologies. The distinction between saying and showing was fundamental in both his earlier and his later philosophy. For instance, Wittgenstein wrote:

What expresses *itself* in language *we* cannot express by means of language.
Propositions *show* the logical form of reality.
They display it.
Thus, one proposition '*fa*' shows that the object *a* occurs in its sense, two propositions '*fa*' and '*ga*' show that the same object is mentioned in both of them . . .
What *can* be shown cannot be said (TLP 4.121–4.1212).

As a first attempt to explain the distinction, one might say that something can be *said* if it would be possible for a hearer to grasp the content of what was being communicated to him without knowing its truth-value; or, to put it another way, it can be said that *p* only if a questioner can formulate a question 'Is it the case that *p*?' without yet knowing the answer to it. For Wittgenstein, something can be *said* only if it could be passed on to somebody as a piece of new information. And what can be said cannot be shown, and what can be shown cannot be said (TLP 4.1212).

To illustrate Wittgenstein's thesis that tautologies show the logical or structural properties of their components, we may give the following example. Suppose we take the three propositions 'If it is Sunday, the shops are shut', 'It is Sunday', 'The shops are shut'. We can form out of them a tautology thus: 'If if it is Sunday the shops are shut, and it is Sunday, then the shops are shut.' It is perfectly clear that the tautology does not say anything about the world in the way in which each of the three constituent propositions does. But, Wittgenstein would say, it does show something about the formal properties of language. It shows that 'The shops are shut' follows from 'If it is Sunday, the shops are shut' and 'It is Sunday.' But why, one might ask, can't this be *said*? Indeed haven't I just this moment *said* it?

The answer must be as follows. For anyone to understand what I have just written, he must take what appears in quotation marks as English sentences, and not just as a succession of meaningless marks. But, if he is to do so, he must already know English, and therefore know the rules for the use of the English expressions which make up the quoted sentences. But if he knows these rules then he already knows that the third sentence follows from the other two; and therefore when I purported to be giving him information I gave him no information at all.

To clarify this, it may help to introduce a distinction Wittgenstein drew (but did not always observe) between signs and symbols (TLP 3.326, 3.32ff.). If we consider a word or a proposition – spoken or written – from the point of view of its perceptible qualities, such as its shape or sound, then we are considering the *sign*; when we try to grasp the meaningful use of the expression, its rules for application, we are dealing with the *symbol*. It is possible for the same sound or mark to be used in language in different ways – e.g. 'den' as a German article and as an English noun; or in English 'bear' as a noun and as a verb. In that case we have the same sign but two different symbols. It is important to note that in order to specify the symbol we do not have to say anything about *semantics*: we do not have to say anything about its reference, or the kind of object it can stand for in the world (TLP 3.33). This is what was wrong with the theory of types: Russell in drawing up his syntactic rules was forced to speak about the things the signs mean (TLP 3.331). But that something belongs to a certain type is something that cannot be said: it cannot be said, for example, that M is a thing (as opposed e.g. to a class). This is something which must be *shown* by the symbol 'M' – not of course by the *sign* 'M' but by the symbol, the sign with its syntactical rules. We cannot speak of types, we can speak only of symbols; but what the theory of types tried to say, the symbols can show (TLP 3.332–3–333; NB 108).

How do the symbols show what the theory of types tried to say? Consider the sentence 'Socrates is a different type of thing from mortality.' This is a piece of nonsense, but what it tries to say can be brought out in the following manner. In 'Socrates is mortal' 'Socrates' is a proper name, but 'mortal' is not; what symbolizes is not only the expression 'mortal', or 'is mortal', but the fact that '. . . is mortal' stands to the right of a proper name. Similarly, in 'John loves Mary', 'loves' alone is not a symbol, but the fact that 'loves' stands between two names in a certain order is what symbolizes. (If 'loves' alone were the symbol, then 'John loves Mary' and 'Mary loves John' and 'loves Mary John' would all be the same proposition, being composed of the same symbols.) And what this shows is what we might try to express, for example, by saying that there is a difference of type between objects, relations and properties (NB 108–9).

Our reformulation, however, has not altogether avoided falling into the forbidden language of semantics, for in distinguishing between what *symbolizes* and what does not one invites the question 'And *what* does it symbolize?' Any answer to this would be open to the same objections as the theory of types, since 'symbolize' is a verb which attempts to cross the boundary between language and the world. We should rather distinguish between accidental and essential features of the symbol, and try to draw the distinction between essence and accident within the realm of syntax (NB 109; TLP 3.334–3.341). Every symbol will have accidental as well as essential features. For instance, it is an accidental feature of the English language that the order of names flanking the verb 'loves' is significant; in Latin it would be the termination of the names which mattered, and 'Mariam amat Joannes' and 'Joannes amat Mariam' would say the same. But every language must contain some feature for distinguishing between the subject and object of the verb, and the essential part of the symbol will be what all symbols which can fulfil the same purpose have in common (TLP 3.341).

Every proposition shows, but does not say, various things about itself. For instance, 'John loves Mary' shows, but does not say, that 'John' is to the left of 'Mary'. This accidental, arbitrary feature can also be said by another proposition. But the logical, non-arbitrary properties which every proposition must have cannot be said by any proposition (NB 110).

Every proposition shows these logical properties (TLP 4.121), but the propositions of ordinary language show them only obscurely, partly because of the occurrence of similar signs belonging to different symbols. What the philosopher of logic can do is to construct a symbolism which does not use the same sign in different symbols, a symbolism which would obey the rules of logical grammar – unlike English, in which, for instance, 'is' signifies in three different ways, and in which 'identical' has the linguistic, but not the logical, syntax of an adjective (TLP 3.323).

Besides signs which look alike but belong to different symbols, ordinary language contains signs which look different but signify in the same way and indeed have the same meaning. This is true not only of ordinary language but also of the formalized languages of Frege and Russell (NB 100). Consider the propositions 'not both p and not q' and 'either not p or q'. Both of these have the same truth-table; they are true and false in exactly the same circumstances as each other. If we regard the sense of propositions compounded with connectives like 'and' and 'or' as being exhausted by the expression of their relation to the truth-possibilities of the more elementary propositions which make them up (TLP 4.4) then we can say that 'not both p and not q' and 'either not p or q' have the same sense. Either of them is substitutable for the other, and indeed their common truth-table could itself be used as a propositional sign with the same meaning (TLP 3.344, 4.44).

But is it correct to regard compound propositions as nothing more than the expression of agreement and disagreement with the truth-possibilities of elementary propositions? Wittgenstein believed this, but he rightly did not take it for granted. To prove it, he offered a number of arguments in the *Tractatus* and in the *Notebooks* which preceded it. One might be tempted, he says, to think that words like 'not' and 'or' have some independent meaning: hardly, that 'not' denotes some Platonic Nothood, but perhaps that the 'or' in 'John will come or Mary will come' expresses a relation between two states of affairs. At one time he seems himself to have been tempted to think this but he soon gave up the idea, and his first surviving letter to Russell says 'Logic is still in the melting pot but one thing gets more and more obvious to me . . . there are no logical constants' (NB 119). And in the *Tractatus* (TLP 4.0312) he described it as being his fundamental thought that the logical constants do not denote. That is to say, they are not proxies, as other words are, for something in the world. It is important to grasp what he meant by this.

First, Wittgenstein argues that nothing in the world corresponds to the negation sign. To both 'p' and 'not p' correspond the same reality, he says in the *Tractatus* (TLP 4.0621); in the *Notebooks* he had said, using Frege's terminology, that they both had the same reference or denotation (NB 100). By this he meant that it is one and the same fact which verifies or falsifies each of them: if it is the case that p, then the positive fact that p both makes 'p' true and makes 'not-p' false; if it is not the case that p, then 'p' is made false and 'not-p' is made true by one and the same negative fact (NB 94; TLP 2.06). No new element enters into the fact which corresponds to 'not-p', for it is the very same fact as corresponds to 'p'. If we are tempted to think otherwise, it is because we are tempted to confuse p's not being the case, with what is the case instead of p (e.g. to confuse the negative fact that the rose is not red with the positive fact that the rose is white) (NB 94–5). If 'not' introduced something new into a proposition, then 'not not p' would be about something different from 'p'. It seems scarcely credible, Wittgenstein says, that there should follow from a single fact that p infinitely many distinct facts, namely, that not not p, that not not not not p, and so on (TLP 5.43, 5.44). In fact 'p' and 'not not p' say exactly the same; and in an ideal symbolism the sign for 'p' and the sign for 'not not p' would be one and the same (NB 100).

Secondly Wittgenstein urges that the binary connectives 'or', 'and' and so on do not denote relations. He offers arguments for this, though it is, he says, 'obvious to the plain man' (NB 101). First of all, unlike real relations they need brackets to express their scope (e.g. to distinguish '(either p or q) and r' from 'either p (or q and r)'); secondly, they are interdefinable (e.g. 'if ... then' can be defined as 'either not ... or', 'p and q' can be defined as 'not either not p or not q' and so on) (NB 115; TLP 5.461; NB 103; TLP 5.42).

Since the propositional connectives are definable in terms of each other, they would not appear in an ideal notation, as they do in Frege's and Russell's, as primitive signs (TLP 5.42). Like the propositional connectives, the quantifiers too are inter-definable ('for all x' = 'not for some x not'; 'for some x' = 'not for all x not'), so in the ideal symbolism they too must vanish (NB 103; TLP 5.441).

What of the third of the logical constants, the sign for identity ('=')? It is self-evident, Wittgenstein says, that identity is not a relation between objects: to say of two things that they are identical is nonsense, and to say of one thing that it is identical with itself is to say nothing at all (TLP 5.53–5.5303). 'I believe it would be possible wholly to exclude the sign of identity from our notation and always to indicate identity merely by the identity of the signs (in certain circumstances)' he wrote in his notebook in November 1914 (NB 34) and he followed up this suggestion in the *Tractatus* (TLP 5.53). In everyday life one man may have several names, and several men have the same name; it was a principle of the ideal nota-tion that there should not be signs which belonged to more than one symbol. If we followed this, then every object would have a different sign and there would be no need for a sign of identity: a proposition like 'A = B' would always be incorrect, and one like 'A = A' always pointless (TLP 5.5303).

One strand, then, in the thought of the *Tractatus*, a strand which was more or less complete by the end of 1914, was the dismantling of the logical system of *Principia Mathematica*. As we have seen, Wittgenstein's criticism has three main targets: (i) the extra-logical apparatus that has to be added to the formal system, such as the theory of types; (ii) the axiomatic method which disguises the fact that no propositions of logic are more primitive than others, as shown by the truth-table method; (iii) the use of logical constants – the propositional connectives, the quantifiers, the identity sign – as undefined primitives.

What was Wittgenstein to offer in its place? This cannot be set out until we have considered his theory of the nature of elementary or atomic propositions. In *Principia* logic appears as something which concerns the relations between complex propositions built up by connectives and quantifiers out of elementary propositions on the pattern of 'Socrates is human' and 'John loves Mary.' Wittgenstein believed that the problems which arose in connection with the complex propositions could be traced back to the nature of the atomic propositions themselves (NB 120). Indeed, he wrote on 5 November 1914, all the logical constants are already contained in the elementary proposition (NB 27). For, as he later explained in the *Tractatus*, 'Socrates is human' says the same as 'For some x, x is human and $x =$ Socrates' – a proposition containing a truth-functional connective, a quantifier and the identity sign. Since the elementary proposition said the same as the complex one, the symbolizing element in each proposition must be the same (see p. 46); and the analysis of the elementary proposition in the ideal notation would reveal the essence which was common to the two. 'Wherever there is compositeness, argument and function are present, and where these are present we already have all the logical constants' (TLP 5.47; NB 121).

A full account, therefore, of the way in which elementary propositions signify would be adequate to explain the way in which the complex propositions signify. This would show the superfluity, the accidental nature, of the logical constants of the Russellian symbolism. The one real logical constant would be the element, whatever it is, in every elementary proposition which makes it capable of saying the same as, and being equivalent to, propositions containing the pseudo-constants of *Principia*. This element Wittgenstein called 'the general form of proposition'; to describe it would be to describe the one and only primitive sign of logic (TLP 5.472; NB 45).

How then are we to describe the general form of proposition? Wittgenstein believed that he had hit on the key to this problem by the discovery of the pictorial nature of propositions. His notebook for 29 September 1914 records how the idea first dawned on him.

The general concept of the proposition carries with it a quite general concept of the coordination of proposition and situation. The solution to all my questions must be extremely simple.

In the proposition a world is as it were put together experimentally. (As when in the law-court in Paris a motor-car accident is represented by means of dolls, etc.) This must yield the nature of truth straight away (if I were not blind) . . .

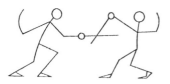

If the right-hand figure in this picture represents the man A, and the left-hand one stands for the man B, then the whole might assert, e.g. 'A is fencing with B.' The proposition in picture writing can be true and false. It has a sense independent of its truth or falsehood. It must be possible to demonstrate everything essential by considering this case. (NB 7)

The next two chapters will show how Wittgenstein followed up this insight.

CHAPTER 4

The Picture Theory of the Proposition

In the *Tractatus* Wittgenstein prefaces his theory that a proposition is a picture with some considerations on the nature of pictures in general (TLP 2.1–2.225). From examples he uses elsewhere it is clear that he would count as pictures not only paintings, drawings, photographs and other obviously pictorial representations in two dimensions, but also maps, sculptures, three-dimensional models, and even such things as musical scores and gramophone records. His theory is perhaps best regarded as a theory of representation in general.

Any representation can be an accurate or inaccurate representation: it can give a true or false picture of what it represents. It is this fact which led Wittgenstein to seek to clarify the nature of the proposition by means of a general theory of representation. In any representation there are two things to consider: (a) what it is a representation *of*; (b) whether it represents what it represents accurately or inaccurately. The distinction between these two features of a representation corresponds to the distinction, concerning a proposition, between what the proposition *means* and whether what it means is true or false – between sense and truth-value.

In the passage quoted at the end of the last chapter Wittgenstein records that he had learnt that in law-courts in Paris motor-car accidents were reconstructed by means of toys and dolls. A collision between a lorry and a pram would be represented by placing together a toy lorry and a toy pram. This would give a three-dimensional picture or model of the accident. Wittgenstein regarded this procedure as throwing great light on the theory of representation and of the proposition.

A particular positioning of the toy pram and the toy lorry may represent the relative positions of pram and lorry at the time of the accident. How is this representation possible? First, the toy pram must go proxy for the real pram, and the toy lorry must go proxy for the real lorry: that is to say, the elements of the model must stand in for the elements of the situation to be represented. This is the pictorial relationship (*abbildende Beziehung*) which makes the picture a picture (TLP 2.1514). But this is not enough: the elements of the model must be related to each other in a particular way. It is the spatial relationship between the toy pram and the toy lorry which represents the spatial relationship between the real pram and the real lorry. If the toys were lying in the store-cupboard they would of course be in a spatial relationship to each other, but this would not represent anything as it does when they are brought into the law-court to go proxy for the vehicles involved in the collision.

The relationship between the elements of a picture – the fact that the elements are related in the way they are – is itself a *fact*, and this led Wittgenstein to say that a picture is a fact. He called the connection of the elements in a picture the structure of the picture (TLP 2.15). Every picture has a structure, but it is not identical with its structure. A picture consists of structure plus pictorial relationship; the picture is the relation between the elements considered as elements having pictorial relationships to objects outside.

We must consider not only the actual structure of pictures, but the features which make such structures possible. The possibility of structure is called by Wittgenstein 'pictorial form' (*Form der Abbildung*). In the case in point the actual spatial relationship of the toys is the structure of the picture, the possibility of this relationship – i.e. the three-dimensional character of the toys – is its form of representation (cf. TLP 2.171). The three-dimensional character is something which the model in court and the actual accident have in common: it is because of this common element that the model in court is able to represent the accident in the road. There must, Wittgenstein thought, be something identical in a picture and what it depicts to enable one to be a picture of the other at all (TLP 2.161). This common element is what is called 'pictorial form'.

Because pictorial form is the possibility of relationship between elements of the picture, and because pictorial form is common to picture and what it pictures, pictorial form is also the possibility that the things represented are related in the same way as the representing elements in the picture (TLP 2.151). Thus a picture represents a possibility in the real world: as for instance an architect's drawing or model shows a possible arrangement of buildings (TLP 2.202).

How does the picture connect with the reality it represents? To this question Wittgenstein seems to give inconsistent answers (TLP 2.151–2.1515). Having explained pictorial form he goes on immediately to say 'That is how a picture is attached to reality: it reaches right out to it' (TLP 2.1511), and this suggests that it is by pictorial form that pictures touch reality. Later, however, he says that it is the pictorial *correlations* between elements of the picture and the objects which 'are as it were the feelers of the picture's elements, with which the picture touches reality' (TLP 2.1515).

The inconsistency is only an apparent one. To select a set of toys as three-dimensional proxies for three-dimensional objects is *eo ipso* to make their three-dimensional properties the pictorial form of the picture. It is the choice of an object *qua* object with a certain pictorial form (i.e. with the possibility of combining with other objects in certain ways to be treated as significant) which makes the connection with reality. (The *shape* of the toys is in this case significant – not their colour or their weight, though in a different case these properties might be significant.) So the connection with reality is made by the person who makes the correlation between the elements of the picture and of reality. How does he do this? At the time he wrote the *Tractatus* Wittgenstein thought this was an empirical matter of no importance for philosophy. Later he came to realize that it was intimately connected with the nature of representation. But in the *Tractatus* he was more interested in discussing pictorial form than in discussing pictorial relationship.

Wittgenstein seems to have thought that for A to be a picture of B, A must be not altogether like B (or it would be B and not just a picture of B) and not altogether unlike B (or it could not picture B at all) (NB 15). What makes A like B, what it has in common with B, is, as we have seen, called by Wittgenstein A's 'pictorial form'. What makes A unlike B, and makes it a picture and not a reduplicated reality, we may call A's 'representational form'.[1] Thus, for instance, in a two-dimensional pencil-sketch of a landscape the pictorial form is the spatiality of the picture, which it has in common with the landscape; the representational form is the black-and-white miniature two-dimensionality which is peculiar to the picture with the conventions of scale, perspective, shading, etc. which this entails (TLP 2.171-3). In the three-dimensional law-court model the three dimensions are all part of the pictorial form but the size and colour remain part of the representational form.

Pictures can be more or less abstract, more or less like what they picture: their pictorial form can be more or less rich. But there is a minimum which must be common between reality and picture if the picture is to be able to portray even incorrectly: this minimum, Wittgenstein says, is logical form (TLP 2.18). What this amounts to is that the elements of the picture must be capable of some combination with each other in a pattern corresponding to the relationship of the elements of what is pictured (cf. TLP 2.0141). What 'combining' amounts to will differ for different representational forms: in a score, for instance, the ordering of the notes on the page from left to right represents the ordering of the sounds in time. The spatial arrangement of the notes is not part of the pictorial form, but

---

1. This appears to be what Wittgenstein meant by '*Form der Darstellung*' (TLP 2.173-4), if he did not mean this expression to be synonymous with '*Form der Abbildung*'.

only of the representational form, for the sounds are not in space. The ordering, however, is common to both; and this common ordering is (it may be surmised) the kind of thing Wittgenstein had in mind when he spoke of logical form. Since every picture must have logical form in common with what it depicts, logical form is part of the pictorial form of every picture; every picture is a logical picture in addition to being e.g. a spatial picture, or whatever other particular kind of picture it may be. Every picture represents a possible state of affairs, which may be called its sense; it is a true picture if its sense agrees with reality, and otherwise a false picture. No picture will itself show whether it is true or false: for this it must be compared with reality (TLP 2.201–2.225).

So much for the general theory of picturing. Wittgenstein goes on to apply this theory first briefly to thoughts and then at greater length to propositions. A logical picture of a fact, he says, is a thought; and in a proposition a thought is expressed in a manner perceptible to the senses (TLP 3, 3.1). Presumably a proposition is not the only perceptible form of expression of a thought: from what has been said elsewhere it would seem that a painting, a sculpture, a musical score would all be expressions of thoughts (cf. TLP 4.014). Since a picture is a combination of elements, the question arises: what are the elements of a logical picture, of a thought? This was put to Wittgenstein by Russell in 1919, and received a rather brusque answer. Since a thought is a fact, Russell asked 'What are its constituents and components, and what is their relation to those of the pictured fact?' 'I don't know *what* the constituents of a thought are' Wittgenstein replied 'but I know *that* it must have such constituents which correspond to the words of Language. Again the kind of relation of the constituents of the thought and of the pictured fact is irrelevant. It would be a matter of psychology to find out.' 'Does a thought consist of words?' insisted Russell. 'No, but of psychical constituents that have the same sort of relation to reality as words. What those constituents are I don't know' (NB 129–30).

In the *Tractatus* we are told little about thoughts. A few conclusions are drawn from the definition of a thought as a logical picture of the facts plus the general theory of picturing. Every picture, of course, is a logical picture; but thoughts are logical pictures *par excellence* since logical structure is the *whole of* their pictorial form. Take away logic, and logical pictures are impossible, so thought cannot represent anything which would contradict the laws of logic; just as we cannot make a spatial representation of something contravening the laws of geometry (TLP 3.03–3.0321). But thought cannot represent logic any more than it can represent illogicality, for no picture can depict its pictorial form, and logic is the pictorial form of thought (TLP 2.172; cf. 4.0312).

If logic is thought's pictorial form, what is its representational form? We are not told; presumably it is the possibility of modelling in the mysterious mental medium mentioned in the letter to Russell. Whatever it is, it cannot be thought about, since no picture can place itself outside its representational form (TLP 2.174).

Only possible states of affairs can be thought of (TLP 3.02). The totality of true thoughts is a picture of the world (TLP 3.01). Since any picture needs to be compared with reality to tell whether it is true or false, there cannot be a thought whose truth is recognizable from the thought itself: hence no thought can be an *a priori* truth (TLP 3.04–3.05).

Thought appears in the *Tractatus* mainly as the link between propositions and states of affairs. To illustrate this, Wittgenstein often uses the metaphor of geometrical projection. The propositional sign (the spoken or written sentence), when it is used, is a projection of a possible state of affairs; the method of projection is to think of, i.e. to form a logical picture of, the possible state of affairs which is the sense of the proposition (TLP 3.5, 3.11–3.12). It is the thought which makes the sign into a symbol, which makes the propositional sign into a proposition; so much so that sometimes Wittgenstein speaks of a proposition as actually being a thought (TLP 3.5–4) and not just, as seems more natural, as being the expression of a thought (TLP 3.2). The projection lines, as it were, run from the sentence to the state of affairs *via* the thought in the mind. In an ideal language the elements of a sentence would correspond to the elements of the thought which in their turn correspond to the objects involved in the possible state of affairs (TLP 3.2). The projection lines would, so to speak, be very simple. In everyday language, however, the form of the thought is disguised in the sentences, for language is no more designed to reveal the form of the thought than clothing is designed to reveal the form of the body (TLP 4.002). The understanding of ordinary language depends on enormously complicated conventions: a great deal is added in thought to each proposition and not said (NB 70). The projection lines are not simple, but as complicated as the human organism. Philosophical analysis is needed to make the elements of propositions correspond to elements of thought and reveal the real logical form behind the appearances of ordinary speech (TLP 4.0031).

The picture theory of the proposition grew out of a contrast which Wittgenstein drew and gradually deepened between propositions and names. This historical fact is reflected in the order of the propositions of the *Tractatus*, where the ways in which the pictorial nature of the proposition marks it off from non-pictorial names are spelt out (TLP 3.14ff.) long before the theory that a proposition is a picture is explicitly enunciated (TLP 4.01). The steps of the development of the contrast are worth retracing.

For Frege names and propositions alike had both sense and reference. When Wittgenstein wrote the 'Notes on Logic' in 1913 he accepted that propositions have a reference, but instead of treating the truth-value of the proposition as its reference, he counted as the reference of a proposition the fact that corresponds to it (NB 94, 111). Thus the reference of 'p', if 'p' is true, is the fact that p; if 'p' is false it is the negative fact that not-p. But if one explains the reference of propositions in this way then there is an important contrast between the relation between names and what they refer to, on the one hand, and the relation between propositions and what they refer to, on the other. For in order to understand a proper name, like 'Wellington', I must know whom or what it refers to; but I can perfectly well understand a proposition without knowing whether it is true or false, i.e., on this account, without knowing its reference (NB 94). For Wittgenstein in 1913, then, propositions, though they have reference, are already sharply distinguished from names. Later he thought it less misleading to say that a false proposition has no reference at all (NB 24); but he continued to speak of a reality 'corresponding to' a false proposition (TLP 4.0621).

What we understand, when we understand a proposition, is not its reference, but its *sense* (NB 94, 111). We have to know what would be the case if it were true and what would be the case if it were false. Both of these elements are necessary: as Wittgenstein puts it, 'Every proposition is essentially true-false. Thus a proposition has two poles (corresponding to case of its truth and case of its falsity); we call this the *sense* of a proposition' (NB 94). This differentiates it from a name. A name can have only one relationship to reality: it either names something or it is not a significant symbol at all. But a proposition has a two-way relation: it does not cease to have a meaning when it ceases to be true. Wittgenstein summed this up cryptically by saying 'names are points, propositions arrows' (NB 97; TLP 3.144). Propositions unlike names have *direction*.

'From this' Wittgenstein wrote 'it results that "true" and "false" are not accidental properties of a proposition such that, when it has meaning, we can say it is also true or false: on the contrary to have meaning means to be true or false; the being true or false actually constitutes the relationship of the proposition to reality, which we mean by saying that it has meaning (*Sinn*)' (NB 112).

So that is one difference between a name and a proposition:

to understand a name is to understand its reference, to understand a proposition is to understand its sense. But another, important, difference is this. To understand the reference of a name, one has to have the reference explained to one (TLP 4.026); to understand the sense of a proposition one does not have to have its sense explained to one (TLP 4.02). Only when we are dealing with an unfamiliar language with the aid of a phrasebook do we take the meanings of propositions as single units: real understanding of propositions arises from understanding of their constituent parts, the words that make them up (TLP 4.024–5). If we know the meaning of 'a' and 'b' and if we know what 'xRy' means for any xs and ys, then we also understand 'aRb' (NB 94).

It is to the fact that a proposition can communicate a new sense with old words – to the fact that we can understand a proposition which we have never heard before, and whose truth-value we do not know – that Wittgenstein appeals to prove that a proposition is a picture, and depicts the facts that it describes (TLP 4.016–4.021, 4.03). What he meant by calling the proposition a picture can, I believe, be summed up in eight theses, which I shall first enunciate and then discuss one by one.

(1) A proposition is essentially composite.

(2) The elements which compose a proposition are correlated by human decision with elements of reality.

(3) The combination of such correlated elements into a proposition presents – without further human intervention – a possible state of affairs.

(4) A proposition stands in an internal relation to the possible state of affairs which it presents.

(5) This internal relationship can only be shown, it cannot be informatively stated.

(6) A proposition is true or false in virtue of being compared to reality.

(7) A proposition must be independent of the actual state of affairs which makes it true or makes it false.

(8) No proposition is *a priori* true.

Let us consider these in turn.

(1) *A proposition is essentially composite.* The point was made long ago by Plato (*Sophist* 262a ff.) that a sentence must consist of more than one word, and that not all combinations of words made up sentences: one noun plus one verb, he thought, was the minimum. Wittgenstein is making basically the same point. A proposition, unlike a name, must have parts. Names in English, of course, have parts, represented by syllables and letters; but these parts are not essential to their role as symbols: 'N' will do as well as 'Napoleon' for a name, and the 'nap' in 'Napoleon' has no separate significance (TLP 3.3411). But a proposition must consist of parts which can occur in other propositions. Even '*ambulo*' is composite, Wittgenstein says, for in '*ambulat*' the same stem gives a different sense with a different ending, and in '*dormio*' the same ending gives a different sense with a different stem (TLP 4.032).

But not every collection of words makes a sentence: as Plato said 'walk runs flies' and 'lion stag horse' are no sentences. A mere set of names cannot express a sense (NB 105; TLP 3.141–3.142); the words must be put together in the appropriate way, 'concatenated' like the links in a chain (TLP 4.22) or 'articulated' like the limbs of a body (TLP 3.141). Indeed, according to Wittgenstein, what constitutes the propositional sign is precisely the fact that its elements are put together in a determinate way (TLP 3.14ff.). A proposition is a fact, not a complex object.

'Symbols are not what they seem to be' Wittgenstein wrote in 1913. 'In "aRb" "R" looks like a substantive but it is not one. What symbolizes in "aRb" is that "R" occurs between "a" and "b"' (NB 99). For instance, in 'John loves Mary' the symbol is not just 'loves', but the fact that the word 'loves' occurs to the left of one name and to the right of the other.

Again, in 'John smokes', what symbolizes is that '. . . smokes' occurs to the right of a name. This is why, for instance, 'John Plato' has no meaning: because there is no convention which assigns significance to 'John''s being to the left of a name, or 'Plato''s being to the right of one (NB 115). Of course the particular relationships mentioned belong to the conventions of the English language; but any symbol which is substitutable for 'loves' and 'smokes' must stand in *some* special relationship to the names it goes with, if it is to be capable of performing the same symbolic task. A special relationship between the signs 'a' and 'b' is therefore necessary in order to express a relationship between the objects a and b. It might even, if our conventions were different, be sufficient, for instance, if we had a convention that the fact that the sign 'a' occurred to the left of the sign 'b' meant that a was older than b, then 'Socrates Plato' would be a sentence expressing that Socrates was older than Plato. Thus generalizing, Wittgenstein says: we must not say 'The complex sign "aRb" says that a stands in the relation R to b, but that "a" stands in a certain relation to "b" says *that* aRb' (TLP 3.1432; NB 105). So facts are symbolized by facts, or rather: that a certain thing is the case in the symbol says that a certain thing is the case in the world (NB 105). In this way the picture theory connects with the earlier criticism of the theory of types (see p. 47 above).

(2) *The correlation of the elements.* The correlation between the elements of a picture and the elements of what has to be pictured, as we have seen, constitutes the pictorial relationship of the picture. Among the elements of the proposition are the simple unanalysable signs, the names (TLP 3.202, 3.26). A name has as its reference an object; it is the proxy in the proposition for the object (TLP 3.203, 3.22, 4.0312). The connection between a name and what it names is a matter of arbitrary convention (NB 25; TLP 3.315, 3.322); the correlation between the two is a matter of psychology (NB 104, 111, 99). Because the choice of signs is arbitrary, if a certain combination of signs fails to make sense, this will not be because of anything illegitimate in

the sign itself, but because we have failed to make a correlation between it and reality – we have failed to make it a symbol (TLP 5.4733). That, for instance, is why 'Socrates is Plato' or 'Socrates is identical' is nonsense (NB 2; TLP 5.473). We can, however, be mistaken about whether we have made an appropriate convention or not (TLP 5.4733).

A proposition, however, is not just a set of names, and in addition to correlating the names with objects we have to correlate relationships between the names in a proposition with relationships between objects in facts. This correlation too is made by the arbitrary laying down of a rule (NB 99). 'One name' wrote Wittgenstein in his notebook on 4 November 1914 'is representative of one thing, another of another thing, and they themselves are connected; in this way the whole images the situation – like a *tableau vivant*. The logical connection must, of course, be one that is possible as between the things that the names are representatives of, and this will always be the case if the names really are representatives of the things' (NB 26; TLP 4.0311). The names really will be representative only if they have the appropriate syntactical form.

(3) *Non-arbitrary representation.* 'In this way' Wittgenstein wrote in his notebook the following day 'the proposition represents the situation – as it were off its own bat' (NB 26). The correlation of names and objects is arbitrary, and arbitrary too is the stipulation that a certain relationship between names will represent a certain relationship between objects; but once these conventions have been made there is no need of a further convention to say that these names in this relationship signify those objects in that relationship. This is how it is possible to understand a proposition previously unheard, while each new name needs a special explanation (TLP 4.026).

(4) *Internal relation between proposition and situation.* 'A proposition communicates a situation to us, and so it must be *essentially* connected with the situation. And the connection is precisely that it is its logical picture' (TLP 4.03). Every proposition has accidental as well as essential features; the accidental

features result from the arbitrary conventions of the particular language to which it belongs; the essential features are those without which it could not express its sense (TLP 3.34). The essential features are the logical form, the logical multiplicity, which it must have in common with the situation it presents. In the proposition there must be exactly as many distinguishable parts as in the situation represented (TLP 4.04). The relation between the proposition and situation is not causal or contingent, but internal. An internal property or relation is defined by Wittgenstein as one which it is unthinkable that its possessor should not possess (TLP 4.123). The logical structure of a proposition is an internal property of it: it is unthinkable that the proposition should remain the same proposition and have a different logical structure. Similarly, possible situations have internal properties, and these are expressed by the internal properties of the corresponding propositions (TLP 4.124); the proposition 'describes reality by its internal properties' (TLP 4.023).

(5) *Internal relation shown not said.* Earlier we remarked that for Wittgenstein something can be *said* only if a hearer could be able to grasp the content of what was being communicated without knowing its truth-value. It follows that the possession of an internal relation is not something that can be said: if it is unthinkable that a thing should lack the property F, then it cannot informatively be said that it has it. Among the internal relations which have to be shown rather than said are those between propositions and the situations they represent (NB 25). The proposition that the cat is on the mat says that the cat is on the mat; but it cannot say, but only show, *that it itself says that the cat is on the mat* (TLP 4.022). '"The cat is on the mat" says that the cat is on the mat' does not, indeed, look particularly informative. Moreover, though the proposition can represent the cat's being on the mat, it cannot represent what is in common between that situation and itself, to wit, the logical form (TLP 4.12). Logical form is mirrored in propositions, not represented by them; that is to say, it is shown by them and shared by them (TLP 4.121).

(6) *Comparison with reality*. Every proposition describes a possible state of affairs, but not every proposition describes an actual state of affairs. Given any proposition, however, we know that either it or its negation describes an actual state of affairs: as Wittgenstein put it 'A proposition determines reality to this extent, that one only needs to say "Yes" or "No" to it to make it agree with reality' (TLP 4.023). But there is no way of finding out from the proposition itself *which* to say – in order to do this, to find out whether the proposition is true or false, we must compare it with reality (TLP 4.05; 2.223). In calling the verification of a proposition 'a comparison with reality' Wittgenstein is of course using the language of the picture theory; he believed that unless a proposition were a picture (picturing reality, give or take a 'yes' or 'no') we would not know where to look in the world in order to verify the proposition (TLP 4.06; NB 8).

(7) *Independence of reality*. 'The proposition must *contain* (and in this way show) *the possibility of its truth*. But not more than the *possibility*' Wittgenstein wrote shortly after he first propounded the picture theory (NB 16). This follows from the fundamental idea that a proposition has two poles, of truth and falsehood: this would be impossible unless the proposition were independent of the actual state of affairs which, if it is true, gives it its truth. What a picture represents it represents independently of its truth or falsity (TLP 2.22). A proposition does not actually contain its sense; if it did, it could not be false, since the actuality of its sense is what makes the proposition true (TLP 3.13).

(8) *No* a priori *truth*. This is a corollary of (7). A proposition could be true *a priori* only if it were possible to recognize its truth by inspection of the proposition itself without comparison with the world (TLP 3.05). But this can never be possible unless a proposition itself contains the state of affairs which would verify it, and this is prohibited by (7). As Wittgenstein wrote in his *Notebooks* 'In order for a proposition to be capable of being true it must also be capable of being false' (NB 55). In

other words, all genuine propositions are contingent propositions. Logical propositions can be seen to be true from the
symbols alone (NB 127; TLP 6.113); this shows they are only
'propositions' by courtesy. 'There are' he wrote already in
1914 'no such things as analytic propositions' (NB 21). In the
Prototractatus he wrote that all analytic propositions are tautologies (PTLP 4.44602), and in the *Tractatus* 'The propositions
of logic are tautologies. Therefore the propositions of logic
say nothing. (They are the analytic propositions.)' (TLP 6.1–6.11.)
Though logical would-be propositions can be called 'true'
(the tautologies take the truth-value 'true' for every truth-
combination in the truth-table) (TLP 4.464, 4.46), strictly speaking this is incorrect. A tautology is not a picture, not a
proposition, and cannot be called 'true' because it is 'made
true' ('*wahr gemacht*'), not compared with reality (NB 8, 55;
TLP 4.4611ff., 6.125).

In stating the elements of the picture theory I have not used
the word 'picture', because I think that the logically interesting
features of the theory are independent of the question whether
it was helpful or misleading to encapsulate it in the slogan
'A proposition is a picture.' What makes the picture theory
of the proposition something more than a comparison is the
fact that all the theorems enunciated above remain true, so
Wittgenstein believed, if for 'proposition' one substituted the
word 'picture'. But, as his examples show, he was more or
less consciously extending the use of the word 'picture' when
he applied it to a musical score; and in the *Prototractatus* he
was equally extending that of 'proposition' when he wrote 'A
theme in music is a proposition' (PTLP 3.16021), though he
gives no indication of what a theme pictures or how it is to
be compared with reality.

Wittgenstein compares the proposition in the *Tractatus* not
only to a picture, but also to a ruler; a picture, he says, is 'laid
against reality like a ruler' (TLP 2.1512). This leads to the
difficulty that a ruler, unlike a picture, applies to reality a whole
scale and not merely a 'yes–no' question. The way in which a

law-court model is compared with reality (TLP 2.223) is such that there are only two possibilities: either reality agrees with the model (the accident did happen in this way; the colliding vehicles were in this position) or it does not. When a ruler is laid against an object to be measured, indefinitely many possibilities are open: the end of the object may touch the 99-cm mark, the 100-cm mark, the 101-cm mark, etc. . . . Wittgenstein concealed this difficulty when he wrote the *Tractatus* by pretending that only the two points on the scale which touch the edges of the object to be measured really concern it (TLP 2.15121: only the outer graduating lines contact the object to be measured (cf. WWK 63)). But later he was to go back on this and realize that in some ways a ruler was a more apt comparison for a proposition than a picture was. This we shall see in chapter six.

Wittgenstein was of course aware that a proposition did not seem at first sight like a picture (TLP 4.011). The elements of a proposition do not look like the elements of reality they represent; and there is not a one–one correlation between words and elements of reality. For instance, in the sentence 'Socrates taught' neither word seems to denote an element of reality, since Socrates, being complex and mortal, and teaching, being abstract and universal, seem implausible candidates for being ultimate, unanalysable objects of the world.

The first point Wittgenstein considered comparatively unimportant. There are other cases of pictures, he suggested, where the elements don't look like what they represent: musical notation does not look like notes, nor does phonetic notation look like phonemes, since notes and phonemes, being sounds, don't look like anything. The essence of the pictorial relation between phonetic signs and sounds is the existence of rules for deriving one from the other (TLP 4.014, 4.0141). This example is helpful, but not altogether clear since it is not obvious what is supposed to be a picture of what. The derivation rules connect score, record and sound: is each supposed to be a picture of the other? Surely not: score and record must surely be supposed to be a picture of the sound: it is the sound, at least, which we are most interested in. But Wittgenstein does not here make clear what, in addition to A's having logical structure, and pictorial relation to B, is needed for A to be a picture of B rather than the other way round. It must be that the pictorial relationship which makes the picture into a picture (the correlation of the elements) is in some way a one-way correlation; but this is not, at this stage of Wittgenstein's life, at all spelt out. The problem is indeed aggravated when he says (in order to dispel the apparent lack of similarity between picture and proposition) that the pictorial nature of the proposition would become clear if we imagined a proposition made up not of words but of spatial objects, whose spatial relationship expressed its sense (TLP 3.1431). Given suitable conventions (e.g. using an inkpot as my name, and the table as the name of my chair) that this inkpot is on this table may express that I sit in this chair (NB 98). In such a case one is very curious to know exactly how the convention establishes which is to be the picturing and which the pictured fact. By the time Wittgenstein came to investigate such questions he had had to modify the picture theory in significant ways.

The second point was even in the *Tractatus* treated as an important one. The non-pictorial appearance, Wittgenstein thought, is due to the fact that the real form of a proposition need not be its apparent one; its surface grammar may not be the same as its logical grammar (TLP 3.325, 4.0031). If a proposition were fully articulated, as it already is in thought and as it would be if written out in an ideal language, then to each element of the propositional sign would correspond a single object in the world (TLP 3.2). Thus its pictorial nature would leap to the eye.

It became one of the important tasks of the *Tractatus* to spell out the relationship between such a language and ordinary language, to indicate how everyday propositions were to be analysed so as to remove their non-pictorial appearance, and to describe the structure of the world in so far as the nature of language revealed this as a precondition for the possibility of propositions. To these topics – which constitute the metaphysics of logical atomism – the next chapter will be devoted, and in considering them we shall see more fully what the *Tractatus* took to be the essence of a proposition.

CHAPTER 5

The Metaphysics of Logical Atomism

Though most of the *Tractatus* is devoted to the nature of language, its earliest pages contain a series of pronouncements about the world. Both historically and logically the theses about the world follow those about language, but their dependence is masked by their presentation at the beginning of the book. In this chapter I will try to set out the theses and make explicit their relation to the logical matters we have been discussing hitherto. For convenience, and following Russell, I shall call Wittgenstein's metaphysical doctrine 'logical atomism' though this is not a name he used himself and its use should not disguise the differences between the thought of the two philosophers.

To each pair of contradictory propositions, there corresponds one and only one fact: the fact which makes one of them true and the other false. The totality of such facts is the world (TLP 1.1). Facts may be positive or negative: a positive fact is the existence of a state of affairs; a negative fact is the non-existence of a state of affairs (TLP 2.06). A state of affairs (a *Sachverhalt*) is a combination of objects or things. An object is essentially a possible constituent of a state of affairs (TLP 2.011), and its possibility of occurring in combination with other objects in states of affairs is its nature (TLP 2.0123), its internal properties (TLP 2.01231) and its form (TLP 2.0141). Since every object contains within its nature all the possibilities for its combination with other objects, if any object is given, then all objects are given (TLP 5.524), and if all objects are given then all possible states of affairs are given (TLP 2.0124).

Objects are simple, without parts, but they can combine into complexes (TLP 2.02–2.0201). They are ungenerable and indestructible, because any possible world must contain the same objects as this one; change is only an alteration in the configuration of objects (TLP 2.022–2.0231, 2.0271). Objects may differ from each other in logical form (i.e. they can enter into different possible states of affairs) or in external properties (i.e. they are *de facto* in different actual states of affairs), or they may be merely numerically distinct (i.e. though indiscernible they are not identical) (TLP 2.0233–2.02331). The objects make up the unalterable and subsistent form, substance and content of the world (TLP 2.021, 2.023, 2.024, 2.025).

Objects combine into states of affairs, in which they stand in a determinate relation to one another 'like the links of a chain' (TLP 2.023). The way in which they are connected is the structure of the state of affairs (TLP 2.032). The form of a state of affairs, we are told, is the possibility of its structure (TLP 2.033).

States of affairs, we are told, are independent of one another (TLP 2.061); from the existence or non-existence of one of them it is impossible to infer the existence or non-existence of another. Since facts are the existence and non-existence of states of affairs, it follows that facts too are independent of each other (TLP 1.21). The totality of facts, of reality, is the world.

These first pages of the *Tractatus* are extremely obscure. Pronouncement predominates over argument and technical terms are piled up and reduplicated (form and content = substance; facts = reality; essence = nature = form). The criterion for identity of states of affairs is left fatally undetermined, and, most baffling of all, no examples are given of objects. To be sure, Wittgenstein having said that objects are in a space of possible states of affairs, goes on to say 'A speck in the visual field, though it need not be red, must have some colour: it is, so to speak, surrounded by colour-space. Tones must have *some* pitch, objects of the sense of touch *some* degree of hardness, and so on' (TLP 2.0131). But it is clear that these are analogies and not instances. Just as a speck in the visual field must be in a colour-space (i.e. have some position on the spectrum), so an object must be in a logical space (i.e. have the possibility of combining with others) (TLP 2.013, 1.13).

Logical space, it should be explained, is the sum of the possible-and-existing states of affairs plus the possible-and-non-existing states of affairs (TLP 1.12–1.13, 3.42). Specks in the visual field, sounds, tactile feelings and other immediate data of experience which philosophers mean when they talk about sense-data are clearly not indestructible objects common to all possible worlds. Nor are the objects whose names figure in the logicians' standard propositions – men, dogs, tables and chairs ... We are left to make what we can of the cryptic remark 'Space, time, and colour are forms of objects' (TLP 2.0251).

The lack of examples is not accidental. Wittgenstein believed in the existence of simple objects and atomic states of affairs not because he thought he could give instances of them, but because he thought that they must exist as the correlates in the world for the names and elementary propositions of a fully analysed language. Why he thought this, we shall see in a moment. But in order to illuminate what he says about objects and states of affairs, it may be well to try to give a concrete interpretation for his theses. I suggest that the game of chess, importantly modified, provides as near as we can get to a model for the way the world is conceived in the *Tractatus*.

Imagine that the objects of the world are the chess-pieces and the squares of the chessboard. Then states of affairs will be the relations between the pieces and the squares. That a certain piece is or is not on a certain square will be a positive or negative fact. The world, all that is the case, will be the position on the board at any given time. In order to represent the indestructibility of the *Tractatus* objects we must imagine the rules of chess altered so that it is not permitted to *take* pieces. With this alteration, we can interpret many of the early propositions of the *Tractatus* in terms of our example.

The world will be, as the *Tractatus* says, the totality of facts, not things (it is the position, not just the board plus the pieces). Logical space will be chess-space, i.e. the set of possibilities allowed by the rules of chess (TLP 1.13). It is essential to the chess-pieces that they should be possible holders of positions on the board, and to the squares that they should be possible positions for chess-pieces. That is all there is to them essentially. In the rules nothing is accidental: if a piece can occur in a state of affairs (e.g. if a particular bishop can stand on a black square) then this is written into the rules for its use (TLP 2.012). The rules for the positioning of the pieces give their logical form; pieces may differ in logical form (a knight from a rook) or be merely numerically different (two pawns). The internal properties of pieces (e.g. a bishop's being able to move diagonally) may be contrasted with their external ones (e.g. a bishop's being now on QR4). A king, away from the board and the other pieces, is unimaginable: chess-pieces cannot be thought of away from the rules and the game (TLP 2.0121). The chess-pieces are simple: of course actual chess-pieces are made of wood or ivory and have shapes and parts; but so far as the rules go their composition is accidental and hard atoms would do as well.

Where the analogy limps is that the atomic facts of chess are not independent of each other in the way that *Tractatus* states of affairs are (TLP 1.13, 2.061). This is because two pieces cannot be on the same square, so that from the fact that the king is on KR1 there follows the non-existence of many states of affairs (e.g. of the queen's-being-on-KR1); and again because one piece cannot be on two squares, so that from the same fact there follows the non-existence of many other states of affairs (e.g. of the king's being on QR1). Moreover, the rules of chess govern the positioning of the pieces indirectly, since they govern directly the moves in the game, which are changes from one state of affairs to another rather than states of affairs themselves. The *Tractatus* has very little to say about change.

Despite these defects, the chess analogy throws light not only on Wittgenstein's view of the world but also on his account of the relation between the world and language. The report of a chess-game can be given in such a way that it conforms to Wittgenstein's picture theory of the proposition. The normal way of reporting a game of chess is by reporting the moves (as 'P–K4' reports that a pawn moved to K4). But this method, of course, presumes in the reader a knowledge of the opening position for a game: it is in fact a method by which one is given a recipe for constructing the $n + 1$th position from the nth position. Another possible, clumsier, but more complete way of reporting a game would be to describe the position of pieces after each move. And this could be done, most obviously, by the sort of picture of a chessboard which is used in setting chess problems, as illustrated by the fragment below.

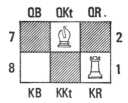

Here the description is by a picture; the picture of the bishop represents the bishop, the symbol for the rook represents the rook and the symbols for the squares represent the squares; that the symbol for the bishop is *within* the symbol for QKt7 represents the bishop's being *on* QKt7.

Here the two-dimensional relation between the symbols represents the three-dimensional relation on the chessboard: two-dimensionality is its representational form. But it would be possible for the report to be less obviously pictorial: e.g. we might report the same fragmentary position as above in an obvious notation thus: WR/KR1 and BB/QKt7. The three-dimensional nature of our chess-sets is itself, of course, inessential to the game: what is essential to the game is that the elements corresponding to the board and pieces should have the same logical form (same possibilities of combination) as ours do. This logical form is (both in Wittgenstein's theory and in fact) something which any apparatus for reporting chess must share. A single stationary uniform red ball, for instance, is not going to enable anyone to report a game of chess. But it will be a different matter if he is allowed to bounce the ball – say, once for a pawn, twice for a knight; a hundred times for QR1, a hundred and one for QR2 and so on. The bouncing-system, provided it has the same number of possibilties as there are possible chess situations, will have the logical multiplicity, the logical form, necessary for it to be a picture of the game of chess.

There are reasons to believe that the propositions which make up Wittgenstein's logical atomism form an incoherent whole: if so, then it is not too alarming that it should be so difficult to think of examples to illustrate them. What is important is rather to understand the logical reasons which led him to postulate the existence of simple indestructible atoms and atomic states of affairs. He summarized one reason himself in the *Investigations* as follows.

One is tempted to make an objection against what is ordinarily called a name. It can be put like this: *a name ought really to signify a simple*. And for this one might perhaps give the following reasons: The word 'Excalibur', say, is a proper name in the ordinary sense. The sword Excalibur consists of parts combined in a particular way. If they are combined differently Excalibur does not exist. But it is clear that the sentence 'Excalibur has a sharp blade' makes *sense* whether Excalibur is still whole or is broken up. But if 'Excalibur' is the name of an object, this object no longer exists when Excalibur is broken in pieces; and as no object would then correspond to the name it would have no meaning. But then the sentence 'Excalibur has a sharp blade' would contain a word that had no meaning, and hence the sentence would be nonsense. But it does make sense; so there must always be something corresponding to the words of which it consists. So the word 'Excalibur' must disappear when the sense is analysed and its place be taken by words which name simples. It will be reasonable to call these words the real names. (PI I, 39)

Wittgenstein was to reject this argument later on the grounds that it was false to say that a name ceased to have meaning when its bearer was destroyed (PI I, 40) and that the notion of 'simplicity', in abstraction from particular contexts, was empty (PI I, 47). But it is worth while to trace in the *Notebooks* and the *Tractatus* the genesis of the argument summarized and criticized in the *Investigations*.

The basic consideration which lay behind Russell's theory of descriptions and behind the atomism of the *Tractatus* is this. Whether a sentence has meaning or not is a matter of logic. Whether particular things exist or not is a matter of experience. But logic is prior to all experience. Therefore whether a sentence has meaning or not can never depend on whether particular things exist. The three premises of this argument are plausible, and were and are widely held. They are, for instance, implicit in the almost universal rejection of the ontological argument for the existence of God.

If this counter-argument is accepted the conclusion lays down a condition which any system of logic must meet. To meet this condition Russell's theory offers us a way of talking about any describable object which will make sense whether or not it exists. But the theory of descriptions involves the use of quantifiers, and quantified sentences presuppose simpler sentences containing names instead of quantifiers. 'For some x, x is F' is taken to mean: some sentence in which the predicate F is attached to a name is true. So if the condition above is to be met, there must be some provision to secure that the names which are to occupy the argument places in the quantified propositions cannot fail to have reference. Russell attempted to secure this by stipulating that they should refer to objects which were epistemologically guaranteed (objects of immediate acquaintance, e.g. sense-data); Wittgenstein by having them refer to objects which were metaphysically guaranteed, indestructible simples.

As has been said, Wittgenstein admired Russell's theory of descriptions, but his own application of it involved considerable modification and adaptation. For one thing, Wittgenstein's convention that identity should be expressed by identity of sign instead of a sign for identity meant that the clauses in Russell's analysis which secure uniqueness needed some alteration. 'There is one and only one king of France' is translated by Russell as 'For some x, x is king of France, and for all y, if y is king of France, then y is identical with x.' Wittgenstein writes this, without the identity sign, as 'For some x, x is king of France; and it is not the case that for some x and for some y, both x is king of France and y is king of France' (TLP 5.5321). On this pattern, 'The king of France is bald' will be 'For some x, x is king of France and x is bald; and it is not the case that for some x and for some y, both x is king of France and y is king of France.'

Unlike Russell, Wittgenstein was particularly interested in descriptions formed by the use of two-place predicates. In Russell's analysis above, '. . . is the king of France' is treated as a one-place predicate; but clearly it can be further analysed so that 'France' appears as a name, and '. . . is the king of . . .' as a two-place predicate. The analysis will then be, on the *Tractatus* pattern, 'For some x, xRa; and not, for some x and for some y, xRa and yRa.' This pattern of analysis can be extended in two ways: we can consider the analysis not only of expressions of the form description–relation–name (like 'the man who rules France') but also of the form description–relation–description (like 'the anointed of the Lord' or 'the man in the moon') and even of the form name–relation–name. Examples of the last form are not easy to come by in ordinary language, but one was given above on p. 39: 'Austria-Hungary', regarded as a definite description of the country which consists of the union of Austria with Hungary. In his *Notebooks*, on 5 September 1914, Wittgenstein jotted down a notation for such sentences using '$\varphi(a)$' in the way I have hitherto used 'a is F'.

$$\varphi(a) . \varphi(b) . aRb = \text{Def. } \varphi[aRb]$$

In this notation the expression in square brackets '[aRb]'

means the object consisting of a standing-in-the-relation-R to b – in the case in point, Austria-Hungary. It was clearly sentences analysed along these lines which he had in mind when in the *Investigations* he criticized the idea that 'My broom is in the corner' means 'My broomstick is in the corner, and my brush is in the corner, and the broomstick is fitted in the brush' (PI I, 60).

Thus in the *Tractatus* (2.0201) he wrote, echoing a remark from the 'Notes on Logic' (NB 99) 'Every statement about complexes can be analysed into a statement about their constituent parts, and into those propositions which completely describe the complexes.' Wittgenstein's adaptations have perhaps taken us far from Russell's original theory of descriptions, but the fundamental element remains in common, that a proposition containing a description of something that does not exist is treated as a false, not a meaningless, proposition (TLP 3.24).

It is not difficult, and it is in accordance with philosophical tradition, to accept the idea that names are simple signs in the sense that they are signs which do not have significant parts. But when Wittgenstein talks of names as 'simple signs' he means rather that they are signs *for* simple objects, as we saw in the passage above from the *Investigations* and in TLP 3.2–3.303. Why, we may ask, can there not be simple signs for non-simple objects, as indeed all the names in English seem to be? The *Investigations* recalled an argument that, if so, some meaningful propositions would turn out meaningless. The *Tractatus* argues that if simple signs denote complex objects then the propositions in which they occur would have an indeterminate sense (TLP 3.24; PTLP 3.20106; TLP 3.23). This argument is obscure: it is not clear from these passages what 'indeterminacy of sense' is, nor what is wrong with it. The argument is spelt out at slightly greater length in the *Prototractatus*.

The analysis of signs must come to an end at some point, because if signs are to express anything at all, meaning must belong to them in a way which is once and for all complete . . . if a proposition is to have sense, the syntactical employment of each of its parts must have been established in advance. For example, it cannot occur to one only subsequently that a certain proposition follows from it. Before a proposition can have a sense, it must be completely settled what propositions follow from it. (PTLP 3.20102–3; NB 64)

The theme 'analysis must come to an end' is a recurrent one in the *Notebooks*, and throughout 1914 Wittgenstein worried about the relation between logic and analysis. Is logic really concerned with the analysability of the functions with which it works (NB 4)? Wittgenstein found it hard to answer this question.

On the one hand, Russell's work had shown that analysis was possible, and analysis seemed necessary since it seemed impossible to construct the syntax of unanalysed subject-predicate sentences without knowing their analysis. For instance, we cannot tell what follows from a sentence without analysing it, just as Russell's analysis was needed to make clear that 'The king of France exists' follows from 'The king of France is wise' (NB 4). Indeed the task of philosophy seems to be precisely the giving of such analyses (NB 12). Typical philosophical problems show this. Is 'A is good' a subject-predicate proposition? Is 'A is brighter than B' a relational proposition? Is a point in the visual field a simple object (NB 3)?

On the other hand it is not at all clear how such questions are to be answered. Self-evidence is very dubious, and logic cannot depend on experience, so that one cannot have to depend on acquaintance with the fact corresponding to a proposition in order to know how the proposition is to be analysed (NB 3). It seems that if analysis is to be possible at all whatever is essential for it must be given by the unanalysed propositional sign itself (NB 3). But, if this is so, then analysis seems to be superfluous. After all, if we can identify unanalysed subject-predicate sentences, must we not already know what the logic of subject-predicate sentences is? For an apparent subject-predicate sentence is one which *appears to have* the logic which a completely analysed subject-predicate sentence *does have*.

So it seems that all the logician has to do is to investigate this logic, and not worry about analysability. We can, after all, apply logic to ordinary propositions like 'Socrates is a man' without knowing what structure is possessed by Socrates or mortality (NB 69). Indeed, questions of analysability, like questions of type, cannot really be posed: it cannot be said either of a thing or of a complex that it is not further analysable, for the expression 'not further analysable' is, as Wittgenstein puts it, 'on the Index' (NB 9). Still, the nagging question remains: how does what we try to express by this get shown? Perhaps the answer is that analysability shows itself simply by our providing further definitions; but that such analysability should not prevent us from treating a proposition exactly as if it were unanalysable (NB 10).

But how is it possible for logic to be applied to unanalysed subject-predicate or relational propositions (NB 66, 69)? To apply logic to a proposition I must know the syntactical treatment of its names. But in order to know this I must know the composition of what the proposition is about: 'The syntactical employment of the names completely characterizes the form of the complex objects which they denote' (NB 61). For instance the sense, and indeed the form, of the proposition 'This watch is shiny' depends on the complexity of what I mean by 'this watch' (NB 61).

Does this mean that in order to mean something by 'The watch is shiny' I have to know how the watch is in fact constructed? Apparently not: when I say that the watch is not in the drawer, it does not follow from what I say that some wheel, which I did not know to be in the watch, is not in the drawer (NB 64). That is not something which is said in the proposition, not something that belongs to its sense; but if it is to tell us anything at all, then it must be clear what it asserts and what it leaves open. 'If a proposition tells us something, then it must be a picture of reality just as it is, and a complete picture at that.'

There will, of course, also be something that the proposition does *not* say – but what it does say it says completely and it must be susceptible of sharp definition (NB 61).

One thing that analysis will bring out is how far the complexity of an object determines the sense of a proposition and how far possibilities of different complexities are left open (NB 63–4). Where something is left open, generalizations will appear (i.e. expressions containing quantifiers, as in Russell's theory). 'What I do not know, I do not know, but the proposition must show me what I know' (NB 63). In this way a proposition like 'This watch is lying on the table' can contain a lot of indefiniteness, vagueness, and yet have a perfectly clear sense (NB 69, 70). It might be, for instance, equivalent to: there is a complex of wheels, springs, hands and other parts connected together in some way or other, and lying on the table.

Thus the sense of the proposition 'The watch is lying on the table' is more complicated than the proposition itself. There is enormously much added in thought to each proposition and not said (NB 70). For instance, no date is given in the proposition (NB 66). But there is nothing wrong in leaving such things unsaid; one can make use of the enormously complicated conventions of our language (NB 70). Even such a proposition is a clear statement of something definite (NB 4); it has a sense without the definitions of its component parts being attached to it (NB 46), and what we mean by it must be precise (NB 68). The propositions that human beings use have a sense just as they are and are not waiting for future analysis to acquire a sense (NB 62). Analysis only brings out a sense already there.

Yet, against this, if the proposition 'The watch is lying on the table' has a clear sense, then I must, in every possible set of circumstances, be able to say whether the proposition is true or false. There could, however, be positions of the watch in which I would not be certain whether to say it was lying on the table. All this would show, Wittgenstein suggests, is that I did not know what I meant in general by 'lying'; that what I meant on *this* occasion was some particular relation which the watch actually has to the table, and which I might indicate by pointing to 'the appropriate complex' (NB 68, 70). This does not seem to be a very satisfactory answer: if it is the watch–table complex itself which gets pointed to, then it seems that Wittgenstein is allowing a fact to be a picture of itself. Moreover, suppose the proposition is false: in that case there will not be the appropriate complex to point to to give the proposition its meaning. But perhaps by 'the appropriate complex' Wittgenstein does not mean the complex I am talking about, but some other complex which is appropriately related.

It cannot, I think, be said that Wittgenstein resolved these problems in his *Notebooks*, and the pages in which he worried over them are among the most difficult he ever wrote. There seems to be a persisting ambiguity in the notion of a complete analysis of a complex. Does it mean an analysis in which the proposition would contain as many elements as the state of affairs it depicts (as suggested by the entries for 12 October 1914, 20 October 1914, 18 December 1914, etc.)? Or does it mean an analysis in which the proposition would contain as many elements as I know there to be in the state of affairs (as suggested by NB 64)? If the former then it seems as if I cannot utter the simplest proposition without a fantastic amount of information about the composition of the universe; if the latter then it seems irrelevant to discuss, as Wittgenstein does, whether spatial objects are infinitely divisible. Perhaps the difference between the two was masked for him because he frequently chose as an example of something that might be a simple a point in the visual field. The visual field being a phenomenal item, what there is in the visual field is the same as what I know to be in the visual field; and so the question whether there are infinitely many points in the visual field (NB 64–5) is the same as the question whether I see infinitely many points. But the same is not true of his other example of candidates for simple objects: the material particles of physics (NB 20, 67).

In the *Tractatus* he does not so much resolve as skirt round the problems left unsolved in the *Notebooks*. This makes it surprising that he should there be so emphatic that in order to secure definiteness of sense there must be simple objects – and objects that are metaphysically, not just epistemologically simple (TLP 2.0211, etc.). He opts for one side of the constant dialectical argument. In the fully analysed proposition there are as many names as there are objects (TLP 3.2), and every proposition has one and only one complete analysis.

We are given no information in the *Tractatus* as to what kind of thing simple objects are – specks in the visual field and the material points are no longer put forward as candidates. It is not even clear whether the simples would be particular individuals or universal types. Among the examples listed in the recantation in the *Investigations* both categories appear: individuals such as bits of wood, molecules, atoms, colour-patches, segments of curves; universals such as colours, type-letters (PII, 47–8, 58). But this lack of clarity accords with Wittgenstein's insistence that it is only *a priori* that he knows of the existence of simples, not that he can give any examples. The question 'Are there unanalysable subject-predicate propositions?' cannot even be asked (TLP 4.1274).

To states of affairs which are concatenations of simple objects there correspond elementary propositions which assert the existence of states of affairs; elementary propositions are concatenations of names for simple objects (TLP 4.21–4.221). The world can be completely described by listing all elementary propositions, and then listing which of them are true and which false (TLP 4.26). For the true elementary propositions will record all the positive facts, and the false elementary propositions will correspond to all the negative facts, and the totality of facts is the world (TLP 2.06, 1.1).

Since we cannot give any examples of names for simples, we cannot give any examples of elementary propositions either, since these consist of concatenations of names. None the less, Wittgenstein believed, all propositions – all the propositions of ordinary language, that is, that are genuine propositions, and not pieces of nonsense, or attempts to say what can only be shown – are truth-functions of elementary propositions (TLP 4.4, 5). Once I am given all elementary propositions I can simply ask what propositions I can construct out of them, and then I will have all the propositions there can be (TLP 4.51).

It is natural to understand this as meaning that all propositions can be constructed out of the elementary propositions plus the logical constants 'and', 'or', etc., as 'p or q' is constructed out of 'p' 'or' and 'q'. But Wittgenstein would regard this as misleading, as suggesting that the logical constants added something that was not already there in the elementary propositions. The way in which a truth-function of elementary propositions is produced out of the elementary propositions is an *operation* (TLP 5.3). 'Operation' is Wittgenstein's technical term for what has to be done to one proposition to make another out of it (TLP 5.23). Negation is an operation (TLP 5.2341; NB 39). It does not, of course, consist simply in adding the word 'not' or a twiddle to a proposition; given different conventions either of those procedures might have quite a different effect (TLP 5.512). It consists in reversing the sense of a proposition – changing all the 'T's in its truth-table to 'F's and vice versa. If, as Wittgenstein suggests, we take the truth-tables themselves as propositional signs (TLP 4.44), then all truth-operations (i.e. all operations producing truth-functions out of elementary propositions (TLP 5.234)) can be regarded as modifications of the pattern of 'T's and 'F's in the table. Indeed every truth-function can be expressed as the result of successive applications to elementary propositions of a single pattern of modification, as Wittgenstein showed, in the following manner.

Suppose that we write '$N(p)$' for the negation of 'p', '$N(p, q)$' for the negation of 'p' and of 'q', '$N(p, q, r)$' for the negation of 'p', of 'q' and of 'r', and so on for any number of propositions in the brackets (TLP 5.502–5.52). This will represent an operation which consists in constructing a truth-table with 'F's in every line but the last. We can see this if we construct the truth-tables in the normal way.

p	N(p)		p	q	N(p, q)		p	q	r	N(p, q, r)
T	F		T	T	F		T	T	T	F
F	T		F	T	F		F	T	T	F
			T	F	F		T	F	T	F
			F	F	T		F	F	T	F
							T	T	F	F
							F	T	F	F
							T	F	F	F
							F	F	F	T

This shows an operation which can be applied to any number of propositions. But it does not make it at all clear how *every* proposition is a result of successive applications of the operation N(. . .) to elementary propositions, or how the use of this operation gives us the most general form of transition from one proposition to another (TLP 6.001ff.).

We can see this better if we consider Wittgenstein's observation that all possible truth-functions of a given number of elementary propositions can be set out in a simple schema (TLP 5.101). There are, for instance, sixteen possible truth-functions of two propositions, as can be seen from the following table.

p	q	1	2	3	4	5	6	7	8	9	10	11	12	13	14	15	16
T	T	T	F	T	T	T	F	F	F	T	T	T	F	F	F	T	F
F	T	T	T	F	T	T	F	T	T	F	F	T	F	F	F	T	F
T	F	T	T	T	F	T	T	F	T	F	T	F	F	T	F	F	F
F	F	T	T	T	T	F	T	T	F	T	F	F	T	F	F	F	F

Some of these are familiar – No. 5, for instance, is 'p or q' and No. 15 is 'p and q'. No. 1 and No. 16 are the 'degenerate' truth-functions, tautology and contradiction – the truth-functions which are true for all, and no, values of their arguments respectively. But for our present purposes the most interesting ones are 10 and 11, for these columns, as will be seen, are the same as those for p and for q; so that the symbol constructed by this truth-table presents the proposition 'q' as a truth-function of the two arguments 'p' and 'q'. This shows that we do not need to have truth-tables of different sizes to represent propositions of different complexity. Indeed, if there are n elementary propositions, then a truth-table with 2^n lines will contain in it 2^{n^n} propositions, whether elementary or composite, just as in the table above the four lines give room for all the sixteen possible truth-functions of two arguments.

Let us now imagine that we have a universe – as Wittgenstein would say, a logical space – with n possible states of affairs. Then our truth-table with 2^n lines will contain every possible proposition about that universe (it will also, of course, contain tautologies and contradictions, which are not strictly speaking 'about' that universe, but this does not matter). Among the propositions on the right-hand side will be the elementary propositions, each now expressed as truth-functions of all the elementary propositions there are. Two things will be true of the elementary propositions thus expressed. (1) Each elementary proposition will contain the name of all the objects there are in the universe, for if we are given all the elementary propositions we are given all the names, and each elementary proposition is expressed as a function of all the elementary propositions. (2) Each elementary proposition will appear as a conjunction of itself and a tautology – for instance, in the table above, 'p', as a truth-function of 'p' and 'q' is equivalent to 'p and (q or not-q)' (cf. TLP 4.465).

It remains to show how every proposition which appears in the table can be reached by the repeated application of the operation N to the elementary propositions. Let us consider the simple case of the table with only four lines and two elementary propositions. To apply the operation to a single proposition, one writes 'T' for 'F' and 'F' for 'T'. To apply it to two propositions one writes 'T' whenever two 'F's occur and otherwise 'F'. To apply it to three propositions one writes

'T' whenever three 'F's occur, otherwise 'F'. So we start with the two elementary propositions 10 ('*p*') and 11 ('*q*'). Applying the operation N to 10 we get 7 ('not-*p*'), and applying it to 11 we get 6 ('not-*q*'). If we apply it to 10 and 11, we get 12 ('neither *p* nor *q*'); if we apply it to 12, we get 5 ('*p* or *q*'). If we apply it to 6 and 7 we get 15 ('*p* and *q*'); if we apply it to 15, we get 2 ('not both *p* and *q*'). If we apply N to 2 and 15 (or, for that matter, to 10 and 7, or to 11 and 6, or to 5 and 12) we get 16 (contradiction); if we apply it to 16, we get 1 (tautology). If we apply it to 12 and 15 we get 8 ('*p* or *q* but not both'), and then applying it to 8 we get 9 ('*p* if and only if *q*'). We are now left with just four to get: 3, 4, 13 and 14. One way to get 13 would be to apply N to the trio 9, 11 and 12. 13 is '*p* and not *q*'; the negation of 13, reached by one application of N to it, is 4 ('if *p* then *q*'). 14 ('*q* and not *p*') can be reached by applying N to 9 and 10, and from it by one application of N we can reach its negation 3 ('if *q* then *p*'). Thus our task is complete, and each of the sixteen propositions can be shown as a result of successive applications of N to the elementary propositions 10 and 11 or to the results of previous applications of N to them. Thus, if we write an 'N' for each application of the operation, 7 is N(10), 6 is N(11), 15 is N(N(10), N(11)), 2 is NN(N(10), N(11)) and 16 is N((N(10), N(11)), NN(N(10), N(11))). 16 is also, more simply, N((10), N(10)). As this last example shows, the same proposition may be reached in more than one way and expressed in more than one way by the N notation: in a case like double negation, for instance, operations may vanish, in the sense that the iterated application of an operation will bring one back to where one started, to the base of the operation.

We have shown informally how the truth-functions of two arguments can be constructed by means of the operation N from the elementary propositions. This does not amount to a formal proof of this possibility even in the simple case of the four-line truth-table, still less for truth-tables of larger size. Still less does it offer a proof, or even a suggestion, as to how the applications of the operation can be arranged in a formal series as Wittgenstein says they can (TLP 6; but cf. TLP 6.001). Neither does Wittgenstein offer any proof. He merely says: 'It is obvious that we can easily express how propositions may be constructed with this operation, and how they may not be constructed with it; so it must be possible to find an exact expression for this' (TLP 5.503), and 'Every proposition is a result of successive applications to elementary propositions of the operation' (TLP 6.001). So far as concerned truth-functions Wittgenstein's confidence was no doubt based on the fact that the logician Sheffer had shown that all truth-functional connectives were reducible to joint denial, which has affinities with Wittgenstein's 'N'. (His work is mentioned in the 'Notes on Logic', NB 102.)

Wittgenstein, however, went further, and maintained not just that every truth-function of elementary propositions could be constructed out of them by means of repeated application of the operation N, but that every proposition was a truth-function of elementary propositions, so that the formula for constructing truth-functional propositions out of elementary propositions was the form of propositions in general (TLP 5.3). This is a very surprising claim. It cannot, of course, be contested directly. Since neither Wittgenstein nor a critic can point to any example of an elementary proposition, one does not know quite how to assess the claim that a proposition like 'Snow is white' is a truth-function of elementary propositions. But it seems possible to contest the claim indirectly by pointing out that propositions of ordinary language seem able to occur within other propositions of ordinary language without doing so truth-functionally. Thus 'Snow is white', besides occurring truth-functionally in 'It is not the case that snow is white' occurs non-truth functionally in 'It is possible that snow is white' or 'James believes that snow is white' (TLP 5.541, etc.). Moreover, 'For all x, x is white', though related to 'Snow is white' (it entails it), does not seem to be a truth-function of it. Despite all this, Wittgenstein said 'In the general propositional form propositions occur in other propositions only as bases of truth-operations' (TLP 5.54).

This theory involves, first of all, treating the quantifiers as truth-functions, and therefore as the result of applications of the operation N to elementary propositions. In the bracket following the N, in Wittgenstein's notation, are given the propositions to which the operation is to be applied. These propositions can be listed, as for instance in 'N(snow is white, soot is white)', which is equivalent to 'Neither snow is white nor soot is white' or, if you like, 'Neither snow nor soot is white.' This is the procedure we have adopted hitherto, except that we have been using schematic letters instead of English propositions. But the propositions to which the operation is to be applied could be indicated in another way: we could replace a list by an indication that all propositions of a certain pattern are to be included. For instance, we might write N(x is white) to mean that the operation was to be applied to all propositions formed out of an appropriate noun and the predicate 'is white' (TLP 5.501). It would then be equivalent to N(snow is white, soot is white, gold is white . . .) which again would be equivalent to 'Neither snow nor soot nor gold nor . . . are white'. In fact, Wittgenstein says, it would be equivalent to 'It is not the case that for some x, x is white' or 'For no x, x is white' (TLP 5.52), i.e. 'Nothing is white.' Since the universal quantifier 'for all x' can be defined as 'not, for some x, not . . .' Wittgenstein has thus introduced quantified propositions as truth-functions of elementary propositions in accordance with his general principle. The universal quantifier differs from the particular quantifier by being a different truth-function of the same propositions; they differ from the propositional connectives solely in the way in which the propositions to which the truth-operation is to be applied are specified. The generality is shown by the 'x' in the argument place (TLP 5.523).

What Wittgenstein's method amounts to is this: universally quantified statements are taken as long conjunctions, and existentially quantified statements are taken as long disjunctions.

And in some cases this method seems reasonable enough. 'All the Apostles were Jews' may fairly be taken as equivalent to 'Peter was a Jew and James was a Jew and John was a Jew . . . and Judas was a Jew' and 'There was an Apostle who was a traitor' as 'Peter was a traitor or James was a traitor or John was a traitor . . . or Judas was a traitor.' But this seems reasonable because we are tacitly presupposing the knowledge that Peter, James, John, etc. are all the Apostles there are. If we wanted to make this explicit, we would have to do so by another quantified statement, e.g. 'Peter was an Apostle, and James was an Apostle . . . and Judas was an Apostle, *and no other object was an Apostle*' (cf. WWK 38). To render 'No other object was an Apostle' in the way in which we tried to render 'All the Apostles were Jews' one would have to list all the objects in the universe and deny, of each of them, that it was an Apostle. This, if the universe contains an infinite number of objects, may well be an impossible task. So it looks as if the viability of Wittgenstein's method turns on the finitude of the number of objects in the world, on whether the dots in a proposition such as 'N(snow is white, soot is white . . .)' are 'mere dots of laziness' which could be filled in had we but world enough and time, or are the mark of an infinite, unfillable gap.

If this is a fair statement of the case, it looks as if Wittgenstein is going to need an axiom of finitude in order to get quantification theory off the ground just as Russell needed an axiom of infinity to get number theory off the ground. And this seems a disquieting result for a system which grew out of dissatisfaction with *Principia*. Moreover, elsewhere in the *Tractatus* Wittgenstein treats it as an open question whether the world is finite; at least, he thinks it conceivable in some sense that every state of affairs might be composed of infinitely many objects (TLP 4.2211). Strictly speaking, of course, it is senseless to speak of the number of all objects (TLP 4.1272). What the axiom of infinity was meant to say would be expressed in a perspicuous language by there being an infinite number of names with different meanings (TLP 5.535). But if it is to be, in some sense, an open question, unsettleable by logic, how many names there are, it does not seem that Wittgenstein can consistently introduce a quantifier notation which will work only if the number of names is finite.

But is it fair to say that his notation does this? He does not, after all, say that the propositions to which the N-operation is to be applied in quantified propositions must be *listed*: this is how quantifiers differ from other truth-functional operations; the propositions are not listed, but given as all the values of a certain function. The totality of propositions (and therefore of names) occurs no more essentially in a quantified proposition than in an unquantified proposition. Every elementary proposition can be represented, as we have seen, as a truth-function or all elementary propositions (TLP 5.524). Every proposition carries with it the whole of logical space; neither truth-functional operators nor quantifiers introduce anything new (TLP 3.42).

In terms of the analogy with chess earlier introduced, we might say that, for Wittgenstein, every elementary proposition about the position of one piece on one square presupposes the whole chessboard and all the pieces. It does not, of course, *say* anything about the other pieces or squares (e.g. it does not say where the other pieces are) but as it only makes sense as part of the game of chess it presupposes the whole of 'chess space', of the board and the pieces and the rules. Any elementary proposition – e.g. that the king is on square K1 – could be represented as a conjunction of itself with a set of tautologies: e.g. 'The king is on K1 and either the queen is on Q1 or the queen is not on Q1 and either the king's bishop is on Q1 or the king's bishop is not on Q1 . . .' Since the number of pieces and squares is finite it would in this case be perfectly possible to construct in this way a proposition which said the same as the simple one 'K/K1' and yet which mentioned every piece and every square and every possible position. This would bring out quite clearly how the proposition determined only one place in logical space, and yet gave the whole of logical space. The tautologies compounding the proposition would make up, as it were, a logical scaffolding: the scaffolding by whose aid the picture is built up (TLP 3.42).

The fact that an elementary proposition p says the same (has the same truth-conditions) as the conjunction of itself with a tautology (p and q or not-q) was appealed to by Wittgenstein as showing that the truth-functional connectives do not add anything which is not already there in the elementary proposition. The same is true of all logical operations. Elementary propositions themselves contain all logical operations. For 'a is F' says the same thing as 'For some x, x is F, and $x =$ a.' The sole logical constant is what *all* propositions, by their very nature, have in common with one another. That is the general propositional form (TLP 5.47). So if Wittgenstein's system breaks down because we cannot assume that the number of objects is finite, it does so from the very beginning, and not just when quantifiers are introduced.

For Wittgenstein, then, the propositional connectives and the quantifiers are already present in the elementary propositions. What of identity, the third logical constant? The way in which this is present becomes clear if we recall from an earlier chapter[1] that, for Wittgenstein, in a perspicuous language a sign for identity would be replaced by identity of sign (TLP 5.53). In such a language anything which is now expressible by a conjunction of an elementary proposition and an identity statement would be expressible by an elementary proposition (TLP 5.531). Thus identity would enter into the elementary proposition as the one–one relation between sign and signified in a perspicuous language. Thus all the logical relations between propositions will be reducible to the possibility of their construction out of each other by the N-operation. The rules for this construction will be what they have in common with each other, the general propositional form (TLP 5.47).

But does not the N-operation presuppose truth-tables, containing 'T's and 'F's? What do these letters stand for?

1. Cf. p. 51 above.

Unless they can be dispensed with in the way that the logical constants can, Wittgenstein cannot be said to have succeeded in showing that there are no logical constants and that molecular propositions say nothing that is not said by the elementary propositions. 'It is clear' Wittgenstein says (TLP 4.441) 'that a complex of the signs "F" and "T" has no object (or complex of objects) corresponding to it.' This is because truth and falsehood are not accidental, extra, properties of a proposition which are added on to its having meaning; to have meaning means to be either true or false, and the being either true or false constitutes the relation of the proposition to reality which is meant by saying that it has sense (NB 112). To determine the sense of the proposition is to determine in what circumstances it is true (TLP 4.063). It is, of course, important that the truth-table contains only the two values 'T' and 'F' and no third value. But that every proposition is either true or false is not, according to Wittgenstein, a piece of substantial information, on a par with (e.g.) 'All roses are either white or red' (TLP 6.111). It is something which is part of the nature of proposition, like the familiar postulate of determinateness of sense.

We must make a distinction, however, between the 'T's and 'F's which occur in the truth-tables under the molecular propositions and those which occur under the elementary propositions, since the 'T's and 'F's under the molecular propositions – or rather the table of which they are part – actually determine the sense of the molecular propositions, given the sense of elementary propositions; but the table does not determine their sense, and the 'T's and 'F's under them presuppose that it is already determined. This is done, not by comparison with any other proposition, but by the rules for the simple signs of which they are composed, plus the manner of their composition, as set out in the picture theory. It seems, then, that if Wittgenstein's account of the nature of the proposition is to be complete, the explanation of the general form of proposition in terms of the N-operator needs to be supplemented with an account of the form of elementary propositions.

'In giving the general form of a proposition,' Wittgenstein said in 1914 'you have to explain what kind of ways of putting together symbols for things and relations will correspond to the things having those relations in reality' (NB 112).

In the *Tractatus* Wittgenstein says that to give the general propositional form one must give 'a description of the propositions of *any* sign-language *whatsoever* in such a way that every possible sense can be expressed by a symbol satisfying the description, and every symbol satisfying the description can express a sense' (TLP 4.5). He then goes on to say, rather disappointingly, 'The general form of a proposition is: This is how things stand.' It is hard to see how this is a description of a symbol at all, and harder to see how it matches the account of the general form of proposition given in TLP 6 in terms of the operation N. However, 'This is how things stand' is probably better translated 'This state of affairs exists', so that Wittgenstein is here saying the same as at TLP 4.21 'An elementary proposition asserts the existence of a state of affairs' (*Sachverhalt*). In giving this as a general form of proposition Wittgenstein does not mean to say that all propositions are elementary propositions: in the *Prototractatus*, having given the general form of proposition, he goes on at once to say 'This form must be contained in all propositions in some way or other'. (PTLP 4.303). TLP 4.5 and TLP 6 can be reconciled in the following manner: every proposition is the result of an N-operation on propositions asserting the existence of states of affairs (elementary propositions being truth-functions of themselves) (TLP 5).

Since 'state of affairs' has a technical meaning for Wittgenstein – a state of affairs being a combination of simple objects (TLP 2.01) – the statement that the general form of proposition is 'This state of affairs exists' is not as empty as it at first sounds. But can logic say any more than this about the possible structures of elementary propositions? Wittgenstein raises this question at TLP 5.55, and brings out its difficulty. On the one hand, we cannot give a list of the names of all the objects in the world; but what possible forms of elementary propositions there are depend on what possible combinations of objects there are; so it seems that it cannot be a matter of logic to decide whether, for example, there are unanalysable twenty-seven-term-relational propositions (TLP 5.55, 5.5541, 5.5561). On the other hand, it seems equally absurd to suppose that to be answered such questions must await experience: experience can tell me whether propositions are true, but it cannot be a matter of experience whether a certain proposition has sense (TLP 5.551, 5.553). Wittgenstein's answer is that what elementary propositions there are is decided by the *application* of logic, not by logic nor by experience (TLP 5.557). Logic presupposes that there is a world, that names have reference and that elementary propositions have sense (TLP 5.552, 6.124), but what is presupposed is not a matter of experience since experience is itself limited by the totality of objects (TLP 5.5561). Logic does not presuppose the existence of particular objects nor does it lay down what elementary propositions have sense. It concerns the system by which we can give meaning to symbols; but what particular symbols there are depends neither on logic nor on experience but upon the creative activity of human beings (TLP 5.555–5.556). To attempt to give *a priori* a list of elementary propositions leads to nonsense (TLP 5.5571). Elementary propositions cannot be ordered in a formal series like molecular propositions (TLP 5.556).

A fully analysed proposition, then, will be an enormously long truth-function of elementary propositions: every possible elementary proposition will occur in the truth-function, and every name in the language. This seems a far cry from the humble propositions of everyday life, such as 'My watch is lying on the table', from which the analysis began. None the less, Wittgenstein insists that all the propositions of our everyday language, just as they stand, are in perfect logical order (TLP 5.5563). What would occur in the full analysis of them is presumably already present in the thought of someone who utters them with understanding; for a fully analysed sentence would contain a name for every object in the thought it expressed (TLP 3.2). But of course they are not present in thought in such a way as to be objects of consciousness: we produce our sentences without any idea how each word symbolizes or what its meaning is, just as people speak without knowing how the individual sounds are produced (TLP 4.002).

Not all sentences produced by English-speakers, however, count as propositions of everyday life which are in perfect logical order: many of them are only pseudo-propositions which analysis would reveal to be nonsensical, as attempts to say what can only be shown. The last seventeen pages of the *Tractatus* (the 6s) are devoted to a brisk demonstration of how the propositions of logic (6.1s), mathematics (6.2s), the *a priori* part of natural science (6.3s), ethics (6.4s), philosophy (6.5s) are all in different ways pseudo-propositions.

The only propositions which deserve a place in logic-books are tautologies, which say nothing but exhibit the logical properties of genuine propositions (TLP 6.121). Even these would be superfluous in an ideal language (TLP 6.122). Other propositions in logic-books are at best (like the axiom of infinity) attempts to say what could only be shown (TLP 5.535), and at worst pieces of nonsense resulting from a bad symbolism or from the discrepancy between the logical and grammatical syntax of English (TLP 5.132, 6.1264). As instances of such cases Wittgenstein gives 'For all x, $x = x$', 'There is only one zero' and laws of inference like *modus ponens* (TLP 4.1272, 5.534, 4.243).

The theory of inference, which was once the central concern of logic (TLP 6.1224), is very briskly despatched. If 'p' can be inferred from 'q', this must make itself clear in the propositions 'p' and 'q' themselves. Laws of inference such as *modus ponens* ('From "p" and "if p then q" infer q') are superfluous; moreover they cannot be expressed as genuine propositions (TLP 5.132, 6.1264). All the propositions of logic are tautologies, and the proof of one logical proposition from another consists simply in the calculation which turns one tautology into another. The proof that one non-logical proposition follows from another consists in showing that in certain combinations they yield a tautology: for instance, we can show that '*q*' follows from 'if *p* then *q*, and *p*' by combining them to form the tautology 'If, if *p* then *q*, and *p*, then *q*' (TLP 6.1221). But the calculation of tautologies is a superfluous mechanical device: in a perspicuous notation the formal properties of propositions and their logical relations could be recognized by mere inspection of the propositions themselves (TLP 6.122).

Mathematics is next considered. Mathematics consists of equations, and equations mean that the signs on either side of the '=' can be substituted for one another. But if this is so, it must be manifest in the two expressions themselves, and hence the equation is an attempt to say what shows itself, and therefore a pseudo-proposition. In real life we make use of mathematical propositions only in passing from one non-mathematical proposition to another one (TLP 6.2–6.23).

The natural sciences do consist for the most part of genuine propositions: indeed at TLP 4.11 Wittgenstein says, rather surprisingly, that the totality of true propositions is identical with the corpus of natural sciences. (What has happened, one wonders, to such disciplines as history?) But science contains, or might be thought to contain, in addition to particular laws of physics which speak, however indirectly, about the world, general laws of an *a priori* kind – e.g. the law of causality, the law of least effort, the axioms of Newtonian mechanics. These, Wittgenstein says, are not really propositions, but *a priori* insights into the forms in which the genuine propositions of science can be cast (TLP 6.32–6.3431; NB 42). The law of induction, on the other hand, is a genuine proposition whose falsehood is thinkable, since the happening of one event never necessitates the happening of another. It is, for instance, a merely uncertain hypothesis that the sun will rise tomorrow (TLP 6.31; 6.363ff.). The only necessity is logical necessity, and the only impossibility logical impossibility (TLP 6.37, 6.375). There are impossibilities which look like non-logical impossibilities, for instance, the impossibility of a thing's being red and green all over; but the language of physics shows this to be a kinetic impossibility (a particle cannot have two velocities at the same time), which is in fact a logical impossibility (a particle cannot be in two places at the same time, for we should call particles that were in two places different particles) (NB 81; TLP 6.375).

In ethics and aesthetics, again, there are no genuine propositions. No proposition can express the meaning of the world or of life, for all propositions are contingent; if there is any genuine value its value cannot be a contingent matter (TLP 6.41). There can indeed be propositions expressing the pleasant and unpleasant consequences of one's actions; but these are irrelevant to any genuine ethical imperative which cannot be concerned with a mere contingent sanction for disobedience (TLP 6.422). Survival after death, for instance, even if there were reason for expecting it, would be a contingent matter which could not contribute to the solution of any 'problem of life'. All we can say is that a man is fulfilling the purpose of existence if he no longer needs to have any purpose except to live. That is why the solution of the problem of life is seen in the vanishing of the problem. The problem, 'Is life worth living?', vanishes when the urge to ask the question is dispelled (TLP 6.52ff.; NB 73).

Among the propositions which involve attempts to say the unsayable are, surprisingly, statements about people's knowledge, beliefs and perceptions. In 1914 Wittgenstein told Moore that 'The relation of "I believe p" to "p" can be compared to the relation of "'p' says p" to "p": it is just as impossible that I should be a simple as that "p" should be' (NB 118). This rather obscure remark can be illustrated as follows. If I say that grass is green, then the saying is done by the issuing of the words 'Grass is green' from my mouth. This event is articulate, divisible, in just the same way as the proposition is: the utterance of a proposition is obviously no more and no less composite than the proposition uttered. Something analogous must be true, Wittgenstein is arguing, of my thinking that grass is green: the mental event which is that particular thought must have the same articulateness as the proposition. He summed this up in the *Tractatus* by saying that 'A believes that p', 'A has the thought p' and 'A says p' are of the form '"p" says p' (TLP 5.542). But '"p" says p' must be a pseudo-proposition, since a proposition shows its sense and cannot say that it has it (TLP 4.022). Similarly, belief propositions must be pseudo-propositions – or more precisely they will be the conjunction of a genuine proposition and a spurious one. The proposition that Jones believes that grass is green will be a conjunction of (1) the proposition that certain mental elements in Jones's mind are related in a certain way, and (2) the pseudo-proposition that their correlation in that way says that grass is green. The proposition that Jones believes (or knows) that either grass is green or grass is not green, however, is even more bogus; for everyone's mental elements cannot help but be related in this way: anyone who knows what 'Grass is green' means, and thus has the appropriate mental elements, knows *eo ipso* that either grass is green or grass is not green (NB 94); so to say that they stand in this relation is not to make a significant assertion. For this reason Wittgenstein can say that from the proposition that A judges that a is in a relation R to b if correctly analysed, the proposition 'aRb or not aRb' must follow. Thus it is impossible to judge a piece of nonsense (TLP 5.5422; NB 96, 97). And thus also he can say 'A knows that p is the case', if 'p' is a tautology, is, like a tautology, itself senseless (TLP 5.1362).

Finally, as we saw in the first chapter, the propositions of philosophy and of the *Tractatus* itself fall under the axe which cuts off pseudo-propositions. Philosophy is not a corpus of propositions but an activity, the activity of analysis, the activity of making thoughts clear and sharply bounded (TLP 4.112). More precisely, the activity of analysis applied to non-philosophical propositions – to the propositions of everyday speech that are in perfect logical order, to the propositions of natural science – makes them sharp; applied to philosophical propositions it reveals them as nonsensical. There is only one way in which a proposition can be nonsensical, namely, when it contains a sign to which no meaning has been given. It is sometimes obvious that this is so – as, for instance, in the propositions 'The good is more identical than the beautiful' or 'Socrates is identical' – no meaning has been given to 'identical' as a property-word or as an adjective of comparison (TLP 4.003, 5.473, 5.4733). But it may take a more or less prolonged process of analysis to reveal this, as in the case of the propositions to be found in philosophical works and in the *Tractatus* itself. The meaningless propositions of the *Tractatus* are attempts to say what can only be shown; but this does not make them useless, because their very failure, and the way in which they break down, is instructive. 'My propositions serve as elucidations in the following way: anyone who understands me eventually recognizes them as nonsensical, when he has used them – as steps – to climb up beyond them. (He must, so to speak, throw away the ladder after he has climbed up it.) He must transcend these propositions and then he will see the world aright' (TLP 6.54).

CHAPTER 6

The Dismantling of Logical Atomism

After the *Tractatus* Wittgenstein retired from philosophy for ten years. He published nothing more in his lifetime except a paper to the Joint Session of the Aristotelian Society and the Mind Association entitled 'Some Remarks on Logical Form'. He wrote this in 1929 soon after his return to Cambridge, and disowned it by the time it was due to be delivered. It cannot be said to contain any ideas which he thought worth preserving, but it is useful as an indication of the state of his thought a decade after the completion of the *Tractatus*.

The paper begins with a brisk restatement of some of the main themes of logical atomism. 'Every proposition has a content and a form. We get the picture of the pure form . . . if we substitute variables for the constants of the proposition' (cf. TLP 3.315). Propositions in general are truth-functions of simpler propositions; but analysis must lead to propositions which are immediate connections of terms, 'atomic propositions', which are the kernels of every proposition. It is the task of philosophy to discover and understand these atomic propositions, and to devise a clear symbolism for their expression. Ordinary language disguises logical structure, allows the formation of pseudo-propositions – Wittgenstein offers as an example 'The Real, though it is an *in itself*, must also be able to become a *for myself*' – and uses single terms with a variety of different meanings. We must replace it by a symbolism which gives a clear picture of the logical structure, excludes pseudo-propositions and uses its terms unambiguously. We can only do this by a logical investigation of phenomena themselves, almost *a posteriori*; we cannot conjecture the forms of atomic propositions *a priori* from the structure of propositions in ordinary language. The few forms of ordinary language correspond to many different logical forms. Such forms as

'This paper is boring', 'The weather is fine', 'I am lazy', which have nothing whatever in common with one another, present themselves as subject-predicate propositions, i.e. apparently as proposition of the same form (RLF 31–3).

In this lecture Wittgenstein's most significant modification of the doctrines of the *Tractatus* was the abandonment of the claim that elementary propositions were independent of each other. He was led to this by a consideration of statements of degree, that is to say statements concerning properties which admit of gradation, such as the length of an interval, the pitch of a note, the brightness or redness of a shade of colour. It is characteristic of these properties that one degree of them excludes any other. One shade of colour cannot simultaneously have two different degrees of brightness or redness, one note cannot have more than a single pitch or volume. 'The important point' Wittgenstein wrote 'is that these remarks do not express an experience but are in some sense tautologies. Every one of us knows that in ordinary life. If someone asks us "What is the temperature outside?" and we said "Eighty degrees" and now he were to ask us again, "And is it ninety degrees?" we should answer "I told you it was eighty."' (RLF 34.)

Wittgenstein had recognized, when he wrote the *Tractatus*, that it was contradictory to say that a point in the visual field had two different colours at the same time. At that time he had taken this as proving that a proposition assigning a colour to a point in the visual field was not an elementary proposition, since the logical product of two elementary propositions could not be a contradiction (TLP 6.3751). It followed that a statement assigning a hue to a speck had to be further analysed; and the same must be true of any statement expressing the degree of a quality. He seems to have believed that statements of degree could be analysed into a conjunction of single statements of quantity and some supplementary statement, roughly in the way in which one can describe the contents of one's pocket by saying 'It contains a penny, a shilling, two keys, and nothing else' (RLF 35).

Now Wittgenstein came to see that it was impossible to regard statements of degree as analysable in this way. Suppose that the entity E has a certain brightness. How shall we analyse the proposition 'E(2b)' which says that E has two degrees of brightness? If we try to analyse it as the conjunction 'E(b) and E(b)', this says no more than 'E(b)'; if, on the other hand, we try to distinguish between the units and consequently write 'E(2b) = E(b') and E(b'')', we assume two different units of brightness; and then, if an entity possesses one unit, the question could arise, which of the two – b' or b'' – it is; which is obviously absurd (RLF 35).

Wittgenstein drew the conclusion that statements which attributed degrees to quality *were* elementary propositions, since they could not be analysed. In consequence, as he put it, 'Numbers must enter into the structure of the atomic propositions themselves.' Atomic propositions will involve functions of the form 'E has n degrees of property P' which will give a true proposition only for one value of the variable n. Since not more than one such proposition can be true at a time, atomic propositions will no longer be independent of each other.

The admission that atomic propositions may exclude each other in this way leads to a complication in the manner in which non-atomic propositions are to be dealt with. Let us suppose that 'p' is the proposition that a point in the visual field is red and 'q' is the proposition that the same point is blue. Then we can construct according to the normal rules for truth-tables the following symbol for their conjunction:

p	q	p and q
T	T	T
T	F	F
F	T	F
F	F	F

But the top line of this table represents an impossible combination – an attempt, as it were, to put both redness and blueness where there is only room for one of them. This sort of thing could never happen if all elementary propositions were independent, as stated in the *Tractatus*; but if elementary propositions can exclude each other in this way, then the rules for the construction of truth-tables will have to be supplemented by further rules of syntax in a perfect notation. 'These will have to tell us that in the case of certain kinds of atomic propositions described in terms of definite symbolic features certain combinations of the 'T's and 'F's must be left out. Such rules, however, cannot be laid down until we have actually reached the ultimate analysis of the phenomena in question.' 'This' Wittgenstein said in the last sentence of his lecture 'as we all know, has not yet been achieved' (RLF 37).

In conversations with other philosophers in Vienna in 1929 and 1930 Wittgenstein returned to the problem of colour exclusion and the modifications it necessitated in the *Tractatus* system.

Thus, for instance, at Christmas 1929 he said to Waismann:

I once wrote 'A proposition is like a ruler laid against reality. Only the outermost graduating marks touch the object to be measured.'[1] I would now rather say: a *system* of propositions is laid against reality like a ruler. What I mean is this: when I lay a ruler against a spatial object, I lay all the graduating lines against it at the same time.

It is not individual graduating lines that are laid beside it, but the whole scale. If I know that the object reaches up to the mark 10, I know also immediately that it does not reach to the mark 11, 12

1. What Wittgenstein actually said in the *Tractatus* was 'Only the outermost points of the graduating lines actually make contact with the object to be measured' (TLP 2.15121), but the present passage shows that this means that only the outermost graduating lines concern the object, only they are to be taken into account.

and so on. The assertions, which describe for me the length of an object, form a system, a proposition-system. It is whole proposition-systems of this kind that are compared with reality, not single propositions. For instance, when I say: such and such a point in the visual field is blue, I know not only that, but also that the point is not green, not red, not yellow and so on. I have laid the whole colour-scale alongside simultaneously. That is also the reason why a point cannot have different colours at the same time. For if I lay a proposition-*system* against reality, it is thereby already affirmed – just as in the spatial case – that only one state of affairs can obtain, and not more than one.

All this was something I did not realize when I was working on my book; I then thought that all inference rested on the form of tautology. I had then not yet seen that an inference can also have the form 'A man is two metres high, so he is not three metres high.' That is connected with my believing that the elementary propositions must be independent; that one could not infer from the existence of a state of affairs to the non-existence of another. But if my present conception in terms of proposition-systems is correct, it is in fact the rule that one can infer from the existence of a state of affairs to the non-existence of all others which are described by the same proposition-system. (WWK 63–4; PB 317)

The comparison between systems of propositions and rulers is developed in several places in the *Philosophische Bemerkungen*. Suppose I am looking at something black, and say 'That is not red', how do I know that I am not talking nonsense, that what I am talking about is something that has the possibility of being red? How does 'That is not red' differ from 'That is not abracadabra'? Wittgenstein's answer is that red is another marking on the same ruler as black. I must know, for instance, that 'red' takes the place of 'black' and not, for example, of 'soft' (PB 75). How far can the comparison between colours and points on a scale be taken? Can we, for instance, speak of *directions* in connection with colours, and say that the direction which leads from black to red is different from the one which leads from black to blue (PB 76)? A remark Wittgenstein made to Waismann answers the question in part.

We often imagine, that we carry round with us a kind of memory picture of colours inside us, and that such a memory picture gets compared with a colour which I now see. We imagine that what happens is some sort of comparison. That is not quite so. Imagine the following case. You have seen a quite particular blue, say sky blue, and I now show you various samples of blue. You say 'No, no, it wasn't that, or that, or that – there, that's it.' Is it not as if you had various keys in your head, and I try until I depress a quite particular key, and then the bell rings? Does not the recognition of colour take place like that? Does a bell ring in me, is there a kind of click at the sight of the correct colour? No! On the contrary, I know of a particular blue, not only that it is not the right colour, but also, I know in which direction I must vary the colour in order to reach the right one. If you have to mix the colours, I can guide you by saying: more white, more white, now too much, a little more blue, and so on. That means: every colour presupposes the whole colour system. (WWK 87–8)

Statements about the relationships between colours did not fit easily into the system of the *Tractatus*. Does the fact that colours made up a system belong to logic or to experience? At Christmas 1929 Schlick put Wittgenstein the following problem. Suppose that a man had spent his whole life shut in a red room and could see only red: would he be able to say that there must be other colours too? Wittgenstein replied that either his syntax was the same as ours, including the expressions 'red', 'redder', 'bright red' and so on, in which case he possessed the whole colour system; or else he had a different syntax, in which case he was not acquainted even with a single colour in our sense. If his word 'red' was to have the same meaning as ours, then it must have the same syntax. As so often elsewhere, Wittgenstein compared colour with space. A man forever locked in a room would know that there was space beyond the room, that it was possible to leave the room, even if it had walls of adamant. 'That is no experience: it is included in the syntax of space, *a priori*' (WWK 65–6).

Neither Schlick nor Wittgenstein was really satisfied with this answer, and a few days later they returned to the topic.

'How do I know', asked Schlick 'that such and such rules of syntax hold? How do I know that red and blue cannot be at the same spot at the same time? Isn't this a sort of empirical knowledge?' This time, Wittgenstein replied that it depended on what one meant by 'empirical'. If a piece of empirical knowledge had to be something expressible in a proposition, then this was not a piece of empirical knowledge. But in another sense syntax too could be called empirical. And he quoted with approval a sentence from the *Tractatus*: 'Logic is prior to the question "How?", not prior to the question "What?"' (TLP 5.552). Logic depends on there being something in existence and there being facts; it is independent of what the facts are, of things being thus and so. That there are facts is not something which can be expressed in a proposition. If one wants to call there being facts a matter of experience, then one can say logic is empirical. But when we say something is empirical we mean that it can be imagined otherwise; in this sense every proposition with sense is a contingent proposition. And in this sense the existence of the world is not an empirical fact, because we cannot think it otherwise (WWK 77).

At first sight the existence of the world seems a very different matter from the existence of the colour system; but the connection between the two had been brought out by Wittgenstein in an earlier conversation, a few days previously, on the nature of objects. Logic presupposes, in the *Tractatus*, that there are objects (TLP 5.552, 6.124) but, as we have seen, we are given little clue in that work as to what kind of thing objects are. We are given some illumination by a remark in a conversation of 22 December 1929. Frege and Russell, Wittgenstein said, when they spoke of objects, had in mind things like chairs and tables which would be referred to by substantives in a subject-predicate sentence. But there is no reason at all to imagine that elementary propositions will resemble the subject-predicate forms of ordinary speech: what their fully analysed form will be we cannot foresee, but it may not have the slightest similarity with the logical pattern of normal propositions; they are more likely to be as complex as the equations of physics. Every colour can be represented as a combination of different degrees of the four primary colours red, yellow, blue and green, and so every assertion about colours can be set out by means of symbols showing where the colours can be located on the primary-colour scales. In this way the primary colours become elements of the method of representation. *This* is what objects really are. It is senseless to ask whether objects are more like substances or like properties or relations: objects belong to the method of representation which is more fundamental than the subject-predicate form (wwk 43).

The role which Wittgenstein here assigns to the primary colours is similar to the one he later assigned to units of measurement. In a well-known passage of the *Philosophical Investigations* he mentions the standard metre at Paris as an example of an object which looks as if it *had* to exist, as if it existed necessarily like the objects of the *Tractatus*. This is because of its special role in the technique of measurement. Anything which looks as if it *has* to exist, he says, is part of the language – it is something essential to our mode of representation, not something that is represented (pi i, 50).

Throughout the 1929 conversations and the *Philosophische Bemerkungen* Wittgenstein constantly returns to the comparison between colours and spatial properties – a comparison which is of course implicit in the analogy between the system of colour-propositions and a ruler, and in the notion of 'logical space'. He had, indeed, already said in the *Tractatus* that every coloured object was in a colour-space: 'A speck in the visual field, though it need not be red, must have some colour: it is, so to speak, surrounded by colour-space' (TLP 2.0131). But, when he wrote that, he had failed to see that the possible positions in this space were analogous to the graduating marks on a ruler, and that it was the whole proposition system which got applied like a ruler to reality (wwk 89). The sense in which propositions about length build up a system is this: that when I understand that something is three metres long I understand also what is meant by its being five metres long because I understand *eo ipso* that it is *not* five metres long (WWK 89). Similarly, when I see what colour something is, I see *eo ipso* what colour it is *not*. If I wish to verify the proposition 'The azalea is not blue' I compare it with reality: i.e. I look at the azalea. I see that the azalea is red; and I see immediately, without the need of any inference, that it is not blue (WWK 87). That this is so is not as obvious in the case of colours as in the case of measurement. This is so because we do not literally have a ruler to measure colours and so nothing corresponds to an experience such as seeing the two metres which are left over if one lays a three-metre rule against an object that is five metres long. This, Wittgenstein suggests, is why people are much more impressed by the fact that colours are incompatible than by the fact that lengths are incompatible (WWK 78).

In the *Tractatus* period Wittgenstein had argued that all analytic propositions were tautologies. He had now isolated a class of propositions, or would-be propositions, which though *a priori* were not tautologous. Did this mean that they were, in Kantian terms, synthetic *a priori* judgements? It was thus, as Schlick pointed out, that Husserl had treated them in his *Logische Untersuchungen*. Wittgenstein vigorously rejected this suggestion.

Let us take the assertion: 'No object is red and green simultaneously.' Do I mean by this merely that I have never hitherto seen such an object? Obviously not. I mean: 'I *cannot* ever see such an object', 'Red and green *cannot* be in the same place.' Here I would simply ask: what does the word 'can' mean here? The word 'can' is obviously a grammatical (logical) concept, not a factual one. Assume now that the assertion 'An object cannot be red and green' is a synthetic judgement, and the words 'cannot' mean logical impossibility. Then, since a proposition is the negation of its negation, there must also be the proposition 'An object can be red and green.' This proposition would be likewise synthetic. As a synthetic proposition it has sense, and that means that the state of affairs it depicts can exist. So if 'cannot' means logical impossibility, we come to the conclusion that the impossible is possible after all. The only way out which remains for Husserl is for him to explain that there is a third sort of possibility. To this I would reply: it is possible to invent words; but I cannot think any thoughts to go with them. (wwk 68; cf. pb 78)

The propositions which set out the colour-system, then, according to Wittgenstein, are not synthetic *a priori* propositions. Are they *a posteriori*, empirical ones? Empirical psychologists have conducted researches into the question whether two colours could be seen at the same place. Wittgenstein was willing to admit the possibility that sense could be attached to these researches, but in a straightforward sense colour-exclusion propositions are not matters of experience (wwk 79). What are they then? They are rules of syntax.

The notion of syntax – logical syntax, or logical grammar – begins to acquire great importance at this period of Wittgenstein's life. The notion is already mentioned half-a-dozen times in the *Tractatus* (TLP 3.325, 3.33, 3.334, 3.344, 6.124), but it is not of very great importance there. In the perspicuous notation which the *Tractatus* aimed at, 'the nature of the natural and inevitable signs' would speak for itself (TLP 6.124) and the rules of syntax would be obvious (TLP 3.334).

It was in the spirit of the *Tractatus* that Schlick asked, in January 1930, 'Should not a language be constructed such that the rules of syntax would show themselves in it?' and that Waismann replied

That is the case when we use a system of rulers for description. If the sign-system has the correct multiplicity, then the rules of syntax are superfluous. The use of the words 'north of' depends on certain syntactical rules: I must not say 'A is north of B and B is north of A.' But maps cannot depict this piece of nonsense, because they have the correct multiplicity. (wwk 79)

But Wittgenstein himself was no longer so definite. One could with equal right say that syntax makes a system of the right multiplicity superfluous, as say that a system of the right multiplicity makes syntax superfluous. Signs and syntax complement each other. 'For instance, my notation for the logical constants is neither better nor worse than Russell's. Russell's signs plus syntax achieve exactly the same as my notation. Mine has perhaps only the advantage that it makes a number of things more easily recognizable' (WWK 80).

Perhaps this was not so great a change as it sounds from the doctrines of the *Tractatus*. The main advantage there claimed for Russell's notation over ordinary language, and for Wittgenstein's over Russell's, was that it avoided philosophical misunderstandings and allowed to be clearly shown things which were not perspicuous in the less preferred notation (TLP 3.325). Even in 1918 Wittgenstein would presumably have agreed that the Russellian notation, like ordinary language, was 'in perfect logical order' (TLP 5.5563), i.e. could be used perfectly successfully for a limited purpose. At the end of 1929 he summed up his views on the Russellian notation as follows. Our language is perfectly in order, provided only that we are clear how it symbolizes. Languages which differ from ordinary language are also valuable to the extent that they show us the common features of ordinary languages. For certain purposes, for instance to bring out inference-relationships, an artificial symbolism is very useful. Frege's function-and-argument symbolism is very good when what is needed is to illustrate simple logical relationships. But once we try to deal with real states of affairs, we find that this symbolism is inferior to our real language.

It is, of course, quite wrong to speak of a *single* subject-predicate form. In reality there is not just one, but numerous such forms. If there were only one, then all substantives and all adjectives would be substitutable for each other . . . but it is visible already in ordinary language that this is not so. Apparently I can say 'The chair is brown' and 'The surface of the chair is brown.' But if I replace 'brown' by 'heavy' then I can sensibly say only the first sentence and not the second. That proves that the word 'brown' too had different meanings. (WWK 46)

The rules for the connection of sentences into truth-functions, therefore, now appear as a comparatively minor part of the logical syntax (WWK 74, 80), and Wittgenstein's interest shifted more and more to the other part of logical syntax, the part which governed the construction of the units to which the truth-functional connectives applied. He continued to believe that there were elementary propositions in the sense that analysis would lead to sentences which were an immediate linking of objects without the help of logical constants like 'not', 'and', 'or' and 'if', and to the end of his life he was prepared to define a proposition as something to which the calculus of truth-functions can be applied (PI I, 136). But having ceased to believe that elementary propositions were independent of each other he realized that the rules for truth-functional combination of sentences needed supplementing with rules 'which stem from the inner syntax of sentences' (WWK 80). It was the study of these inner rules, and the internal relations between elementary propositions, which led to the theory of language-games which played such an important part in his later philosophy. Ruler-like proposition-systems are language-games in embryo.

Against Wittgenstein's new view Schlick protested that the truth-functional constants seemed to be more essential to language than the particular rules of syntax. The possibility of constructing conjunctive propositions, he said, seemed to be a much more general, all-embracing fact than the rule of syntax that red and blue could not be in the same place. But Wittgenstein replied that he thought there was no crucial distinction there. The rules for truth-functions were not to be separated from other rules of syntax. 'Both' he said 'belong to the method of depicting the world' (WWK 81).

As can be seen from this quotation, the recantation of the independence of the elementary propositions, and the altered understanding of the nature of objects, though it amounted to the abandonment of atomism, did not carry with it any abandonment of the picture theory of the proposition. The picture theory, so far from being regarded by Wittgenstein as being incompatible with the new doctrine that propositions form systems, was actually used by him to prove that doctrine in a striking conversation of the 5 January 1930.

He discussed the question 'Does every proposition belong to a system?', i.e. 'Does the proposition "a is F" presuppose other propositions of that sort, for instance "b is F"?' He replied that if there were only the proposition 'a is F', then mention of 'a' would be superfluous. It would be enough to write 'F' alone. 'In that case' he said 'the proposition would not be composite. But the essential thing in a proposition is that it is *a picture* and is composite.' So if 'a is F' is to be a proposition, there must also be a proposition 'b is F', that is to say, the arguments of '. . . is F' must form a system.

Similarly, 'a is F' presupposes 'a is G.' The same consideration applies: if there were only one function 'F' for 'a' then it would be superfluous and could be left out. In that case the propositional sign would be simple and not composite. It would not depict (WWK 90).

Take the example of the proposition 'This is yellow.' 'This', which is yellow, must be something I can recognize again even if it is red. If 'this' and 'yellow' formed a unity, they could be represented by a single symbol, and we would not have a proposition (WWK 97).

There was, however, one important modification to the picture theory. Wittgenstein now admitted the possibility of elementary propositions which were incomplete pictures of states of affairs. In the *Tractatus* he had said 'A proposition may well be an incomplete picture of a certain situation, but it is always *a* complete picture' (TLP 5.156). This means: a proposition may leave much undetermined, but what it leaves undetermined must be specified. What is left open would be expressed in the proposition by generalizations, by the presence of quantifiers which in the fully analysed proposition would appear as truth-functions of propositions in which all the possible values of the quantified variable would occur, one

by one. In 1929 Wittgenstein came to doubt whether propositions were always complete pictures, and whether quantifiers
could be explained truth-functionally (wwk 38–41, 44, 51–2).

Consider the proposition 'All the men in this room are
wearing trousers.' On the lines suggested by the *Tractatus*
this is more or less equivalent to 'Schlick is wearing trousers,
Waismann is wearing trousers, and there is no one else in the
room.' It is essential to the complete enumerations that are to
take the place of quantifiers that they should end with an expression such as 'and there is nothing else . . .' But how is this
to be analysed? One might be inclined to say it means 'Carnap
is not in the room, and Feigl is not in the room . . .' and so on.
But *this* enumeration cannot have a closure, for '. . . and that
is all the things there are' is not a genuine proposition (wwk
38). It was suggested above that at the time of the *Tractatus*
Wittgenstein would have said that the completeness of the
enumeration was something which would show itself by all
the names in the language having been used in it; but now he
was less satisfied with the account of the universal quantifier as
a conjunction except when the conjunction was clearly finite.
Statements about all numbers could clearly not be treated as conjunctions of statements about each of the numbers (wwk 45).

Consider the following proposition 'I have seen two pieces
of material of the same colour.' One cannot construe this as
'I saw two pieces of material, and either they were both green
or both blue or . . .' For one can use the sentence without being
able to produce such an enumeration. But neither can it be
construed as 'For some x, I saw a piece of material of the
colour x, and another piece of the colour x.' If this sentence
could be constructed, then it would be possible to form the
sentence 'For every x, I saw a piece of material of the colour x,
and another piece of the colour x' – i.e. 'The two pieces of
material have every colour in common'; but that is a piece of
nonsense. The sentence 'I saw a piece of material of the colour
x, and another piece of the colour x' must itself be a genuine
elementary proposition and not just the raw material for a

proposition to be built out of by a quantifier (wwk 40). Such a proposition is 'an incomplete portrait of a state of affairs' (wwk 40).

As another example of a proposition which was an 'incomplete picture' Wittgenstein gave 'I see a square containing a circle.' He said

I can describe a state of things which consists of a circle of a definite size being in a definite place in the square. For our purposes it does not matter what form of description I choose – whether, for instance, I make use of coordinates – provided that the chosen method of description has the correct multiplicity. If, then, numbers appear in this proposition, which indicate where the circle is and how large it is, it may happen that I put variables in place of the numbers, or perhaps only intervals (e.g. 6–7, 8–9), and then I obtain an incomplete picture. Think of a portrait, in which I leave the mouth out. This can be interpreted in two ways: one, that the mouth is white like the blank paper; secondly, that, whatever the mouth is like, the picture is always correct. (wwk 40; cf pg, 257)

Wittgenstein's discussion of this point is obscure, and sometimes self-contradictory (compare wwk 39 with wwk 44, wwk 45 and wwk 51), but it is clear that the treatment of generality in the *Tractatus* no longer satisfied him. To follow this up fully would take us too far into Wittgenstein's philosophy of mathematics, since it was especially the case of mathematical induction which presented difficulty. But the point is of importance outside the philosophy of mathematics.

The recognition of elementary propositions which were incomplete pictures brought with it as a necessary consequence the possibility of relationships between propositions which were not provided for in the *Tractatus*. For there could be relationships between complete and incomplete descriptions of the same state of affairs. Wittgenstein gives the following example:

If I give a complete picture of this state of affairs I will have to say, for example, that a is 2 m. long, b is 1.5 m. long. Then, that a is longer than b will be something which can only be shown; for it cannot be *said* that two is greater than 1.5, since that is an internal relation. But I can say, for example, that the left-hand stroke is 0.5 m. longer than the right-hand one, and this statement will report an external relation. This is connected with the fact that we now have an incomplete picture of the state of affairs. If we describe the state of affairs fully, then the external relation disappears (WWK 54–5).

Waismann observed that from a complete proposition one could infer an incomplete one: was this form of inference, he asked, tautologous? Wittgenstein replied:

> Tautology is quite incidental. It is only in a certain notation that inference displays itself as tautology. The only important thing are the rules of syntax, which were always employed long before anyone knew what a tautology was. A determinate description looks like this: a certain length is 25 m. An indeterminate one would be: a length is between 20 and 30 m. Let these two descriptions be '*p*' and '*q*'. Then it is laid down through the syntax of the word 'length' that it is impossible that the first proposition should be true and the second false; that is, *p* and not *q* is not permitted.

Suppose we now construct the truth-function 'if *p* then *q*' (or rather a truth-function which is analogous or similar to implication) and allow for the rules of syntax, a tautology will appear (WWK 91).

On the pattern of the notation in the 'Remarks on Logical Form', the rule will be expressed in the following table:

p	*q*	if *p* then *q*
T	T	T
~~T~~	~~F~~	~~F~~
F	T	T
F	F	T

The 'allowing for the rules of syntax' comes out in striking out the second line of the table; the whole expression is a tautology in the sense that the remaining lines all give it the truth-value true. In this notation the correctness of the inference shows itself in the fact that 'if p then q' becomes a tautology. 'But it is quite unnecessary', Wittgenstein said,

to show the correctness of the inference in precisely this way. The correctness of the inference shows itself just as well in the ordinary rules of inference. It is only one of several possible notations, and perhaps its only advantage is its greater clarity. But in themselves the Russellian signs together with the rule for their syntactical application achieve the same object. That inference is *a priori* means only that syntax decides whether an inference is correct or not. Tautology is only one way of displaying matters of syntax. (WWK 92)

The conversations of late 1929 and early 1930, then, so far as concerns their relationship to the *Tractatus*, may be summed up as follows. Wittgenstein continued to believe that a proposition is a picture, that it must have the same multiplicity as the state of affairs it depicts, that it must be composite, that it must be compared with reality in order to be seen to be true or false; he continued to believe in the distinction between showing and saying, and in the existence of internal relations between propositions which could only be shown and not said, and which are the basis of inference from one proposition to another. But he ceased to believe in the independence of elementary propositions, in the possibility of representing generality solely by means of truth-functions; and his conception of the nature of the objects forming the structure of the world underwent a change. The effect of these changes was to make the system of the *Tractatus* more supple and closer to ordinary language. Crudely oversimplifying, one could say that Wittgenstein abandoned the atomism of logical atomism but kept most of its logic. It is time to turn to the more positive, forward-looking developments of the *Philosophische Bemerkungen*.

CHAPTER 7

Anticipation, Intentionality and Verification

In a justly famous passage in the *Philosophical Investigations* Wittgenstein insists on the diversity of the functions of words and warns us against being misled in philosophizing by the uniform appearance of spoken and written words.

It is like looking into the cabin of a locomotive. We see handles all looking more or less alike. (Naturally, since they are all supposed to be handled.) But one is the handle of a crank which can be moved continuously (it regulates the opening of a valve); another is the handle of a switch, which has only two effective positions, it is either off or on; a third is the handle of a brake-lever, the harder one pulls on it, the harder it brakes; a fourth, the handle of a pump: it has an effect only so long as it is moved to and fro. (PI I, 12)

The passage is sometimes used to contrast the later Wittgenstein's realization of the richness and diversity of language with the earlier Wittgenstein's attempt to bring all forms of speech into a uniform pattern; it is also used to contrast the theory of meaning as use, and the comparison of words to tools, with the earlier picture theory of the proposition. In fact the passage occurs, with slight differences in wording, already in the *Philosophische Bemerkungen* (PB 58), and a theory of meaning as use is enunciated on the next page. 'We can say: the sense of a proposition is its point; or, of a word, its meaning is its purpose' (PB 59). The passage in which it occurs, in the second chapter of the *Bemerkungen*, is indeed concerned with a variety of uses of sentences which were neglected in the *Tractatus*, namely, the use of sentences in prescriptions and commands. But so far from being incompatible with the picture theory of the proposition, the considerations it adduces are presented as support for that theory. 'If the proposition is conceived as a prescription for the construction of models, then its pictorial nature becomes even clearer' the chapter begins, 'for, in order that the word can guide my hand, it *must* have the multiplicity of the desired activity' (PB 57).

We can make a broad distinction of uses of language into imperative and indicative uses: uses of language to guide behaviour and uses of language to report facts. When logicians have talked of propositions, as was mentioned in an earlier chapter, they have traditionally had indicative and not imperative sentences in mind. For one reason, they have been interested in applying the calculus of truth-functions to propositions, and it is not at all clear how such a calculus can be applied to a sentence such as 'Pass the salt', which, being a request and not a statement, is neither true nor false. The *Tractatus* is no exception to this, and the picture theory of the proposition is presented in that work as a theory of the indicative proposition. Yet it is clear enough on reflection that the pictorial element of a proposition is separable from its assertoric, or indicative, element. Whatever is pictorial in 'The waters are above the firmament' is equally pictorial in 'Let the waters be above the firmament.' Wittgenstein does himself, at one place in the *Tractatus*, separate out the two elements. 'A proposition *shows* how things stand *if* it is true. And it *says that* they do so stand' (TLP 4.022). One might equally say 'A command *shows* how things stand *if* it is obeyed. And it *says that* they should so stand.' Both an indicative proposition and a command, we might say, contain a description of a state of affairs; the indicative proposition presents the description as an account of how things are, the imperative sentence presents it as an account of how things should be. In the two different uses of language the relation between the description and the world differs. If the description in the indicative sentence does not accord with the relevant state of affairs, then the indicative sentence is faulted as false; if the relevant state of affairs does not accord with the description in the imperative sentence, then it is not the sentence which is faulted but the state of affairs which is regarded as unsatisfactory. (If I give a child the order 'Close the door' and the door remains unclosed, it is not I who am untruthful, but the child who is disobedient.) If it is correct to compare a proposition with a picture, then what should be compared is not the indicative sentence as a whole, but the feature which it has in common with the corresponding imperative sentence. This point was made very clearly by Wittgenstein in the *Philosophical Investigations* (PI I, p: II):

Imagine a picture representing a boxer in a particular stance. Now, this picture can be used to tell someone how he should stand, should hold himself; or how he should not hold himself; or how a particular man did stand in such-and-such a place; and so on. One might (using the language of chemistry) call this picture a proposition-radical.

Using this terminology, we might say that the picture theory is really a theory of the proposition-radical rather than of the proposition. Wittgenstein did not express it so, at the time of the *Philosophische Bemerkungen*. Rather, he said, 'Every prescription can be conceived as a description and every description can be conceived as a prescription' (PB 59). What exactly this means is obscure; but it is clear that he was beginning to distinguish what is common to description and prescription and what distinguishes them from each other. A formal language might distinguish between the sentence-radical and the mood-indicator. Mood is indicated in English by a variety of devices; Frege introduced an assertion-sign which had, as one function, to mark the indicative (PI I, II). The shift of Wittgenstein's interest could be described as the taking of an interest in moods other than the indicative. Commands are, of course, not the only non-indicative forms of speech of philosophical interest: the expression of desire or will in a wish – the optative, as opposed to the imperative, mood – is also of great interest. As Wittgenstein remarked: 'The understanding of a command before executing it is related to the volition of a piece of behaviour before carrying it out' (PB 58). The expression of expectation comes somewhere between a statement about a current state of affairs, and a command for the future. The analysis of expectation began to interest Wittgenstein at this period and continued to fascinate him throughout his life.

In the *Tractatus* what corresponds to an indicative sentence is a thought, a psychological fact about which nothing is said except that it stands in an internal relation to a proposition and a state of affairs, and that it contains objects which would correspond to the elements of a fully analysed proposition (TLP 3.2). Expectation is a special kind of thought presumably, a state of mind which corresponds to a future-tense indicative statement: it too stands in an internal relation to the sentence which expresses it and the state of affairs which, if it occurs, fulfils it. 'Could we imagine a language' Wittgenstein asked 'in which expecting *p* was not described by means of *p*? Isn't that just as impossible as a language in which not-*p* could be expressed without using *p*?' (PB 69.)

Between the *Tractatus* and the *Bemerkungen* Russell had published *The Analysis of Mind*, in the third lecture of which he had presented an account of desire which made it definable in terms of the events which terminated it. 'A mental occurrence of any kind – sensation, image, belief or emotion –' Russell wrote

may be a cause of a series of actions continuing, unless interrupted, until some more or less definite state of affairs is realized. Such a series of actions we call a 'behaviour-cycle' . . . The property of causing such a cycle of occurrences is called 'discomfort' . . . the cycle ends in a condition of quiescence, or of such action as tends to preserve the *status quo*. The state of affairs in which this condition of quiescence is achieved is called the 'purpose' of the cycle, and the initial mental occurrence involving discomfort is called a 'desire' for the state of affairs that brings quiescence. A desire is called 'conscious' when it is accompanied by a true belief as to the state of affairs that will bring quiescence; otherwise it is called 'unconscious'. (*Analysis of Mind*, Allen & Unwin, 1921, p. 75)

Russell's account of expectation was rather different:

Suppose I am believing, by means of images, not words, that it will rain. We have here two interrelated elements, namely, the content and the expectation. The content consists of images of (say) the visual appearance of rain, the feeling of wetness . . . Exactly the same content may enter into the memory 'It was raining' or the assent 'Rain occurs.' The difference lies in the nature of the belief-feeling. (op. cit., p. 250)

Wittgenstein attributed to Russell an account of expectation parallel to his account of desire. 'We might' he said in the *Blue Book* 'explain that a certain tension is said to be an expectation that B will come if it is relieved by B's coming. If this is how we use the phrase then it is true to say that we don't know what we expect until our expectation has been fulfilled' (BB 21).

Wittgenstein attacked this conception in the *Bemerkungen*, and returned to the attack several times later (BB 20; Z 53–63; PI I 437ff.). In the *Bemerkungen* his attack took the form of saying that Russell's method ignored the element of intentionality (*Intention*) in language. This term he appears to have taken from Husserl, who in turn took it from Brentano, and scholastic tradition; but he explains what it means in language drawn from the *Tractatus*. 'The essential thing in intentionality, and in intention itself (*Absicht*) is the picture, the picture of what is intended.' The difference between Wittgenstein's picture-conception and Russell's conception is that on the picture-conception the recognition of an event as the fulfilment of an expectation appears as the perception of an internal relation, whereas on Russell's view recognition is an external relation.

For me there are only two things involved in a thought's being true, namely, the thought and the fact; for Russell there are three things, namely, the thought, the fact, and a third event, which, if it occurs, is the recognition. This third event, rather like the satisfaction of hunger (the two other events being the hunger and the eating of a certain food), this third event could be e.g. the occurrence of a feeling of joy. (PB 63)

Russell's theory, Wittgenstein said, amounted to this: if I give someone an order and what he does then pleases me, then he has carried out the order. But this would be as foolish as to say that if I wanted to eat an apple and somebody gave me a punch in the stomach which took away my appetite, it was this punch which I had really wanted all along.

The fulfilment of an expectation does not consist in the occurrence of a third thing that can be described in some way other than simply as 'the fulfilment of the expectation' . . . For the expectation that *p* will be the case must be the same as the expectation of the fulfilment of this expectation . . . My whole theory is expressed thus: the state of affairs that satisfies the expectation that *p* is expressed through the proposition *p*, and not through the description of a quite different event. (PB 65–6; cf. PI I, 437–45)

'I am expecting to see a red spot' may be a description of my present mental state. 'I see a red spot' describes the expected event, a quite different event from the first. Does it not look as if the first proposition were a description of my mental state via an inessential, alien event? 'Expectation is not described externally by a statement of what is expected, in the way that hunger is by a description of the food which would satisfy it, which can after all only be guessed. The description of expectation in terms of what is expected is an internal description' (PB 68).

It was not only philosophers like Russell, but psychologists like Pavlov, who Wittgenstein thought had missed the point which he was making in saying that expectation contained a picture of what was expected. 'When I wish that *p* were the case, *p* is not the case, and so there must be a proxy for *p* in the state of affairs which constitutes the wish, no less than in the expression of the wish' (PB 66).

The expectation, the thought, the wish that *p* will occur only deserve the name if these processes have the multiplicity which is expressed in *p*, that is to say, if they are articulated . . . Only articulated processes deserve the name of thoughts; or perhaps one could say, only processes which have an articulated expression. Salivation – however exactly measured – is *not* something I would call expectation. (PB 70)

The trouble with all such accounts was that they tried to make the connection between states of mind and their counterparts in the world into causal and external connections; whereas expectation must be internally related to what is expected, connected immediately with reality (PB 72). Wittgenstein sought to show this by appealing to the striking fact that we always know, in the case of an expectation, that it *is* an expectation – for instance, it never happens that I have a mental image before me and ask myself the question 'Is this an expectation or a memory, or a picture unrelated to reality in either of those ways?' (PB 72).

If it is not a difference in causal relations which makes one and the same picture in one case an expectation picture, and in another a memory picture, what is it? Presumably the answer is that in the two cases the picture is *meant* differently: our knowledge of which images are memories and which expectations is part of our knowledge of our own intentions.

But this only raises the question: how is a picture *meant*? 'The intention – the intentionality – never lies in the picture itself, because however the picture is constructed it can always be meant in different ways' (PB 65). The possibility has already been ruled out that how a picture is meant could be something to be settled by a future event (e.g. a feeling of satisfaction when the pictured event occurred). It must be something to be settled in the present. 'The intention expresses itself already in the way in which I *now* compare the picture with reality' (PB 65). But how can I now compare the picture with reality, since it is meant as a picture of a future event? Well, one way in which my intention expresses itself is precisely in the fact that I do not *now* try to verify the proposition which expresses the expectation, just as when I say to someone that it will be fine weather tomorrow, he displays his understanding of what I mean by *not* looking out of the window now (as a child might, who had not yet learnt the word 'tomorrow'). But this is not enough: there have to be other elements in my present knowledge, in my present inclination to behave, to incarnate the picture being meant as an expectation. In the third chapter of the *Bemerkungen* Wittgenstein makes several suggestions along these lines.

Expectation is connected with looking for. My looking for something presupposes that I know what I am looking for, without what I am looking for *having* to exist. I'd once have expressed this by saying that looking for something presupposed the elements of the complex, but not the actual combination I am looking for. And that is no bad comparison. For in speech it expresses itself in the fact that the sense of a proposition presupposes only the grammatically correct use of certain words . . . We expect and wish in signs no less than we think in signs. (PB 67, 69)

So among the present features of my condition which add up to the expectation is my knowledge of the language – not just, however, of the elements and their combination into sentence-radicals (this would be necessary whether the picture was meant as memory or expectation), but also that part of the knowledge of the language which is involved in tenses and moods. To use Wittgenstein's ruler metaphor: it is my *present* possession of the skill of operating with the rulers which enables me now to expect a future event. Future event and present expectation must be in the same logical space: the speech-ruler must be laid on the present point and point forward in the direction of expectation (PB 72).

The passage on expectation in the *Philosophische Bemerkungen* is of great importance for the study of the continuity of Wittgenstein's thought. For, though it is clearly shot through with the early, pictorial view of the nature of language, it already contains in germ the crucial elements of his later philosophy of mind. In his later works he returned to the same topic many times, refining the details of his treatment but not altering the essentials.

In the *Blue Book* Wittgenstein made the point that expectation was not a sensation; or rather, that if one were to use an expression such as 'the expectation that B will come' as the name of a sensation, it would not be possible to explain thereby the meaning of any phrase which is derived from this by substituting a different name for 'B'. Knowing the sensation which is referred to by 'The expectation that Lucy will come' will be no help towards knowing what is meant by 'The expectation that George will come'; for the sensation which occurs when I expect Lucy (delighted excitement) is quite different from the one which occurs when I expect George (unbearable nausea). 'One might say that the phrase "expecting that B will come" (so understood) is not a value of a function "expecting that x will come"' (BB 21).

The *Philosophical Investigations* adds considerations of context to the features which are involved in making a current mental state a state of expectation. 'An expectation is imbedded in a situation, from which it takes its rise. The expectation of an explosion may, for example, arise from a situation in which an explosion is to be expected' (PII, 581; Z 67). The internal relationship between expectation and fulfilment is spelt out in the *Investigations* in the following way. 'I want to say: "If someone could see the mental process of expectation, he would necessarily be seeing *what* was expected" . . . he would not have to *infer* it from the process he perceived' (PI I, 452–3; Z 56). But then he corrects himself: if one sees the *expression* of an expectation, which would be the only possible sense in which one could 'perceive an expectation', then one sees what is expected. Especially, of course, if the expectation is expressed in language: it is in language that an expectation and its fulfilment make contact (PI I, 445). In the *Bemerkungen* there is a similar self-correction. 'Only articulated processes deserve the name of thoughts; or perhaps one could say, only processes which have an articulated expression' (PB 70).

Later Wittgenstein doubted whether one could call a phenomenon such as expectation 'an articulated process'. In the

Zettel, having described behaviour characteristic of a particular expectation, he asks: 'Was my behaviour only a side effect of the real expectation, and was that a special mental process? And was this process homogeneous or articulated like a sentence (with an *internal* beginning and end)' (z 53)? The questions obviously expect the answer 'no'; but Wittgenstein would have continued more sympathetic to the suggestion that expectation was a state whose *expression* must be articulate – the only expression adequate to isolate the expectation of a particular object is a verbal expression, and the verbal expression is as it were 'the movement of a pointer which shows the object of expectation' (z 53).

This verbal expression must be, in a sense, articulate: though here too Wittgenstein was shortly after the *Bemerkungen* to make a small, but important, modification to the *Tractatus* theory. 'I do not think' he told Waismann in September 1930 'that it is correct to say that every proposition must be composite in the verbal sense. Suppose that "*ambulo*" consisted only of the root-syllable. The truth is that every proposition is an instance of a general rule for the formation of signs.' He means that though there has to be composition of a kind for sentences, the elements combined need not both be verbal elements. We might have a convention, for instance, that if the root '*ambul*' were uttered *without* a termination then it was the utterer who was being said to walk. We already have a similar convention in English: if the word 'walk' is uttered in a certain tone of voice without any subject being attached to the verb, then the utterance is normally taken as an imperative, and the subject of the verb as the addressee (wwK 107).

At this point we can see that though much of the picture theory remains, its significance is profoundly altered in various ways. Instead of a proposition being linked to reality by means of a psychological state possessing the required multiplicity, each psychological state is linked to reality by being expressed in a proposition which belongs to a system of the required multiplicity. No picture, not even enriched by lines of projection, can be linked with what it depicts save by a technique of projection, and the technique cannot itself be contained in the picture (z 236, 291). This was stressed from the *Bemerkungen* onwards. Suppose I give someone the instruction '*p*'. If he asks 'What does "*p*" instruct me to do?' I can only tell him, i.e. give him yet another sign. I could, of course, play-act what he is to do; but even here I must get across that he is to imitate me. 'Sooner or later there must come a leap from the sign to what it signifies . . . the assumption that in the order a picture goes proxy for the event does not help, because even so there has to be the transition from the picture to what is depicted' (PB 66–7).

In the *Bemerkungen* Wittgenstein was closer than at any other time of his life to the central positions of logical positivism. The best known of these is the verification principle, which in its starkest form stated that the meaning of a proposition is its mode of verification. Several times in conversation in 1929–30 Wittgenstein subscribed to this principle (wwk 47–8, 79; cf. wwk 244).

'The sense of a question' he wrote in the *Bemerkungen* 'is the mode of its answering . . . tell me how you seek and I will tell you what you seek' (PB 66–7). He was rather more interested in the mathematical analogue of the principle of verification, namely the thesis that the sense of a mathematical proposition is the mode of its proof. The relation of an immediate datum to the ordinary-language proposition it verifies, he wrote, is the same as that of the visible mathematical proof to the equation it verifies. Neither of them is a mere expression of something else, replaceable by a different expression of the same thing. 'Verification is not just one among several indications of the truth, but the very sense of the proposition' (PB 200).

It is in the last chapter of the *Bemerkungen* that the fullest account of the relation between proposition and verification is given. Here Wittgenstein treats 'proposition' and 'hypothesis' apparently as synonymous terms. 'A proposition, a hypothesis, is linked with reality more or less loosely. In the extreme case there is no longer any connection: reality can do whatever it likes without coming into conflict with the proposition. In that case the proposition, the hypothesis, is senseless.' All our signs, in however complicated a manner, refer to immediate experience and not to some extra *Ding an sich*; phenomena are not symptoms for something else which really verifies propositions; they are themselves the reality which make propositions true or false (PB 283).

This is clear enough, and familiar enough. But there are many puzzling features about what Wittgenstein says in this chapter. At one point he says that if the sense of a proposition can never be completely verified, then the proposition has no meaning; 'If a hypothesis cannot be definitively verified, then it cannot be verified at all, and there is no truth or falsehood for it' (PB 283; WWK 47). But a few paragraphs earlier he had said – surely more plausibly – 'All that is necessary for our propositions about reality to have sense is this: our experience must *in some sense* be in agreement or conflict with them. Immediate experience need verify no more than *one* facet of them. This picture is taken immediately from reality, because we say "Here is a chair" when we see only one side of it' (PB 282; cf. 283). How are these passages to be reconciled? On the one hand, he seems to be saying that conclusive verification is necessary if a proposition, or hypothesis, is to make sense; on the other, he seems to be saying that something far less than conclusive verification is adequate.

The solution is given a few pages later (PB 285). Wittgenstein thinks that the definitive verification of a hypothesis is neither possible nor necessary. It is not possible: not in the sense that there is such a thing as conclusive verification, which we can only approach and never succeed in reaching; but rather, that the formal relation which a hypothesis has to reality is something quite different from that of verification – it is a looser relation, though not, as he said at the beginning of the chapter, so loose that it can never conflict with reality. A hypothesis such as 'Here is a book' is related to the particular observations made to verify it in the way that a curve on a graph is related to the points from which it is constructed. 'If our experiences yield the points on a straight line, then the proposition that these experiences are different glimpses of a straight line is a hypothesis. The hypothesis is a method of representing the reality, because a new experience can agree with it or disagree with it, and, it may be, can necessitate an alteration of the hypothesis' (PB 285).

Wittgenstein's main interest in the verification principle in this chapter was in applying it ('our old principle' he calls it) to sentences expressing probabilities. But the preliminary discussion of it from which I have quoted seems to me to be of considerable historical importance. From one point of view it can appear as marking a departure from a strong verification principle in favour of a weak verification principle: to be meaningful a sentence need not be conclusively verifiable, but it must be capable of being confirmed by experience. Or it can be taken as marking a greater interest in falsifiability than in verifiability: the hypothesis is falsified when an alteration of it is necessary. But I think that the revision of the principle now adopted by Wittgenstein is more radical than this, though it is not yet clear-cut and its importance can be seen only with hindsight based on his later work.

First of all, the hypotheses which are not conclusively verifiable are, as we have seen, not things which contingently fall short of being verifiable; they are things which stand in an altogether different relation to reality, so much so that the words 'true' and 'false' should not be applied to them, or can be applied only with a different meaning (PB 285). Secondly, the verification principle in its original form was about propositions: and the question arises whether 'hypotheses' count as propositions or not. On the one hand, as remarked above, Wittgenstein appears to use the two terms in synonymous apposition in these passages, and it is clear from the examples that perfectly ordinary propositions like 'Here is a book' count as hypotheses in Wittgenstein's current sense. On the other hand, if hypotheses are not, in any ordinary sense, true or false, then it seems that they are not, in any ordinary sense, propositions; and indeed there are passages in this chapter where Wittgenstein seems to make a sharp distinction between the two. 'A hypothesis is a law for the construction of propositions . . . a proposition is, so to speak, a cross-section of a hypothesis at a particular point' (PB 285-6). In these passages a proposition seems strictly to be a record of immediate experience. Later Wittgenstein would come to think that it was the propositions of ordinary language he here calls hypotheses which were the genuine propositions. The propositions which at this time he thought were records of immediate experience, involving no element of hypothesis, he later came to regard as not being propositions, or indeed records, at all. The experiences which provide the 'points on the graph' for the propositions are then thought of not as verifying the propositions but as criteria for their truth – that is, as non-inductive evidence for their truth. The later stages of this development will be the subject-matter of later chapters; at present I merely wish to remark that the final chapter of the *Bemerkungen* marks a turning point. At the end-point of the evolution verification loses its unique importance. 'Asking whether and how a proposition can be verified is only a particular way of asking "How d'you mean?" The answer is a contribution to the grammar of the proposition' (PI I, 353).

At the end of the *Bemerkungen* one important feature of verificationism remains: 'According to my principle, two suppositions must be identical in sense, if all possible experiences which confirm the one confirm the other also – if no decision on the grounds of experience between the two is conceivable' (PB 282). Does this principle, applied to reports of mental states and events, lead to behaviourism, the view that ascriptions of mental states and events are at bottom ascriptions of behaviour? In Waismann's *Theses* of 1930, based largely on the *Tractatus* and discussions with Wittgenstein, behaviourism is exhibited as the consequence of the verification principle.

A sentence cannot say more than is established by its verification. If I say 'My friend is angry' and ascertain this by his displaying certain perceptible behaviour, then I *mean* by it nothing more than that he is displaying this behaviour . . . The method of verification is not a means, or vehicle, but the sense itself. I can say 'I will drive to A' or 'I will walk to A', and there we have two different means of transport in space. But I cannot say 'I can verify the proposition in one of two ways.' (WWK 244)

Wittgenstein, in the sixth chapter of the *Bemerkungen*, applies his principles to the particular case of pain (PB 94). First he says 'The two hypotheses, that other men have toothache, and that other men behave exactly as I do but have no toothache, could be identical in sense. That is, if I had learnt the second form of expression, I would speak in pitying tones about men who have no toothache, but behave as I do when I have it.' Later he says more decisively 'The two hypotheses, that others have pain, and that they do not have pain but only behave as I do when I have it, must be identical in sense if all possible experiences which confirm the one confirm the other also – if no decision on grounds of experience between the two of them is conceivable' (PB 95).

The second of these formulations looks backward to the 'old principle' – the sense of a proposition being given by its verification in experience. The first of them looks forward to the theory of language-games: the theory that the sense of a proposition is given not just by its verification, but by its connection with a host of non-linguistic activities of which verification is only one and commiseration, for example, is another. Neither formulation, by itself, commits one to behaviourism. One might accept even the second, more verificationist, formulation and explain it along non-behaviourist lines, saying that there were possible experiences which confirmed one and not the other, e.g. the experiences to which one would appeal in trying to settle, in a real case, whether someone was really in pain or just pretending. Or one might say that though no experience could settle between the behaviourist and the mentalist position this showed not that the two positions came to the same but that the difference between them was somehow given prior to experience, so that the two positions were not really hypotheses.

Wittgenstein appears to have been attracted by both these conflicting views of the second formulation. 'It is not possible to believe something which one cannot somehow imagine verified. If I say I believe that someone is sad, I as it were see his behaviour through the medium of sadness, from the point of view of sadness' (PB 89). Here the first sentence seems to support the first interpretation (one can believe someone is sad, so one can verify it); the second to support the second (belief in the sadness is in some way prior to the observed sad behaviour, a form of observation).

Wittgenstein's positive account of these matters became clearer later, as we shall see. What he is at this point most concerned to do is to argue against a position which seems both to follow from, and to be destructive of, verificationism. The position goes like this.

(1) 'I am in pain' is a proposition which I verify by inner observation of myself.

(2) 'He is in pain' says the same thing about him as 'I am in pain' says about me.

(3) Therefore 'He is in pain' is a proposition which is verified by inner observation of him. (From 1 and 2)

(4) I cannot inwardly observe him: I cannot stand to his pain in the relation that he stands to it, or that I stand to mine.

(5) Therefore 'He is in pain' cannot be verified. (From 3 and 4)

(6) Therefore 'I am in pain' cannot be verified. (From 2 and 5)

(7) Therefore 'I am in pain' is meaningless. (From 6 and the principle of verification)

Premisses 1, 2 and 4 can seem intuitively obvious; yet coupled with the verification principle they seem to lead to the conclusion that the reports of immediate experience which, on verificationist views, provide the underpinning for the verification and therefore for the meaningfulness of all other propositions, are themselves meaningless. Faced with this difficulty, Wittgenstein's reaction is to question premisses 1, 2 and 4 rather than the verification principle. He came to believe that they were all false; and he continued to believe this long after he had ceased to be centrally interested in verificationism.

(1) Words like 'observe', 'perceive', Wittgenstein says, belong to the ordinary 'physicalist' language for dealing with tables, boxes and other physical objects (PB 88). If one talks of perceiving one's pain, then pain is represented as something which can be perceived in the way a matchbox is perceived. (If this were the appropriate expression, then it would not be the pain but the perception of pain which would be the unpleasant thing (PB 94).) But the form of speech 'I perceive x' belongs to the physicalist language, and cannot be applied in phenomenological contexts, where x is a sense-datum, without the sense of both 'I' and 'perceive' changing (PB 88). The experience of pain is not the experience that a person called 'I' has something: in pain I can distinguish intensity, localization, etc., but not the possessor of pain (PB 94).

In contrast with what he later came to think, Wittgenstein is still content to say that 'I am in pain' is a proposition which gets compared with reality. For he says '"I am not in pain" means: if I compare the proposition "I am in pain" with reality, it is shown to be false' (PB 92). But the comparison does not involve any identification of myself as the subject of the sentence: I could, like some oriental despot, adopt a convention according to which when I am in pain I said 'There is pain' and when someone else, A, is in pain, I say: 'A is behaving as Kenny behaves when there is pain' (PB 89). This language, containing no first person, can do all that our present language does; and the difference between first and third person in our language comes out only in a difference between the application of the language. As he put it in considering the same hypothesis in the Waismann conversations, if I have toothache, I can say 'Now there is toothache', and that is the end of the verification; but someone else, A, can say 'Kenny has tooth-ache' – or better 'Kenny is behaving as A behaves when there is toothache' – and this proposition is no longer the end of the verification (wwᴋ 50). The difference between the two formu-lations comes to the same as that in our own language he later expressed by saying 'Psychological verbs are characterized by the fact that the third person of the present is to be verified by observation, the first person not' (z 472). Now if 'I am in pain' had the logical form, the logical multiplicity it appears to have, this replacement by 'There is pain' would not be possible.

(2) Given these differences between the first- and third-person uses of psychological verbs it already follows that 'He is in pain' does not, despite appearances, say the same thing about him as 'I am in pain' does about me; for 'I am in pain' is not strictly *about* me. Wittgenstein adds other reasons for the denial of (2). 'Does it make sense to say "I am in pain, but I do not notice"? In this sentence one could certainly replace "I am" with "he is". And conversely, if the propositions "He is in pain" and "I am in pain" stand on the same level logically, I must be able to replace "he is" with "I am" in the sentence "He is in pain which I do not feel"' (ᴘʙ 91). Moreover, 'I am in pain' when *I* utter it is a sign of a different kind from the same sentence in the mouth of another; for in another's mouth it does not convey its message unless I know whose mouth uttered it. The propositional sign consists not only in the sounds, but in the fact that such and such a mouth produced them (ᴘʙ 93).

(3) Wittgenstein regards it as a total confusion to say that one cannot observe another's pain because one cannot have another's pain. In the first place, having a pain is not observing pain, as remarked above; in the second place 'I cannot have your pain' does not rule out any genuine possibility. It would be bizarre, but quite imaginable, that I should feel pain in your

body (e.g. be sensitive to injuries in your tooth or your leg); it would be possible, and indeed often happens, that I feel the same pain as you in the sense of feeling a pain in the same place and of the same intensity, etc. But if pain is conceived as a sense-datum, as something which it is unthinkable anyone else should have, then it cannot be informatively said that I have it as opposed to others (PB 90–91). *Having* toothache is not a relation between two terms, a person and a pain; for this to be so each term of the relation would have to be identifiable separately from the holding of the relation, which is obviously not the case (PB 91). There is, as Wittgenstein says, using *Tractatus* terminology to make an *Investigations*-like point, not the necessary logical multiplicity in the feeling of pain to justify the 'my' in 'I feel my pain.'

'Our language', Wittgenstein says, 'uses the expression "my pain" and "his pain"; and also the expressions "I am in pain" and "He is in pain." An expression such as "I feel my pain" or 'I feel his pain" is nonsense. And it is on this, it seems to me, that the whole controversy about behaviourism finally rests' (PB 94). And despite the behaviourist-sounding suggestion from which we began, he goes on to draw a conclusion which seems designed to show that behaviourism is self-refuting. Let us suppose that behaviourism is the doctrine that others do not feel pain but only behave the way I do when I feel pain. Then either this is a genuine hypothesis, in which case there will be some conceivable experience which will settle whether behaviourism is true, or there will be no conceivable experience to settle between behaviourism and mentalism; in that case behaviourism must be being asserted on *a priori* grounds. But to assert behaviourism one must say that others feel no pain; but this presupposes that it makes sense to say that they feel pain; so it cannot be ruled out *a priori* that they feel pain.

The argument in the *Bemerkungen* is obscure and frequently ambiguous. But it contains many of the essential elements which we shall later see fully developed in the private-language argument of the *Philosophical Investigations*.

CHAPTER 8

Understanding, Thinking and Meaning

During the early 1930s Wittgenstein wrote copiously. The preface to the *Philosophische Bemerkungen* was written in November 1930. Between July 1930 and July 1932 he wrote into notebooks entitled 'Remarks on Philosophical Grammar' many brief paragraphs, philosophical reflections, arguments and aphorisms on several topics. Out of these notebooks he made a selection which he worked into a consecutive text late in 1932 or early in 1933, and which he revised partially but drastically at the end of 1933. Despite these revisions he was never satisfied with the text as it stood. Many of the paragraphs contained in the manuscript were used, modified or unaltered, in the *Philosophical Investigations*. But the work as a whole was not published until 1969 when it appeared posthumously as *Philosophische Grammatik*.

The *Philosophische Grammatik* is by far Wittgenstein's longest work. Its first part, entitled 'The Proposition and its Sense', is about as long as, and covers some of the same ground as, the *Philosophical Investigations*. The second part, 'On Logic and Mathematics', is about as long as, and covers some of the same ground as, *The Remarks on the Foundations of Mathematics*. The final revision of the first part is almost contemporary with, and in many respects very close to, the English notes which Wittgenstein dictated to his class in Cambridge during the session 1933–4 and which circulated under the title *The Blue Book*. It occupies a central place in his thought, firmly linking the earlier philosophy to the later philosophy. At different times of his life Wittgenstein employed different slogans about meaning: that a proposition has meaning in virtue of being a picture, that the meaning of a proposition is the mode of its verification, that the meaning of an expression is its use. All of these slogans appear in the

Grammatik, apparently quite happily reconciled with each other. Many of the characteristic ideas of the *Philosophical Investigations* – the notions of language-game, family likeness, criterion, the distinction between meaning and bearer, cause and reason; the criticisms of the conception of understanding as an inner process, and of the attempt to explain language on the basis of ostensive definition – are found in this book in embryo or fully fledged. Some of the most famous passages of the *Investigations* – for instance, the discussion of St Augustine's naïve theory of language – turn out to be excerpted from the *Grammatik*; and on the other hand some passages of the *Grammatik* which were not excerpted cast light on baffling passages of the *Investigations*. (Compare, for instance, PG 54 and PI I, 559.)

The first part of the *Grammatik* can be regarded as an attempt to answer the question: what is it that gives significance to the sounds and marks on paper which make up sentences in language? By themselves the symbols seem inert and dead; what is it that gives them life (PG 40, 107; PI I, 430)? The obvious answer is that they become alive by being meant by speakers and writers and understood by hearers and readers. This obvious answer is indeed the true one; but, Wittgenstein believed, it is almost always misleading, because we have a confused picture of what meaning and understanding are.

We think of meaning and understanding, and thought in general, as processes which are simultaneous with, and accompany, the speaking, hearing, writing, and reading of language. Unlike the written or spoken syllables, however, the elements of these processes – so we think – are invisible and inaudible; the processes are not material, but take place in the spiritual recesses of the mind. Against this Wittgenstein argues that meaning and understanding are not processes at all, and that the criteria by which we decide whether someone understood a sentence, and what he meant by it, are quite different from the criteria by which we discover what mental processes are going on while someone is talking or writing (PG 148; Z 236).

Moreover, Wittgenstein argued, the notion of mental process is itself one which needs clarification. Someone who talks of mental processes may mean something analogous to an experience, something which a conscious subject can report upon after introspection. Or he may mean an event in a hypothetical mechanism postulated to explain the observable intelligent behaviour of a human being, an event of which the owner of the mind may not be conscious. Neither of these ways of viewing mental processes is altogether free from confusion; and very often the two ways are combined in a manner which generates further confusion. For instance, a mental event is postulated as part of a quasi-mechanical theory (e.g. an act of the will is postulated as a cause of a voluntary action), and it turns out that the owner of the mind was not, in the ordinary way, conscious of any such event. It is then suggested that the event *did* occur – it *was* presented to consciousness – but was too sudden, or brief, to be properly observed by the inner eye of introspection. Wittgenstein tried to dispel these confusions by patient examination of particular cases. His handling of detailed examples is vivid and convincing, and these qualities will be lost in summary; on the other hand a summary may hope to give what is conspicuously lacking in the *Grammatik*, a clear overall view of where the argument is moving.

First, then, what is meant by saying that understanding, and meaning, are not mental processes? What kind of thing *is* a mental process? Saying the ABC to oneself in one's head is an example of the kind of thing which might be meant by the expression 'mental process': it is a *process* in the sense that it has a beginning, a middle and an end; it takes a certain time, which I might measure on a stopwatch; it can be interrupted after I have only got a certain way, say to K; it can be simultaneous with, and last a longer or shorter time than other processes such as the burning of a match. It is a *mental* process in the sense that it is not in any ordinary way perceptible to others (unlike my saying the ABC aloud); it is only by asking me that others could find out I was doing it.

When I say 'The weather is fine', and mean and understand what I am saying, then my meaning it is not a mental process of this kind which accompanies what I say, in the way in which I might accompany my climbing up stairs with silent counting of my steps. It is true that when we hear a sentence in a language we know, there are mental events – feelings, images, etc. – which differ from those which occur when we hear a sentence in a language we do not know. Similarly a man who knows the rules of chess will have different experiences when he watches a game from someone who does not know the rules (e.g. he will be excited, admiring, contemptuous, etc.) (PG 41, 49–50). But these experiences will vary from case to case, and cannot be regarded as themselves constituting the understanding.

Again, if someone shows me a series of numbers, and I suddenly realize how to continue it, it is idle to look at my experience at the moment of realization with a view to grasping the essence of understanding. Many different things may happen – I may think of a formula, or recognize a familiar feature of the series, or simply think 'That's easy!' – and none of them are either necessary or sufficient to constitute understanding (PG 65; PI I, 151–5). What is relevant to understanding, in the three cases, is not the experiences a man has but his abilities: can he speak the language, can he play the game, can he continue the series correctly (PI I, 181)? And an ability is not a process. '*When* do you know how to play chess? All the time? Or just while you are making a move? And the *whole* of chess during each move? – How queer that knowing how to play chess should take such a short time, and a game so much longer!' (PG 51; PI I, 151.)

We are tempted to think of the understanding of a sentence as a process like the translation of it into another language (PG 74), but anyone who is tempted to think of meaning as a process which accompanies speech should try to perform that process without the speaking (PI I, 332; PG 155; BB 42). 'Make the following experiment' says Wittgenstein '*say* "It's cold here" and *mean* "It's warm here". Can you do it? And what are you doing as you do it?' (PI I, 510.)

Indeed understanding cannot really be thought of as a process at all. 'When do we understand a sentence?' Wittgenstein asks. 'When we have uttered the whole of it? Or while we are uttering it? Is the understanding an articulated process like the speaking of the sentence; and does its articulation correspond to the articulation of the sentence? Or is it non-articulated, accompanying the sentence in the way in which a pedal point accompanies a melody?' (PG 50.) To understand a word, like knowing how to play chess, is a state rather than a process. But even calling it a state is possibly misleading. If it is a mental state, it is not a psychological state like pain or depression or excitement. Such states last over periods, and can be continuous or interrupted; but one cannot know uninterruptedly what a word means (PG 48; PI p. 59).

One way in which we can be misled by thinking of knowledge and understanding as mental states is this. We see particular displays of knowledge and exhibitions of understanding: knowledge of how to play chess is exhibited in the actual playing of chess; understanding of a word, e.g. in the execution of an order containing it. We think of knowledge as a precondition of its exercise: we think of the understanding of an order as a precondition of obeying it (PG 132; PI I, 430ff.). We are then tempted to imagine knowledge and understanding as states of a hidden system or mechanism of which we see only the outward operation. We picture knowledge as the reservoir from which its exercise flows like visible water; we think that when words are meant and not just spoken, then they are coupled to something within us, instead of just running idle (PG 49; PI I, 507; BB 118).

We may think, perhaps, of the mental processes and states postulated to account for intelligent behaviour and meaningful use of language as being not totally inaccessible to introspection. Normally, we may think, we are not conscious of a mental process of meaning going on in our minds as we talk:

but may this not be simply because the mechanism of the mind operates very swiftly, as it were, so that its movements are invisible in the same way as the movements of the needle in a sewing-machine (PG 105)? Perhaps, if only we introspected with greater attention, we feel, or if we could get the machinery to run in slow motion, we would be able to see in every case something like the situation when a halting German-speaker forms English sentences in his mind when he talks, or at least a semi-permanent state of mind, like a mental light being switched on (BB 34-5, 43).

The mechanism we thus imagine is a *mental* mechanism in two senses. First, as mentioned above, because it is not accessible to empirical investigation: it could not be discovered, for instance, by opening up the skull of a thinker (PG 82-3). Secondly, because if it is to explain all that it has to explain, the mechanism must be constructed out of a very strange type of material, which we imagine as gaseous and ethereal (PI I, 109). 'The mechanism of the mind . . .' we think

can bring about effects which no material mechanism could. Thus e.g. a thought (which is such a mental process) can agree or disagree with reality; I am able to think of a man who isn't present; I am able to imagine him, 'mean him' in a remark which I make about him, even if he is thousands of miles away or dead. 'What a queer mechanism' one might say 'the mechanism of wishing must be if I can wish that which will never happen.' (BB 3-4; cf. PG 99f., 154)

Now Wittgenstein believed that this notion of a mental mechanism was a confusion based on a misunderstanding of the functioning of the language of reporting mental states. An explanatory mechanism might, of course, be postulated to account for the intelligent use of language by human beings. Some physiologists, no doubt, hope eventually to be able to locate in the brain states and processes which will correspond to, and account for, the human use of thought and language. But, if such a hope were fulfilled, what the physiologists would discover would not be the mental mechanism we imagined. For it would not be a private mechanism discoverable by attentive introspection: it would be just a mechanism within the skull, discoverable by sophisticated, but not at all ethereal, empirical methods; and the principles of its operation would not be those of a quasi-supernatural medium, but those of electricity, biochemistry, or whatever turns out to be the appropriate physical system (cf. BB 7–9). Such an explanation, Wittgenstein thought, might be possible; though he insisted that there was no *necessity* that there should be a physiological counterpart of thought. 'No supposition seems to me more natural' he wrote

than that there is no process in the brain correlated with associating or with thinking; so that it would be impossible to read off thought-processes from brain-processes . . . It is thus perfectly possible that certain psychological phenomena cannot be investigated physiologically, because physiologically nothing corresponds to them. I saw this man years ago: now I have seen him again, I recognize him, I remember his name. And why does there have to be a cause of this remembering in my nervous system? Why must something or other, whatever it may be, be stored up there *in any form*? Why *must* a trace have been left behind? Why should there not be a psychological regularity to which no physiological regularity corresponds? If this upsets our concept of causality then it is high time it was upset. (z 608–10)

Again, a psychologist might attempt to construct an explanatory model of the workings of the mind on the basis of certain empirical results of psychological investigations. The model would be part of a psychological theory, Wittgenstein suggested, in the way in which a mechanical model of the ether could be part of a theory of electricity (BB 6). As an example of a model of this kind we might instance Chomsky's idea that the mind possesses innately certain organizing principles of universal grammar as an abstract system underlying behaviour. The existence or non-existence of such a model is to be argued for in terms of its necessity or adequacy in explaining certain human linguistic activities and skills (in particular the construction of well-formed sentences of varying degrees of complexity).

It differs from a physiological model in that it carries no commitment to a localization in the body nor to a specific mechanism of incarnation. It differs also from our naïve notion of a mind-model in that it is not supposed to be, even in principle, available to introspection in a gaseous internal medium.

Wittgenstein did not wish to rule out the possibility of either type of explanation of behaviour. The notion of a mental mechanism, which he thought was the result of confusion about language, was different from either of the two notions outlined above. It is a picture which we conjure up to enable us, as it were, to grasp the *nature* of thinking, rather than to provide empirically testable hypotheses about causal connections. It is a metaphysical fiction, not a scientific hypothesis. It is not, however, irrelevant to the scientific investigation of thought, since it may, if uncriticized, misrepresent the nature of the phenomena to be explained.

Wittgenstein's criticism of the notion takes two principal forms. First he shows that even if there were something as like as it is possible to be to the mental mechanism we uncritically imagine, this would not in any way solve any of the puzzlement we feel about meaning, understanding and thought. Secondly he shows that the criteria for deciding whether and what someone understands, means and thinks are quite different from the sort of criteria by which we decide whether mental processes are taking place.

To illustrate his first procedure, consider one very popular form of the mental-mechanism doctrine, according to which the understanding of the meaning of a word consists in calling up an appropriate image in association with it, and the utterance of a word is comparable to striking a note on the keyboard of the imagination (PI I, 6, 449). We may think, for instance, that in order to understand the order 'Bring me a red flower' one must have a red image in mind, and that it is by comparison with this image that one ascertains which flower to bring. But this cannot be right: otherwise how could one obey the order 'Imagine a red patch'? On this view, before obeying one would have to conjure up a red patch to serve as a pattern for the red patch one is ordered to imagine; which is absurd (BB 3; cf. PG 96).

In order to rid ourselves of the illusion that the possession of a red mental image could explain the ability to understand the meaning of 'red', Wittgenstein suggests that we replace the visual image with the actual seeing of a red bit of paper. If the redness of the image explains the understanding of the meaning of 'red', then surely the more vivid redness of the red sample will do so even better (BB 4). But once we adopt this suggestion, we see that the image explains nothing: for if it is to be explained how someone knows what 'red' means, it is equally to be explained how he knows that his sample image – whether mental or physical – is red. 'As soon as you think' Wittgenstein says 'of replacing the mental image by, say, a painted one, and as soon as the image thereby loses its occult character, it ceases to seem to impart any life to the sentence at all' (BB 5). Of course, it is true that often as we talk mental images pass through our minds. But it is not they which confer meanings on the words we use. It is rather the other way round: the images are like the pictures illustrating a text in a book. It is no more necessary, in order to understand a sentence, that one should imagine anything in connection with it, than that one should make a sketch from it (PI I, 396).

The criteria by which we decide whether someone understands what is going on and the criteria by which we decide what imagery someone is having are quite different. This is particularly so in the cases of understanding music and of understanding poetry, which Wittgenstein frequently compares to the case of understanding a sentence (PG 41; PI I, 527). But the point is a general one. To understand a sentence involves understanding a language; and to understand a language is to master a technique (BB 5): such mastery, unlike images, can be tested, and checked up on by others. This is one important difference between the criteria for having images and understanding. In the case of my mental imagery what I say about it is authoritative; no one else can correct my reports, and the nearest he can come to correcting them is to point perhaps to internal inconsistencies in what I say about them. But others may very well know better than I whether I understand a sentence or an expression: I may wrongly think that I know what is meant by 'absolute motion' or that I mean something by a sentence which on examination turns out to be senseless (PG 130; PI I, 513–17; Z 246, 250). Moreover, the criteria for the possession of images are parasitic on those for the possession of understanding. For to find out what images a man has we must ask him; but if what he says is to tell us what his images are, then he must understand the words he uses. It is futile, therefore, to try to explain understanding by means of mental images.

We saw already that meaning cannot be timed and clocked as various mental processes can. In this connection Wittgenstein was fond of telling a joke about a French politician who said that it was a characteristic of the French language that in it words occur in the order in which one thinks of them (PG 107; PI I, 336). That this is a joke shows that there is something wrong in treating thought as an articulate process like saying.

In the *Blue Book* Wittgenstein summarized the results of his investigation thus.

If we scrutinize the usages which we make of such words as 'thinking', 'meaning', 'wishing', etc., going through this process rids us of the temptation to look for a peculiar act of thinking, independent of the act of expressing our thoughts, and stowed away in some peculiar medium . . . The scrutiny of the grammar of a word weakens the position of certain fixed standards of our expression which had prevented us from seeing facts with unbiassed eyes. (BB 43)

In particular, we are not misled by the analogy between the forms of expression 'to say something' and 'to mean something', which though they have a superficial grammatical similarity are quite different at the level of what we might call 'depth grammar' and do not refer to two parallel processes (BB 35; PI I, 664).

Though 'to mean', 'to understand', 'to think' all differ at the level of depth grammar from verbs like 'to say', 'to whistle', yet the depth grammar of each of them has its own distinctive features, and Wittgenstein in the *Grammatik*, the *Blue Book* and the *Investigations* devotes considerable pains to teasing out the differences between them and related concepts, and the different circumstances appropriate to the use of each of them.

Thinking is much more like a process than understanding is. Thinking out a problem silently is something in which one can be interrupted, even if it may not be a process divisible into clockable parts. Often, of course, we think in language, saying things silently to ourselves: indeed we can think by writing or speaking (BB 6). This does not mean that there are 'meanings' going through our minds in addition to the verbal expressions: the language is itself the vehicle of thought (PI I, 329). But it is perhaps comparatively rare for full-blown sentences to pass through our minds; often a thought goes through one's head like lightning, the solution of a problem suddenly flashes on us 'with the speed of thought' and so on. This does not mean that inward thought has mysterious properties unshared by outer speech: I can see or understand a whole thought in a flash, Wittgenstein says, in exactly the sense in which I can make a note of it in a few words or a few pencilled strokes (PI I, 318–19). What gives the flash, or the notes, a content corresponding to a complicated thought is not anything that happens at the time, but all kinds of circumstances before and after, just as in the case of the man who suddenly sees how to complete an algebraic series (PI I, 323; PG 65).

What is the relation between thought and language? Can one think without speaking? The way to answer this is not to introspect and wait for an occurrence of speechless thought as an astronomer might wait to observe an eclipse. It is rather to consider the different types of thing we call 'thinking', the different types of occasion in which the verb 'to think' is used.

The verb is sometimes used to mark a difference between two types of speaking: speech with thought, and unthinking speech. It is clear enough in this case that thought is not something that can occur without speech, any more than the expression of a piece of music could occur without the music. But we can quite often say of someone that he had the thought that *p*, without our meaning that he said '*p*' aloud or to himself. Wittgenstein gives an example: 'I might act in such a way while taking various measurements that an onlooker would say I had – without words – thought: If two magnitudes are equal to a third, they are equal to one another' (PI I, 330).

However, it can be said of me that I thought something without words only where the thought is one which I could have expressed in some way. Some thoughts – e.g. about God and the creation of the world – seem to be incapable of expression except in language: one cannot take seriously the testimony of a deaf-mute to the effect that he had such thoughts before he learnt language (PI I, 342). There are thoughts which only a language-user can have, as well as thoughts which animals can share: a dog can believe that his master is at the door, but not that his master will come the day after tomorrow, because he cannot master the complicated language in which alone such a hope can be expressed (PI II, 174).

Sometimes, when writing a letter for instance, we strive to find the right expression for a thought. This suggests the picture that the thought is somehow already there, and we merely have to find its expression in words. But if we look at the particular cases to which this description is appropriate, we may find many different things happening. 'I surrender to a mood, and the expression *comes*. Or a picture occurs to me and I try to describe it. Or an English expression occurs to me and I try to hit on the corresponding German one. Or I make a gesture, and ask myself: what words correspond to this gesture? And so on' (PI I, 335). Once we consider these detailed cases, we are less likely to think that in every case in which we express a thought in language there is present in advance an unexpressed thought which we have to translate into language. If we still believe this, it is because of a philosophical belief that wherever there is a single verb applicable to a large number of different situations there must be a single activity taking place common to all those different situations. But this philosophical belief is, Wittgenstein argues, an illusion.

We can imagine people who can only think aloud, as there are people who can only read aloud; but it is not possible to imagine people who spoke only to themselves and never aloud, since our criterion for someone's saying something to himself involves what he tells us about himself (PI I, 331, 344–8).

Thus if we single out various things which might be meant by the question 'Is thought possible without language?' we find a number of different cases, in each of which the answer comes straightforwardly. Instead of finding a single, overall connection of thought with language, we find a number of different interlocking connections. But, though closely connected, the concepts of thinking and speaking are quite unlike each other. To say that thinking is an incorporeal process, while speaking (like eating) is a corporeal one is misleading: not because it makes the two concepts seem too unlike, but because it makes them seem too similar (PI I, 339).

Understanding differs from thinking in several ways. As we saw, it is possible to be mistaken about whether one understands or not; one cannot make the same kinds of mistake about whether one is thinking or not: indeed it is not easy to imagine a mistake here at all (PI I, 328). Understanding, as already mentioned, is more like a state, less like a process, than thinking. In English, of course, 'think' can be used as a synonym for 'believe', where German distinguishes between *denken* and *glauben*; and belief *is* a state (P I p. 190ff.). But even in English, where the same word is used, if one is to avoid philosophical confusion it is important to distinguish the different uses (PI I, 574). Wittgenstein suggests an example which brings out the difference very succinctly. 'When I sat down on this chair, of course I *believed* it would support me. The *thought* of its collapsing never crossed my mind' (PI I, 575; italics mine).

'Understanding' itself covers many different cases, which Wittgenstein examined in detail in chapters I–III of the *Grammatik*. We are inclined to think of understanding as the important thing, and the signs which we use in communicating with each other as inessential and variable means of transferring this mental state from one person to another. But this is a mistake. The relation of signs to understanding is not a causal one like the relation between a drug and a state of hallucination. The relation between signs and understanding is an internal one, and differences in ways of operating with signs mean differences in understanding itself (PG 39, 46, 167). If I have asked someone a question, I am content if he gives me an answer – I do not say: but he has only given me words, signs, how shall I know what he means? If I did say this, the reply would be 'How is *he* to know what he means, when he has nothing but the signs either?' (PG 40; PI 503–4).

We understand a sentence when we are able to translate it into another synonymous one in the same or a different language; we can show understanding by being able to translate a word into a gesture, or a gesture into a word (PG 40–42). There is a difference between this sort of understanding, the understanding which is given by a mastery of a language, and the understanding which depends on familiarity with context. For instance, I understand the sentence 'After he had said this, he left her as on the previous day' in the sense that I know English, and could translate the sentence into other languages; but I don't understand what it means in the way in which I would if I met it in the pages of a novel (PG 43; PI I, 525).

We speak of understanding a sentence in the sense in which it can be replaced by another which says the same; but also in the sense in which it cannot be replaced by another . . . In the one case the thought in the sentence is something common to two different sentences; in the other something that is expressed only by these words in these positions. (Understanding a poem.) (PG 69, PI 531)

Do all these differences make differences of meaning, different senses of 'understand'? No, Wittgenstein replies. These kinds of use of 'understanding' make up its meaning, make up the concept of understanding. We must not think that where there is a concept like 'understanding' all the cases it applies to must have some common property. The different cases may be related to each other through intermediaries, in the way that links of a chain are related to distant links in the same chain. Two members of the extension of a concept may be close to each other and have common features; distant ones may have nothing more in common with each other and yet belong to the same family.

The notion of family likeness was enunciated in the *Grammatik* and developed in the *Blue Book*. Entities which we commonly subsume under a general term, Wittgenstein wrote, need not have anything in common;

they form a family the members of which have family likenesses. Some of them have the same nose, others the same eyebrows and others again the same way of walking; and these likenesses overlap. The idea of a general concept being a common property of its particular instances connects up with other primitive, too simple, ideas of the structure of language. (BB, 17, cf. also BB 87, 124; PI I, 67; PG 75)

The primitive conception of language which Wittgenstein is criticizing is one in which all words are conceived on the pattern of simple types of common noun and proper name. As a spokesman for the primitive conception of language in the *Grammatik* and the *Investigations* Wittgenstein took St Augustine, who at the beginning of his *Confessions*, described how he learnt language as a child.

When my elders named some object, and accordingly moved towards something, I saw this and I grasped that the thing was called by the sound they uttered when they meant to point it out. Their intention was shown by their bodily movements, as it were the natural language of all peoples . . . Thus, as I heard words repeatedly used in their proper places in various sentences, I gradually learnt to understand what objects they signified. (*Confessions* I, 8; PI I, 1; cf. PG 56; BB 77)

This account, in Wittgenstein's view, is oversimple in two principal ways. First of all, it concentrates excessively on names, and ignores other kinds of words which are used very differently from names, as if a man were to describe chess and forget about the pawns (BB 77). Secondly, even in the case of names, it misunderstands the meaning-relation: it regards the meaning of a name as being the object it stands for, the object with which it is correlated by means of ostensive definition. By contrast, Wittgenstein stresses the multiplicity of different types of word and different uses of language; and he brings out the comparatively limited role played by ostensive definition in bringing about the understanding of language. I shall dwell on each of these points in turn.

There are some words in our language which are clearly not names of objects: for instance, exclamations such as 'Away!' 'Ow!' 'Help!' (PI I, 27). We may be inclined to regard these as unimportant fringe cases, but in fact, Wittgenstein suggests, consideration of them is vital for an understanding of the nature of language. Even among words that look like names, it is clear enough that a word like 'five' functions rather differently from a word like 'apple' – to know what 'five' means one has to be able to *count*, and there is nothing quite like that presupposed by knowing the meaning of 'apple' (PI I, 1; BB 79). We are sometimes inclined to account for this by saying that while 'apple' and 'five' are both names, they are names of different kinds of object: apples are tangible, numbers intangible objects. But that is not quite right: a number may just as well be defined by pointing as a word like 'apple' may: one can define 'five' by pointing to five apples (PG 25; PI I, 28; BB 79). But the use of the words *after* they have been defined is totally different.

To illustrate the diversity of types of word in language

Wittgenstein uses many similes and metaphors. Language is like a toolbag: the functions of different words are as different as that of hammer, chisel, square and gluepot (PG 31; BB 67; PI I, 11). Language is like the cabin of a locomotive, with a row of similar handles but the most diverse modes of operation (PB 13; PG 58; PII, 12). Language is an ancient city with different types of building and different kinds of street and square; irregular and maze-like at the centre, ever growing out into the regimented suburbs of the symbolisms of scientific disciplines (PI I, 18; BB 81). Words on the page all look alike; but their representative functions are as different as those of lines on maps (frontiers, street-lines, meridians, grid-lines, etc) (PG 58). Words have as many different uses as money, which can buy a cow, a title, a seat at the theatre, rapid travel, or life itself (PG 63).

In order to grasp the meaning of words, we should not look for an object for which they stand, but should study the diversity of their functions. Frequently, at this time, Wittgenstein repeats two slogans. The first is, that the meaning of a word is its use in a language (e.g. PG 60; PI I, 43). The second is that the meaning of a word is what the explanation of the meaning explains (e.g. PG 60; BB 1).

Instead of saying that the meaning of a word is its use in a language, Wittgenstein sometimes says that it is its use in a calculus (PG 63, 67) or in a language-game (PG 67). In the next chapter we shall have to see in detail what Wittgenstein meant by 'language-game': for the moment we can use a definition given in the *Blue Book*: language-games are ways of using signs simpler than those in which we use the signs of our highly complicated language (BB 17). Augustine's description of language is valid only for a language-game much simpler than our language: one which might itself function as part of a more complicated language or as a complete primitive language, e.g. one in which a builder has a repertoire merely of the four words 'block', 'pillar', 'slab', 'beam', which he uses to call to an assistant to pass the stones in the order in which he needs them

(PG 57; PI I, 2). But it is possible to find very simple language-games for which Augustine's account is already inadequate: e.g. a greengrocer is given a bit of paper with the words 'five apples': he compares the word 'apple' with the labels on different shelves, he finds it to agree with one of the labels, counts from I to the number written on the slip of paper, and for every number counted takes a fruit off the shelf and puts it in a bag (BB 16; PII, I). Here the explanation of the use of 'five' is something for which there is no place in Augustine's account.

In the *Blue Book*, in glossing the slogan that the meaning of a word is what the explanation of the meaning explains, Wittgenstein said that explanations of the meaning of words could roughly and provisionally be divided into verbal and ostensive definitions. Verbal definition, since it takes us from words to words, in a sense gets us no further: so it can look as if ostensive definition is what takes us the real step towards learning the meaning (BB I). It is very natural to think that one can learn the meaning of a word simply by becoming acquainted with what the word stands for. We learn language, it may seem, by giving names to objects, to human beings, say, and shapes, colours, pains, moods and so on (PI I, 26). The essential part of the learning process appears to be the encounter with the object: others may teach us what words mean, but they must do so by putting us in a position where we ourselves can become acquainted with the object which is the meaning of the word to be learnt (PI I, 362). Once such acquaintance is secured, it seems, the learner has only to fix his attention on the appropriate object and associate the word with it and henceforth he knows its meaning. Once you know what the word stands for, we feel, you understand it, you know its whole use (PI I, 264).

Wittgenstein criticized this view of the operation of ostensive definition in chapters II and IV of the *Grammatik*, in the *Blue Book* at the beginning, and most decisively in the first part of the *Investigations* (see especially PI I, 27–35). He insists that acquaintance with the object for which a word stands is not the same thing as knowledge of the word's meaning: the meaning of a word is not the thing that 'corresponds' to the word. We must beware of confusing the bearer of a name with the meaning of a name (PG 63–4). 'When Mr N. N. dies, one says that the bearer of the name dies, not that the meaning dies' (PI I, 40). Though bearer and meaning are distinct, the meaning of the name is sometimes explained by pointing to its bearer: that is precisely what an ostensive explanation is (PI I, 40). But if such explanation is to be successful the learner must not only be acquainted with the bearer, but also grasp the role in language of the word to be defined. Thus, if I know that someone means to explain a colour-word to me, the ostensive definition 'That is called "sepia"' will help me to understand the word (PI I, 30; PG 88). But the ostensive definition will not suffice by itself, because it can always be variously interpreted. For instance, suppose that I explain the word 'tove' by pointing to a pencil and saying 'This is called "tove".' The explanation would be quite inadequate, because I may be taken to mean 'This is a pencil' or 'This is round' or 'This is wood' or 'This is one' or 'This is hard' and so on (PG 60; BB 2). So in the acquisition of the understanding of a word acquaintance with the word's bearer is not so important as mastery of the word's general use.

Knowing that what I am now seeing is called 'tove' does not by itself enable me to answer the question 'And what else am I to call "tove"?' Wittgenstein illustrated the point by an analogy with chess. If someone points to a piece and says 'This is the king' this does not tell me the use of the piece – how to move it, its importance, etc. – unless I already know the rules of the game and am merely unfamiliar with the shape of the piece (PI I, 31). When we learn a foreign language we are in this position: learning that 'rouge' means 'red' presupposes that I know the place in language occupied by the word 'red' and enables me to slot 'rouge' into the same place. But when I learn my first language I have to master a whole complicated system of the identification, classification and naming of colours if I am to know the place into which 'red' fits. Augustine, says Wittgenstein, 'describes the learning of human language as if the child came into a strange country; and did not understand the language of the country; that is, as if it already had a language, only not this one' (PI I, 32).

CHAPTER 9

Language-Games

The theory of meaning as use is closely connected with the concept of a language-game. In the *Tractatus* there is no mention of language-games, but the connection between meaning and use is already made. At 3.32 Wittgenstein distinguishes between sign and symbol. The sign is what is sensibly perceptible in the symbol, and two different symbols may have their sign (spoken or written sounds) in common. Where this is so they signify in different ways. In order to recognize the symbol in the sign, one has to look at the significant use (TLP 3.327). If a sign has no use it is meaningless; on the other hand if everything behaves as if a sign had meaning, then it does have meaning (TLP 3.328). Part of its use, it appears, is its logical syntax. We are told 'A sign does not determine a logical form unless it is taken together with its logical syntactical employment': but employment must involve something in addition to logical form, because use is sufficient and necessary for meaning, whereas in logical syntax the meaning (*Bedeutung*) of a sign must never play a role (TLP 3.33). What is lacking is presumably the correlation between signs, with their logico-syntactical properties, and the reference of signs. This correlation, Wittgenstein then believed, was a psychological matter: it was no part of the task of the philosopher, the theorist of symbolism, to discover it (NB 129).

In particular the use of a proposition is its application, its employment as a picture, by the correlation of its elements with elements of a possible state of affairs. A thought, a proposition with sense, is a propositional sign (a sentence) applied in thought to the world (TLP 3.5, 4).

After his return to philosophy, as we have seen, Wittgenstein began to think that he had been mistaken in regarding the correlation of names with named objects as a trivial, extra-philosophical matter. Simultaneously he began to regard it as an oversimplification to regard the connection between language and reality as consisting only of two elements, the name-relation and the pictorial nature of the proposition. It was this, among other things, that led to the development of the theory of meaning as use and the exploration of the notion of language-games. As we have seen, he came to believe that a name functions as a name only in the context of a system of linguistic and non-linguistic activities; to explain in detail how this was so was not something that could be left to the psychologist; the description of language-games was one of the main tasks of the philosopher.

In the *Tractatus* Wittgenstein had quoted Frege: only in the context of a proposition does a name have reference (TLP 3.3). In the *Bemerkungen* this is glossed in an interesting manner: it is like saying, he says, that it is only in use that a rod is a lever (BM 140). This is one of the earliest appearances of the comparison between words and tools, which as we have seen plays a dominant part in Wittgenstein's later thought. His first employment of the metaphor of a game appears in a conversation at Schlick's house in June 1930 in a discussion of formalism in mathematics. The passage is striking and deserves quoting at length.

Formalism contains both truth and falsehood. The truth in formalism is that every syntax can be regarded as a system of rules for a game. I have been reflecting on what Weyl can mean when he says that a formalist regards the axioms of mathematics as similar to the rules of chess. I would like to say: not only the axioms of mathematics, but the whole of syntax is arbitrary.

I was asked in Cambridge whether I think that mathematics concerns ink marks on paper. I reply: in just the same sense in which chess concerns wooden figures. Chess, I mean, does not consist in my pushing wooden figures around a board. If I say 'Now I will make myself a queen with very frightening eyes, she will drive everyone off the board' you will laugh. It does not matter what a pawn looks like. What is much rather the case is that the totality of rules of the game determines the logical place of a pawn. A pawn is a variable, like the 'x' in logic . . .

If you ask me: where lies the difference between chess and the syntax of a language I reply: solely in their application . . . If there were men on Mars who made war like the chess pieces, then the generals would use the rules of chess for prediction. It would then be a scientific question whether the king could be mated by a certain deployment of pieces in three moves, and so on. (wwk 104)

The comparison between an axiomatic system and a game of chess is repeated and developed several times in the conversations with Waismann (wwk 163, 170), and it is noted that it was anticipated in Frege's *Grundgesetze der Arithmetik* (wwk 150–51). But there is no general notion of language-game; and indeed the study of language-games is not so much the study of a game-like calculus as a study of the ways in which such a calculus can be *applied*. Nor, so far, is there any reflection on the differences between different games: chess, with its strict formal rules, is always taken as the example.

The *Bemerkungen* is silent about language-games, but in the *Philosophische Grammatik* a whole chapter is devoted to exploring the analogies between arithmetic and chess, and in particular to examining the role of truth and falsehood in arithmetic, and winning and losing in a game (PG 289–95). This treatment is more sophisticated but less picturesque than the one in the conversations with Waismann (cf. PG 294). But the more interesting development in the *Grammatik* is the application of the game-analogy to non-mathematical uses of language.

It is the realization of the variety among games which makes the concept of game a particularly useful one for Wittgenstein to express his new insights into the diversity of linguistic usages. The comparison between language and chess is exploited for several purposes (PG 49f.), but Wittgenstein is now very conscious that chess, with its precise rules, is not typical of all games, and that other less rule-bound games may serve as objects of comparison for languages.

I said that the meaning of a word is the role which it plays in the calculus of language. (I compared it to a piece in chess.) Let us think now of the way in which calculation takes place with a word, the word 'red' for example. The locality of the colour is given, the form and size are specified of the spot or body which has the colour, we are told whether it is pure or mixed with others, whether it is lighter or darker, whether it is constant or changing, and so on. Conclusions are drawn from the propositions, they are translated into illustrations and behaviour; there is drawing, measurement and computation. But let us think also of the meaning of the word 'oh!' If we were asked about it, we would probably say 'oh!' is a sigh; we say, for instance, 'Oh, it is raining again already' and similar things. In that way we would have described the use of the word. But now what corresponds to the calculus, to the complicated game which we play with other words? In the use of the words 'oh' or 'hurrah' or 'hm' there is nothing comparable. (PG 67)

In this passage we can see Wittgenstein passing from his once favoured expression 'calculus' to the new favourite 'game'. The coinage 'language-game' itself has one of its earliest uses on page 62 of the *Philosophische Grammatik* in the course of a discussion of ostensive definition. When children learn the meaning of words by being shown objects and hearing their names pronounced, it is doubtful, he says, whether this is properly called 'explanation'.

The language-game (*Sprachspiel*) is still very simple and the ostensive explanation plays a different role in it from the one it plays in more developed language-games. (The child cannot, for instance, ask 'What is that?') But there is no clear boundary between primitive forms and more complicated ones. I would not know what I can still call 'explanation' and what I cannot. I can only describe language-games or calculuses. Whether they can still be called calculuses is indifferent, as long as we do not allow ourselves to be diverted by the use of a general term from the investigation of every individual case that we want to decide. (PG 62; cf. PI I, 27; BB 82)

The stress on the examination of individual case is renewed when Wittgenstein emphasizes that 'game' – or rather the even broader German word '*Spiel*' – is an analogous term.

There is no characteristic that is common to everything that we call games; but we cannot on the other hand say that 'game' has several independent meanings like 'bank'. It is a family-likeness term (PG 75, 118). Think of ball-games alone: some, like tennis, have a complicated system of rules; but there is a game which consists just in throwing the ball as high as one can, or the game which children play of throwing a ball and running after it. Some games are competitive, others not (PG 68). This thought was developed in a famous passage of the *Philosophical Investigations* in which Wittgenstein denied that there was any feature – such as entertainment, competitiveness, rule-guidedness, skill – which formed a common element in all games; instead we find a complicated network of similarities and relationships overlapping and criss-crossing. The concept of 'game' is extended as in spinning a thread we twist fibre on fibre. 'What ties the ship to the wharf is a rope, and the rope consists of fibres, but it does not get its strength from any fibre which runs through it from one end to the other, but from the fact that there is a vast number of fibres overlapping' (PI I, 65–7; BB 87).

This feature of 'game' is one which Wittgenstein believed it shared with 'language', and this made it particularly appropriate to call particular mini-languages 'language-games'. There were others. Most importantly, even though not all games have rules, the function of rules in many games has similarities with the function of rules in language (PG 63, 77). Language-games, like games, need have no external goal; they can be autonomous activities (PG 184; Z 320). But the comparison of language to a game was not meant to suggest that language was a pastime, or something trivial: on the contrary, it was meant to bring out the connection between the speaking of language and non-linguistic activities. Indeed the speaking of language is part of a communal activity, a way of living in society which Wittgenstein calls a 'form of life' (PI I, 23). It is through sharing in the playing of language-games that language is connected with our life (PG 65).

Why is the philosopher interested in the study of language-games? In order to clarify meaning and to distinguish between sense and nonsense. The right method of philosophy, Wittgenstein had said at the end of the *Tractatus*, consisted in showing the metaphysician that he had failed to give a meaning to certain signs in his propositions (TLP 6.53). He did not then say how this was to be done: now it is to be done by showing him that he is using a word outside the language-game that is its home (PI I, 116). Even the simplest sign, such as a name, is a name only in a language-game; the meaning of a sign is precisely its role in such a game (PI I, 49, 261; PG 130).

'This is what Frege meant too' wrote Wittgenstein in the *Investigations* 'when he said that a word had meaning only as part of a sentence' (PI I, 49). In fact, there is an important difference between Frege's dictum and Wittgenstein's contention, which is to the advantage of the latter. Taken strictly, Frege's thesis seems to be refuted by the use of personal names to call people, by a cry of 'Fire!' or a label 'Poison'. These cases are not counter-examples, and do not need explaining away as ellipses, when confronted with Wittgenstein's thesis. For the words belong to language-games; they have the possibility of tying in with other words even if they are not actually so tied. Indeed in their employment in these ways for their characteristic purposes they are actually being employed in the language-game; this type of employment is part of what goes to make up the game.

The most common form of philosophical nonsense arises not when a word is being used outside any language-game at all, but when it is used in a language-game other than the one appropriate to it (often the language-game misleadingly suggested by its surface grammar) (PG 126). So it is clearly important to be able to know where one language-game ends and another begins. How does one do this? Wittgenstein gives us little help here. Consistently with his general position, he does not give any general account of what a language-game is, nor a criterion of individuation for language-games. He merely makes some general remarks about language-games, and otherwise illuminates the concept principally by giving a fund of examples. The most systematic treatment of language-games comes in the *Brown Book* in which a large number are described or invented, and applied to the treatment of traditional metaphysical problems about the nature of modality and time, as well as the notions of language and guidance by rules. But from that book one could not derive a principle which would enable one to detect what constitutes an illegitimate crossing between games (cf. RFM 50).

The fullest list of language-games given by Wittgenstein is in the *Philosophical Investigations* I, 23. It includes obeying and giving orders, describing the appearance of objects, giving measurements, constructing an object from a description, reporting an event, speculating about an event, forming and testing a hypothesis, presenting the results of experiments in tables and diagrams, making up stories, acting plays, singing catches, guessing riddles, telling jokes, translating from one language into another, asking, thanking, cursing, greeting and praying. Elsewhere in the *Investigations* he gives as examples of language-games: the expression of sensation (I, 288), the reporting of past wishes (I, 654), the description of physical objects and the description of sense-impressions (II, 180), ostensive definition (I, 27, cf. BB 83), the subsequent explanation of one's meaning (II, 217). We hear of 'the language-game with the word "game"' (PI I, 71) and 'the language-game "I mean *this*"' (PI II, 217). Language-games are invented by Wittgenstein as models for philosophical theories – e.g. for Plato's account of naming in the *Theaetetus* (PI I, 48, 60, 64) and for Russell's theory of descriptions as used in the *Tractatus* (PI I, 60). Wittgenstein contrasts what he said in the *Tractatus* about the structure of language with the multiplicity of different language-games. 'How many kinds of sentences are there? Say assertion, question and command? – There are countless kinds: countless different kinds of use of what we call "symbols", "words", "sentences". And this multiplicity is not something fixed, given once for all; but new types of language, new language-games, as we may say, come into existence and others become obsolete and get forgotten' (PI I, 23). 'We remain unconscious of the prodigious diversity of all the everyday language-games because the clothing of our language makes everything alike' (PI II, 224).

Several comments seem in order here. First, it is clear that with this variety of things called 'language-games' we have come some distance from 'the forms of language with which a child begins to make use of words', as language-games were defined in the *Blue Book* (BB 17). It is no longer true, as Wittgenstein then said, that 'the study of language-games is the study of primitive forms of language or primitive language'. It has come to mean the study of any form of use of language against a background context of a form of life.

Secondly, there seems to be an inconsistency in the passage quoted from section 23 of the *Philosophical Investigations*. Wittgenstein says that there are countless kinds of sentence: countless different kinds of use of what we call sentences. The first half of that dictum suggests that two uses make two different kinds of sentence; the second half suggests that one kind of sentence may have more than one use. The second suggestion may well seem happier than the first. No doubt the use of 'Come here' to give an order and to make a request are different uses: but this seems no sufficient reason to say that two different kinds of sentence are involved. It may well be thought clearer and more natural to reserve the distinction between types of sentence for those broad distinctions between types of use which are marked in the syntax of the sentence (e.g. the distinction between imperative and indicative mood).

Wittgenstein would reply that this involves paying too much attention to the surface grammar, and not enough to the depth grammar as revealed in the study of the language-game. None the less, it seems that the traditional distinction between assertion, question and command is on a different level from the other distinctions drawn by Wittgenstein. It is clear, for instance, that these different kinds of sentence could occur inside or outside a joke or a fairy-tale; so that the distinction between them cuts across the distinction between fiction and non-fiction. Wittgenstein is surely right that it is futile to try to assimilate questions to statements (e.g. statements of ignorance, or of desire for information) (PI I, 24). But this type of distinction is quite different from the type of distinction drawn if we are to speak of the language-game with a particular word (like 'game') or of the language-game of measurement. For it is clear that the word 'game', or a set of measurements, could occur in a command, an assertion, or a question.

The point on which Wittgenstein would insist is that it is misleading to lump together all indicative sentences – such as 'The bone is in the cupboard', 'He is asleep', He is dreaming', 'I am in pain', 'I am thinking of my father' – as belonging to the class of assertions. One must pay attention to the differences in the use of these sentences – e.g. what sorts of mistake or doubt are possible in connection with them, whether or how we find out whether they are true – and *this* is what makes up the language-game.

There are two related difficulties in understanding what Wittgenstein means by 'the use' of an expression. First, does 'use' mean 'usage' or 'utility'? Does a word have a use provided that it can fit into acceptable sentences, or does its use have to make some difference in the world? Wittgenstein's two favourite similes point in opposite directions. A game, like chess, has only syntactical rules; what goes on in chess has no effect on the world except indirectly through the consequences of winning and losing. On the other hand, tools are instruments for operating on the world and altering it in various ways. Secondly, is the theory of meaning as use to be applied primarily to words or to whole sentences? Here words seem unlike tools, because tools work on the world in isolation, whereas in general we have to put words together into sentences to affect the world in any way: it looks as if it would be a more helpful metaphor to say that in our language we have a kit for assembling tools rather than a tool-bag. It is the complete sentence that seems to be the move in the game (PG 39). Sentences are made, rather than used, once one has got beyond the phrase-book stage of learning a language.

To this Wittgenstein's reply would be that one gives the use of a piece of language by describing its role in a language-game and that a language-game is a more or less complicated sharable human activity which might, or might not, have a utility which could be grasped and stated outside the game. Language cannot be looked on, as a whole, as a means to some extra-linguistic end – 'the communication of thoughts' cannot be regarded as such an end, because there are so many thoughts which cannot even be thought without language. We do not, in general, think, or use language, because we have found that it pays to do so – any more than we bring up our children because we have found that it pays to do so. But of course particular language-games (e.g. the making of calculations when building boilers) have been found to pay off. But even in these cases, Wittgenstein thinks, it would be misleading to regard calculation as a means chosen to an end (PG 109; PI I, 466–8). As for the distinction between words and sentences, this is a distinction which itself presupposes the existence of fairly complicated language-games, and does not arise in the case of simple games like that of the builders with their building-stones (PI I, 18–19). The concept 'sentence' has not the sharp boundary this objection presupposes (PG 112). Of course we can draw a sharp boundary if we wish, in the same way as a pace can be standardized as 75 cm.; but that does not mean that the non-standardized concept is unusual (PG 113; PI I, 69).

One might, however, be inclined to object that unless a language-game is at least complicated enough to allow a distinction between words and sentences to be drawn, then it does not really deserve to be called a *language*-game at all. Wittgenstein was surely right in thinking when he wrote the *Tractatus* that the articulation of propositions, and the possibility of expressing a new sense with old words, is something crucial for the understanding of language. It is not at all clear that the language-game in which the builders call out 'block', 'pillar' and 'stone' to each other could be, as Wittgenstein says it could, 'a complete primitive language'. Clearly, it cannot be essential to the language-game that the English words, or sounds like them, should be used: but if we imagine the builders calling just 'tweet', 'tweet-tweet', 'tweet-tweet-tweet' to each other is it so clear that we should call what they are doing a language?

Wittgenstein makes several attempts to deal with this objection. At PI I, 18 he says that we should not be troubled by the fact that this language-game consists only of orders; but this hardly meets the objection that what is wrong with it is that it has no syntax. In the *Brown Book* he considers the objection that the imaginary tribes which he endows with language-games speak English, so that the whole background of the English language is presupposed. To answer this, he says, the description of the language-games would have to be very much more complete. 'Whether a word of the language of our tribe is rightly translated into a word of the English language depends upon the role this word plays in the whole life of the tribe; the occasions on which it is used, the expressions of emotion by which it is generally accompanied, the ideas which it generally awakens or which prompt its saying, etc.' (BB 102–3).

He turned to a similar objection in the *Zettel* apropos of the builders' language-game.

You are just tacitly assuming that these people *think*; that they are like people as we know them in *that* respect, that they do not carry on that language-game merely mechanically. For if you imagined them doing that, you yourself would not call it the use of a rudimentary language.

What am I to reply to this? Of course it is true that the life of those men must be like ours in many respects, and I said nothing about this similarity. But the important thing is that their language, and their thinking too, may be rudimentary, that there is such a thing as 'primitive thinking', which is to be described via primitive *behaviour*. The surroundings are not the 'thinking accompaniment' of speech. (Z 99)

These replies do not altogether silence the objection. However, it is open to Wittgenstein to say that it is a misunderstanding to think of the primitive language-game as somehow capturing the essence of language. It is true that he said in the *Blue Book*:

If we want to study the problems of truth and falsehood, of the agreement and disagreement of propositions with reality, of the nature of assertion, assumption and question, we shall with great advantage look at primitive forms of language in which these forms of thinking appear without the confusing background of highly complicated processes of thought. (BB 17)

But in the *Philosophical Investigations* he warned:

Our clear and simple language-games are not preparatory studies for a future regularization of language – as it were first approximations, ignoring friction and air-resistance. The language-games are rather set up as *objects of comparison* which are meant to throw light on the facts of our language by way not only of similarities, but also of dissimilarities. (PI I, 130)

It does not greatly matter, he might say, whether the builders' game is rightly called a language: it has similarities with language, and there is no clear break between these primitive games and more complicated ones: the more complicated ones can be built up from the primitive ones by the gradual addition of new forms (BB 17).

One crucial point of comparison between language and games is that both involve the employment of rules. This must not be misunderstood. We do not, in general, use language according to strict rules – we commonly don't think of rules of usage while talking, and we usually cannot produce any rules if we are asked to quote them (BB 25). The application of words is not everywhere bounded by rules, and many possibilities are left open: we do not, for instance, have a rule ready to say whether something which regularly disappears and reappears can be called a 'chair', and one can use a proper name like 'Moses' without having a fixed definitional description to sub-stitute for it in all possible cases (PI I, 79–81). But the same is true of games: there are no rules in tennis for how high or how hard one throws the ball before serving, yet tennis is a game with rules (PI I, 68, 83). Indeed 'rule' like 'game' is a family-likeness term covering many different but related things: what we call a rule in a game, or language-game, may have very different roles in the game (PG 116–18; PI I, 53).

The rule may be an aid in teaching the game. The learner is told it and given practice in applying it. – Or it is an instrument of the game itself. – Or a rule is employed neither in the teaching nor in the game itself; nor is it set down in a list of rules. One learns the game by watching how others play. But we say that it is played according to such-and-such rules because an observer can read these rules off from the practice of the game – like a law of nature governing the play. (PI I, 54)

It is a mistake, when reading what Wittgenstein has to say about rules, to think of the canonical form of a rule as being a conditional imperative. There are examples of rules of this form in his writings, but they are very rare. Two examples occur in PI I, 567: 'Before starting a game of chess, use the kings to draw lots'; 'Before moving a piece, turn it round three times.' This is a passage in which Wittgenstein is discussing not the nature of rules, but the distinction between essential and inessential ambiguity. When he is discussing the nature of rules, and the nature of language as a rule-guided activity, it is striking that he almost always gives concrete examples of rules: a chart correlating words and pictures (PI I, 48, 86), a schema of arrows (BB 90; PI I, 86), a table with printed letters in one column and cursive letters in the other (BB 123; PI I, 162), a signpost (PI I, 85, 198), a ruled line (PI I, 222–37).

One reason for Wittgenstein's preference for concrete ex-pressions of rules over linguistic ones is didactic: if the concept of rule is to throw light on the nature of language, there is a danger of circularity if the rules used as illustrations are ones which need an understanding of language to apply. A table or a signpost is perhaps more naturally thought of as an expression of a rule than as a rule itself: but in Wittgenstein's view the way to study the nature of rules is to study expressions of rules, just as the way to study sensations and thoughts is to study their expression. In discussing the question 'What is a rule?' in the *Brown Book* Wittgenstein gives the following example. B is to move about according to rules given by A. B is supplied with a table like this:

a	b	c	d
→	←	↑	↓

A gives an order made up of letters in the table, say 'aacaddd'. B looks up the arrow corresponding to each letter of the order, and moves accordingly: thus

This table is a rule, and it might be used in any of the following different ways: the table might be given to B and referred to by B every time he is given an order; he might not look it up, but having become familiar with it call up the images of the arrows corresponding to the letters in A's orders; having become even more familiar with it he might carry out the order without looking up or imagining. It is conceivable that after being shown the table once, B might be able to obey A's orders without any further reference to the table; or that the ability to obey the orders was produced by some training which did not involve the use of the table, or was even innate. In these last two cases, the table might be constructed by an observer watching the behaviour of A and B, without either

A or B being able to produce the table on demand (BB 95-8). This example illustrates the various ways in which, in accordance with the passage quoted above from PI I, 54, a rule can play a role in a language-game.

Wittgenstein repeatedly insists that charts, signposts and the like could never be used as we used them if there were not a natural, primitive, uniform reaction that human beings display towards such things, given certain training. It is a fact of human nature that human beings, unlike dogs, can be trained to look in the direction of a pointing finger (PG 94; PI I, 185); just as it is a fact of nature that dogs, and not cats, can be taught to retrieve (BB 90). This primitive reaction is not interpretation, and the training which produces it is not explanation; rather, the reaction is presupposed by any interpretation, and explanation is only possible after training has been successful (BB 77; PI I, 201). Merely to act on a rule – e.g. to walk in the direction indicated by a signpost, to follow with the eye a pointing finger – is not to give an interpretation of the rule: to interpret a rule is rather to substitute one expression of a rule for another (PI I, 201). The training by which children learn words ostensively (for Wittgenstein calls an ostensive definition, too, the expression of a rule) is strictly analogous to the training of animals by example, reward, punishment and the like; it does not become explanation, and ostensive training does not become ostensive definition properly so-called until the child has e.g. learned the language-game of asking what something is called (BB 77; PI I, 27).

The other feature of rules which Wittgenstein stresses is that a rule is something for repeated application, to be applied in an indefinite number of instances and not just once (BB 96). Obedience to a rule is a practice or custom: it is not something which it would be possible for only one man to do and to do only once in his life (PI I, 199, 202).

Wittgenstein's account is sometimes misunderstood as meaning that it is the agreement of the people who share in the practice of the rule which settles whether or not a rule has been obeyed. This is not quite right. It is either true or false that someone is obeying a rule, and it may be true though everyone thinks it false, and vice versa: 'A kept the rule' and 'Everyone agreed that A kept the rule' have different meanings. Wittgenstein is not saying that to obey a rule is to act in a way which others agree in calling obedient. But unless there was the primitive uniform reaction to certain training with certain paradigms, then the concept of rule, and of agreement and disagreement with rule, could never get off the ground (PI I, 240–42).

It is natural to feel that there is something missing from Wittgenstein's account of the place of rules in games and in language. It is not enough, we feel, to point to the existence of concrete expressions of rules and to facts of human natural history as the background of customary operation with these paradigms. What is to be explained is how, when I follow a rule, my action is guided by, determined by, the rule. We want to be shown how the rule provides either a cause or a reason for my action. Wittgenstein believed that this demand may mask a confusion similar to that which looks for a mental act or process of understanding.

In a case such as the simple language-game quoted above from the *Brown Book* there may, of course, be a genuine causal connection between the table and the behaviour according to the rule: that is to say, the current behaviour is causally connected with the training in the past, and in that training the table was physically used. But this is not the causal connection that we have in mind when we say that being guided by a rule involves having one's behaviour caused by the rule. What we vaguely imagine is some sort of mental mechanism connecting the signs and the behaviour; and we think of the mechanism as being set up by the training with the table. We may think of the mechanism as rather like the ghostly equivalent of a pianola, in which the action of the hammers of the piano is guided by the pattern of the holes in the pianola roll (PG 69; PI I, 157; BB 118). Perhaps one has only to make quite explicit what a mental mechanism would be in such a case for it to be clear that the idea of such a mechanism could never be more than a simile for the phenomenon of being guided by a rule (BB 119). But Wittgenstein demolishes the notion by a very painstaking examination of one of the simplest cases of being guided by a rule, namely, that of reading, not in the sense of understanding what one reads, but simply translating script into sounds and vice versa (BB 119–25; PI 156–78).

Though we cannot give flesh and blood to the notion of behaviour being caused by a rule, still, we may feel, what is essential to being guided by a rule is a certain experience or mental state; a feeling of being guided, a feeling that one is acting *because* of the rule. But this will not do. If we consider various actual cases of being guided, we will find that the experiences characteristic of the cases are widely different from each other (e.g. being led by the hand versus simply following a field-track) (PI I, 172). Moreover, given any particular experience, it is possible to imagine someone having that experience (say, under the influence of a drug) while in fact behaving in a completely irregular manner (BB 112; PI I, 160). Indeed it is difficult to see how having a certain feeling is a way of discovering a causal connection: causation is surely something established by experiments, e.g. by the observation of regular concomitances (PI I, 169).

If a rule cannot be said to exercise a causal influence on behaviour, can it be said that the connection between a rule and an action following it can be explained by pointing to the *reason* why we follow it as we do? Certainly one can give a reason for an action by citing a rule; for instance, one can justify reading certain sounds by pointing to the letters on the page and the rule correlating letters and sounds (PI I, 169). Moreover, one can give a reason for obeying a rule in a certain manner by giving an interpretation of a rule, e.g. in answer to the question 'How do you know you are to obey the rule in *this* way?' But the chain of reasons has an end (BB 15; PI I, 211). If one thinks that every way of grasping a rule involves an interpretation, then it will seem mysterious how a rule can ever show one what to do: for whatever one does can be made out, on some far-fetched interpretation, to accord with the rule. In the game cited above, B might obey the order 'a' by moving to the left; and justify this by saying that he had interpreted the table according to the schema ⤬ ⤬ and not ⬇⬇⬇⬇. It is of course unlikely that someone would read the table like that; but what is and is not far-fetched is just a fact of human nature, and nothing to do with the logical structure and multiplicity of the table. So even if we start with the notion of reasons, we are brought back to the primitive, unreasoned reaction on which the system of rules and reasons is grafted.

Does this mean that the rules e.g. of grammar cannot themselves be justified, and are wholly arbitrary? In the *Philosophische Bemerkungen* Wittgenstein observed that the conventions of grammar could not be justified by a description of what was to be represented in language: one could not say, for instance, that colour-language must have certain conventions because colour had certain properties. For the description of the properties of colour would itself have to make use of the grammatical conventions, and so could not justify them; or if it did not, it would either be a piece of nonsense, or would show that the conventions were superfluous (PB 53, 55). He returned to the thought in the *Philosophische Grammatik*: one is tempted to justify rules of grammar by sentences like 'But there really are four primary colours' (PG 186; Z 331). But one cannot really discuss whether the rules we have for words are the correct ones. There cannot for instance be a question whether our rules for 'not' are the correct ones, and accord with its meaning. For without the rules the word has no meaning; and if we change the rules it has a different meaning, or none (PG 184; PI, p. 147). It is against these temptations that one wants to insist that the rules of grammar are arbitrary. But this is not quite right either. 'Why' Wittgenstein asks 'don't I call cookery rules arbitrary, and why am I tempted to call the rules of grammar arbitrary?'

Because 'cookery' is defined by its end, whereas 'speaking' is not. That is why the use of language is in a certain sense autonomous, as cooking and washing are not. You cook badly if you are guided in your cooking by rules other than the right ones; but if you follow other rules than those of chess, you are playing another game; and if you follow grammatical rules other than such-and-such ones, that does not mean you say something wrong, no, you are speaking of something else. (PG 184; Z 320)

Languages can be invented as instruments for particular purposes (PG 140; PI I, 492, 569) and in this case, it will make a difference which concepts we employ, as it makes a difference for some purposes of measurement whether we use the metric system or feet and inches (PG 193; PI I, 569). But language as a whole is not an instrument for a particular purpose specifiable outside language, and it is in this sense that its rules are arbitrary. 'To say the rules of a game are arbitrary is to say that the concept *game* is not defined by the effects the game is to have on us' (PG 192). 'The rules of grammar may be called "arbitrary" if that is to mean that the *aim* of the grammar is nothing but that of the language' (PI I, 497).

CHAPTER 10

Private Languages

For a decade after the dictation of the *Brown Book* in 1935 Wittgenstein worked simultaneously on his *Remarks on the Foundations of Mathematics* and on the *Philosophical Investigations*. The first, and major, part of the latter work was complete by 1945. As we have seen, a considerable part of the material worked into the text came from passages in the *Bemerkungen* or *Grammatik*, or had close similarities with the notes dictated in the *Blue and Brown Books*. We have already observed the similarities with the earlier work of the passages on primitive language-games (PI I, 1–26), on ostensive definition (PI I, 28–37), on games, rules and family-likeness (PI I, 65–88), on understanding (PI I, 138–55, 179–97), on reading (PI I, 156–78), on following a rule (PI I, 198–242), on thought and speech (PI I, 318–62), on expectation and fulfilment (PI I, 439–65). The last thirty or so pages of part one of the *Investigations* (PI I, 491–693) contain many paragraphs unchanged from the *Grammatik*. Wittgenstein's editors tell us that if he had lived to publish the work himself, he would have suppressed a good deal of what was in this section, and worked into its place material which he wrote in 1947–9, and which now appears as the second part of the *Investigations*. Of the more original material in *Investigations* I there are two sections which we shall consider in some detail. The first is the criticism of logical atomism and the revision of the *Tractatus* philosophy of logic (PI I, 39–64 and 89–137 respectively), which will be considered in the final chapter. The second is the argument against a private language which, with kindred matters, occupies 243–363, and was first adumbrated in some lecture notes on private experience written in 1934–6 and published in 1968. The argument to prove the impossibility of a private language will be the topic of the present chapter.

What is a private language, we may wonder, and why does its possibility matter? A private language, in the sense discussed by Wittgenstein, is a language whose words 'refer to what can only be known to the person speaking: to his immediate private sensations' (PI I, 243). Whether such a language is possible has philosophical importance not so much as a question in its own right as because of its consequences for epistemology and philosophy of mind. As was mentioned in the first chapter, it is entailed by several traditional and influential philosophical theories that a private language is possible; consequently, if private languages are impossible those theories are false. For instance, some empiricist philosophers have thought that the only matters of fact we really know are our own experiences: what we claim to know about the world or about other people is based on our knowledge of our own mental states and processes. The same philosophers have commonly taken for granted that our knowledge of our experiences can be expressed in language, at least to ourselves, and that the possibility of this expression does not presuppose any acquaintance with the external world or other minds. Anyone who accepts this much must believe in the possibility of a private language whose words acquire meaning simply by being linked to private experiences. Indeed he must believe that our actual language is a private language, not in the sense that it is peculiar to a single user, but in the sense that its words have acquired their meaning for each of us by an essentially private process: an internal ostensive definition in which an appropriate sample of experience was attended to and associated with a word. Of course, if words are thought of as acquiring meaning in this way, a doubt may arise whether the samples from which one person has acquired his vocabulary are really like the samples from which another person has done so. Thus this form of empiricism carries with it a version of scepticism which finds expression in such thoughts as the following: 'For all we know, what I call "red" you call "green" and vice versa' (cf. BB 60; PI I, 272). One point of the private-language argument is to refute this version of empiricism with its attendant scepticism; to show that the thought just expressed is a nonsensical one and that the doubts it conjures up are spurious. The programme of the private-language argument can be well summed up in a quotation from the *Tractatus*. 'Scepticism is *not* irrefutable, but obviously nonsensical, when it tries to raise doubts where no questions can be asked. For doubt only can exist where a question exists, a question only where an answer exists, and an answer only where something *can be said*' (TLP 6.51). The *Investigations* shows that the empiricist sceptic must use a private language in order to formulate his question; but in a private language nothing can be said and so no questions can be asked.

Wittgenstein considered that the notion of a private language rested on two fundamental mistakes, one about the nature of experience, and one about the nature of language. The mistake about experience was the belief that experience is private; the mistake about language was the belief that words can acquire meaning by bare ostensive definition. The mistake about language has already been considered: we have seen how Wittgenstein argued against the primacy of ostensive definition, against the idea that bare ostension without training in the use of words could constitute the teaching of a language. His arguments concern public ostensive definition as well as private ostensive definition: they apply to the naming of shapes and colours and men as well as to the naming of pains and moods. But if the arguments are accepted then the private-language theory is refuted before it is stated: at least if it supposes the meanings of names for sensations could be learnt simply by acquaintance with the names' bearers, i.e. simply by having and attending to the sensations. However, a defender of private languages might suggest the possibility of a language which was private in that its words *referred to* private sensations without necessarily being private in that its words were *learnt from* private sensations by bare ostension. A private language, he might maintain, might be learnt from private sensations not by bare ostension but by some private analogue of training in the use of words. This suggestion shows that the critique of the primacy of ostensive definition does not render superfluous the later explicit discussion of private languages. What that later discussion does, in effect, is to show that in the case of the private ostensive definition there *cannot* be any analogue of the background which is necessary if the public ostensive definition is to convey meaning.

After these prolegomena we may consider section 243 in which Wittgenstein introduces the private language. Could we, he asks,

imagine a language in which a person could write down or give vocal expression to his inner experiences – his feelings, moods and the rest – for his private use? – Well, can't we do so in our ordinary language? – But that is not what I mean. The individual words of this language are to refer to what can only be known to the person speaking; to his immediate private sensations. So another person cannot understand the language. (PI I, 243)

Having defined a private language as a language whose words refer to the speaker's immediate private sensations, Wittgenstein goes on to comment on the expressions occurring in this definition, and first of all on the expression 'refer to'. In section 244 he asks 'How do words *refer* to sensations?'

In this passage he appears to have no objection to calling 'pain' the name of a sensation, or to calling 'I am in pain' a proposition. 'We talk about sensations every day' he says 'and give them *names*' and, he asks, 'How does a human learn the meaning of the *names* of sensations?' As one possible answer to this question he suggests that words replace the natural pre-verbal expression of sensation. 'A child has hurt himself and he cries; and then adults talk to him and teach him exclamations and, later, *sentences*' (PI I, 244; italics added).

Elsewhere, however, Wittgenstein has been taken to deny that a word such as 'pain' names a sensation. He says, for instance, 'If we construe the grammar of the expression of sensation on the model of "object and name" the object drops out of consideration as irrelevant' (PI I, 293). This seems to suggest that we should not so construe the grammar, i.e. should not consider a sensation-word like 'pain' as the name of an object. In the *Zettel* Wittgenstein's wayward self says '"Joy" surely designates an inward thing' and his sterner self replies 'No. "Joy" designates nothing. Neither any inward nor any outward thing' (Z 487).

These passages can be reconciled in the light of the attack on the primacy of ostensive definition. The model of 'object and name' which we are to reject is the idea that a speaker understands a name by being acquainted with its bearer. This is clear from the context: at PI I, 293 Wittgenstein is criticizing the theory that one knows what pain is only from one's own case. That theory is one formulation of the idea that it is acquaintance which conveys meaning: it is only one's own pain that one is acquainted with, so it is only from one's own case that one knows what pain is. If this were true, and each man knew what pain was only from his own case, then no one could teach anyone else the meaning of the word 'pain'; each speaker would have to name the sensation for himself by a private ostensive definition.

Wittgenstein considers this suggestion at PI I, 257, and brings the critique of ostensive definition to bear.

What does it mean to say that he has 'named his pain'? – How has he done this naming of pain? And whatever he did, what was its purpose? When one says 'He gave a name to his sensation' one forgets that a great deal of stage-setting in the language is presupposed if the mere act of naming is to make sense. And when we speak of someone's having given a name to pain, what is presupposed is the existence of the grammar of the word 'pain'; it shows the post where the new word is stationed.

This echoes the remarks about public ostensive definition: 'The ostensive definition explains the use – the meaning – of the word when the overall role of the word in language is clear' (PI I, 30). Wittgenstein is not denying that one can give a name to a sensation; he is merely affirming that giving a name pre-supposes stage-setting. Such stage-setting, he will go on to argue, is possible in a public language, but not a private language. Given the stage-setting, the word for a sensation may be ostensively defined no less than the name of a colour of a piece of furniture (BB 69; PI I, 288).

To sum up: if by 'name' one means 'word whose meaning is learnt by bare ostensive definition', then 'pain' is not the name of a sensation; but if by 'name' one means what is ordinarily meant by that word, then of course 'pain' is the name of a sensation (cf. BB 82).

If the word 'pain' does not refer to a sensation by being attached to it by bare ostensive definition, how does it refer? In what way is it connected with the sensation? One possibility, Wittgenstein says, is that it is a learnt, articulate replacement of unlearnt, inarticulate expressions of sensation such as moans and winces (PI I, 244; cf. PE 296, 301). The word 'pain' cannot, as it were, hook on to pain directly; it must be attached to pain through its connections with the natural expressions of pain (cf. PI I, 256-7, 271). To try to connect 'pain' with pain in isolation from unlearnt pain-behaviour would be to try to insert language between pain and its expression. This, Wittgenstein thinks, is absurd: presumably because the verbal manifestation of pain is itself an expression of pain (PI I, 245).

Few people are immediately convinced by Wittgenstein's suggestion that it is only via the expression of pain that the word 'pain' can mean pain. Surely, we want to say, we can have a pain without ever saying or showing that we do; and on the other hand we can say that we have a pain without really having one; the only connection between pain and the expression of pain is that they sometimes coincide. Pain and its expression seem no more essentially connected than redness and sweetness: sometimes what is red is sweet, and sometimes not.

In the face of this objection Wittgenstein immediately agrees that in our language we use the words 'being in pain' in such a way that we can say 'A is in pain but he does not show it.' But he insists that we should have no use for the expression if its application was severed from behavioural criteria. So the relation of pain to pain-behaviour is not the same as the relation of redness to sweetness. It is essential to the language-game with the word 'pain' that the people who play it both behave in the particular way we call expressing pain, and sometimes more or less entirely conceal their pains (cf. PE 286, 290; PI I, 281, 304).

Thus Wittgenstein's position differs from behaviourism. If pain is identified with pain-behaviour, then 'A is in pain' means 'A is behaving in such-and-such a way.' But Wittgenstein rejects this interpretation of his theory that pain-language is connected with pain-behaviour. 'Pain' does not mean crying: the verbal expression of pain does not describe the natural expression of pain, but takes its place (PI I, 244).

If pain and pain-behaviour are separable, how are our words for sensations 'tied up with' our natural expressions of sensations? One way suggested by Wittgenstein is that they are *learnt in connection with* the natural expression (PI I, 244; PE 293, 295). Is this the only possible connection? If so, then an innate knowledge of the meaning of 'pain' would be inconceivable: if only learning connects word and sensation an unlearned connection would be impossible. I think that Wittgenstein did not mean to rule out the possibility of innate knowledge (BB 12, 96–7). But even innate knowledge of the meaning of 'pain' would have to connect with the natural expression of pain in a certain way. Knowledge of the meaning would have to be exercised in use of the word, and the use of the word would have to fit in with the usual symptoms and circumstances of pain – with symptoms such as wincing and circumstances such as injury (cf. PI I, 270). Knowledge of the meaning of 'pain', whether inborn, or conferred by a drug, or a sudden gift of the gods, must always be capable of investigation by such criteria. If some humanoid creatures used a word which had no such connection with the symptoms and circumstances of pain, it would be difficult to see why the word should be translated as 'pain'.

The private language was to consist of words 'to refer to private sensations'. Having discussed in sections 244–5 the expression 'refer to', Wittgenstein turns in 246–55 to the word 'private'. He asks: 'To what extent are my sensations private?', and he distinguishes two senses of the word 'private'. The first sense of privacy has to do with knowledge and the second sense has to do with possession: in the first sense, something is private to me if only I can know about it, and in the second sense something is private to me if only I can have it. To claim that pains are private in the first sense is to say 'Only I can know whether I am really in pain; another person can only surmise it' (PI I, 246); to claim that pains are private in the second sense is to say 'Another person can't have my pains' (PI I, 253). Using words that are not used by Wittgenstein, we may use for the first sense of 'private' the abbreviation 'incommunicable' and for the second sense of 'private' the abbreviation 'inalienable'. The question 'Are sensations private?' breaks up into two questions: (i) 'Are sensations incommunicable?' (ii) 'Are sensations inalienable?' Crudely, Wittgenstein's answer to (i) is 'No' and to (ii) is 'Not in any way peculiar to sensations.'

The thesis that pains are incommunicable is a conjunction of two separable theses: (i) I can know that I am in pain; (ii) Other people cannot know that I am in pain. Wittgenstein rejects both theses. Let us consider the second first (PI I, 246ff.). 'In one way' he says 'this is false, and in another nonsense.' If we take the word 'know' as it is normally used, then the claim is false: other people often know when I am in pain: for instance, if they see me falling into flames and crying out (PE 318). On the other hand, if we take the word 'know' to mean 'know in such a way that doubt is logically excluded' then the thesis is senseless, for there can be knowledge only where doubt is possible (cf. PI II, 221).

One reason why people believe that one man can never know if another man is in pain is the possibility of pretence:

may not a man who appears to be in pain be merely pretending? To this Wittgenstein replies that there are cases in which the supposition of pretence is senseless: for instance, the case of infants (PI I, 249) and animals (PI I, 250). In order to be able to pretend or to lie one needs to master certain skills which infants and animals lack (cf. also PI II, 227–9).

Sometimes people claim that one man can never really know of another's pain because they fail to distinguish between inalienability and incommunicability. They assume that to know pain is to have pain, and because they believe that one person cannot have another's pain, they conclude that one person cannot know another's pain. But the impossibility they have in mind is not a mere matter-of-fact impossibility: they mean that it makes no sense to say that A knows B's pain. If so, Wittgenstein replies, then it makes no sense to say that A *doesn't* know B's pain: the negation of a senseless sentence is itself senseless. 'You did not state that knowing was a goal which you could not reach, and that you have to be content with conjecturing; rather there is no goal in this game.' The statement 'You can't know when A has pain' is analogous to a statement like 'There is no goal in an endurance race' (BB 54).

Wittgenstein rejects also the second part of the incommunicability thesis: 'I can know when I am in pain.' It can't, he says, be said of me at all that I know I am in pain, except perhaps as a joke; other people cannot be said to learn of my sensations *only* from my behaviour, because this suggests that I learn of them. But I cannot be said to learn of them: I *have* them (PI I, 246).

Many people are disconcerted by this remark of Wittgenstein's. It is true, they say, that there is no such thing as *learning* that one is in pain, but that only shows that there are some things we know without having learnt them. If I cannot know of my own sensations, how can I know of anything else? One cannot doubt that one is in pain (as Wittgenstein himself agrees (PI I, 288)), and surely one knows what one cannot doubt! Wittgenstein may be right when he says that doubt here is not just impossible, but actually senseless: but isn't that so much the better? If doubt is not merely psychologically, but logically, impossible, then the corresponding knowledge must be so much more secure.

To a first approximation, Wittgenstein's answer runs as follows. 'I know when I am in pain' can be taken in two ways: as an empirical proposition or as a grammatical one. As a grammatical proposition (a proposition to explain the meaning of a word) it means: it is senseless to say 'I doubt whether I am in pain.' So taken, the proposition is correct (PI I, 247). But those who argue that because we cannot doubt our sensations we must know of them are misled by the form of the proposition into taking it as an empirical proposition (PI I, 251). Where it is senseless to say 'I doubt whether . . .' it is not always true to say 'I know that . . .' This can be seen if we compare the expressions not with 'I am in pain' but with 'Good morning!' or 'Shut the door.' 'I doubt whether good morning' and 'I know that good morning' are equally senseless, as are 'I doubt whether shut the door' and 'I know that shut the door.' Of course, 'I am in pain', unlike the other two completions, has the form of a declarative sentence; but Wittgenstein may fairly insist that this is insufficient to show that it *is* a declarative sentence. The words 'I am in pain' may look like a description of a mental state; but they may in fact be more like a cry of complaint (cf. PI II, 189). If they are, then 'I doubt whether I am in pain' may be senseless in the same way as 'I doubt whether ouch.' If so, then it is clearly out of place to talk of knowledge and certainty. It would be foolish to say 'Since it is not just psychologically but logically impossible to doubt whether good morning, the knowledge that good morning must be so much the more secure.'

Whether Wittgenstein is right about 'I know I am in pain' depends therefore on whether 'I am in pain' is, as it appears to be, a declarative sentence, a description of a mental state. This question will have to be pursued later: it can be waived for the moment since the rejection of 'When I am in pain I know that I am in pain' does not function as a premiss in the argument against private language.

In section 253 Wittgenstein passes from the incommunicability thesis to the claim that pains are inalienable: 'Only I can have my pains.' Is this claim true? 'If they are *my* pains then *I* have them' is a straightforwardly grammatical statement, drawing attention to the connection between the pronoun 'I' and the possessive 'my'; but it tells us nothing particular about pain, since the sentence remains correct no matter what plural noun is substituted for 'pains'. But two questions arise: (i) What is *having* here? and (ii) Granted that if they are my pains I must have them, can anyone else have them in addition to me? (Compare: 'Since it is my bank account, I have it, but my wife shares it too.')

'Which are *my* pains? What counts as a criterion of identity here?' asks Wittgenstein (PI I, 253). The two questions are distinct. One asks for the criterion for the possessor of a pain, the other for the criterion of identity for a pain. The first question is answered in section 302: the possessor of pain is the person who gives it expression. *My* pains, then, are the pains which I express; or perhaps the pains which, if expressed at all, would be expressed by me.

This may seem a strange criterion. Surely my pains are the pains *felt in my body*? Against this Wittgenstein argued repeatedly that one could quite conceivably feel pain in someone else's body (cf. WWK 49; PB 90ff.; BB 49–55).

In order to see that it is conceivable that one person should have pain in another person's body, one must examine what sort of facts we call criteria for a pain being in a certain place . . . Suppose I feel a pain which on the evidence of the pain alone, e.g. with closed eyes, I should call a pain in my left hand. Someone asks me to touch the painful spot with my right hand. I do so and looking round perceive that I am touching my neighbour's hand. (BB 49)

This would be pain *felt in* another's body, and not just pain *caused by injury* to another's body (which would also be conceivable – e.g. if I feel pain in my finger whenever you cut yours (cf. BB 54). So my pain is not necessarily pain felt in my body. My pains are the pains to which I give expression; and the expression of my pain (e.g. pointing to places, treating them with solicitude) may single out a place outside my own body.

Now what of the criterion of identity for pains? How, Wittgenstein asks, are pains such as toothache distinguished from each other (PB 91)? By intensity, and similar characteristics, and location. Suppose that these are the same – suppose that you and I both feel a sharp pain in the upper abdomen one hour after eating the same food – then it is perfectly natural to say that we both feel the same pain. But, it might be thought, this is not strictly correct, since the pains are not felt literally in the same place, but only in corresponding places in two different bodies. Well, Wittgenstein points out, two Siamese twins might feel pain in exactly the same place, namely, the place where they are joined together. Even so, it might be said, the pains are only specifically the same, but numerically distinct; because one pain is Tweedledum's pain and the other is Tweedledee's pain. But this, Wittgenstein says, is to make the possessor a characteristic of the pain itself; in the terminology I used above, it is to make the identity of the possessor part of the criterion of identity for the pain: if there are two possessors then there are two pains. This makes 'Only I can have my pains' a grammatical statement like 'If they are my pains I have them.' It also makes it comparatively uninformative about pain. 'Only I can have my x' is true, not indeed of bank accounts, but of many things besides sensations: for instance, blushes and sneezes. If you blush, then that is your blush and nobody else's; and if you sneeze that is not my sneeze or the President's sneeze. But there is nothing specially occult about blushes and sneezes; their inalienability is a very tenuous sort of privacy. We may allow, then, that pains are inalienable; but this will not make sensations any more private than behaviour.

There is, of course, one sense in which experiences are more private than behaviour: experiences such as pain can be kept secret without being publicly manifested in any way. If one wants to call an experience thus kept to oneself 'private' – e.g. a chess move considered, and discarded, in the imagination – then there clearly are such private experiences, as Wittgenstein expressly admits (PE 292). But if a private experience is one that is kept secret, there is no reason to call an experience that is *not* kept secret a private experience. If a man itches, but does not scratch or report his itch, we may call that a private experience; but if he itches and does scratch, why should we call the itch private? If we take 'private' in this sense, and ask 'Are pains private experiences?' the only possible answer is 'Some are, and some are not.' And from the fact that some experiences are, in this sense, private experiences, it does not follow that all experiences could be private experiences. 'What sometimes happens could always happen' is a fallacy. Some money is forged; but it could not be the case that all money was forged (PI I, 345; PE 314).

In the *Investigations*, then, from 246 to 252 Wittgenstein has argued that pain is not incommunicable; from 253 to 255 he has argued that pain has no special inalienability. At 256 he restates the private-language hypothesis. From what has been said up to this point it follows that *our* word 'pain' does not belong to a private language: from 258 onwards Wittgenstein is going to consider not pain, but pseudo-pain, i.e. a sensation supposed to be like pain but different from pain in being incommunicable. The name of pseudo-pain must be learnt by private ostensive definition. It would be cheating to call this process 'the naming of pain', Wittgenstein argues in 257, since naming is part of a language-game (and the private ceremony is not) and since the language-game with pain presupposes the outward signs of pain (whereas pseudo-pain has no outward expression). In 257 Wittgenstein argues that it is futile to start from pain and attempt to subtract its natural expression; in 258 he discusses the attempt to start from pseudo-pain and add to it a linguistic correlate. This section is the kernel of the private-language argument.

We are to suppose that I want to keep a diary about the occurrence of a certain sensation, and that I associate the sensation with the sign 'S'. It is essential to the supposition that no definition of the sign can be expressed: that is to say, that no definition can be given in terms of our public language. If this condition was not fulfilled, then the language to which the sign belonged would not be a private one. The sign must be defined for me alone, and this must be by a private ostensive definition, by my attending to the sensation and producing the sign.

I speak, or write the sign down, and at the same time I concentrate my attention on the sensation . . . in this way I impress on myself the connection between the sign and the sensation.

Wittgenstein argues that no such ceremony could establish an appropriate connection.

'I impress it on myself' can only mean: this process brings it about that I remember the connection right in future. But in the present case I have no criterion of correctness. One would like to say: whatever is going to seem right to me is right. And that only means that here we can't talk about 'right'. (PI I, 258)

This crucial passage is often misinterpreted. What would it be to remember the connection right? Many philosophers have taken 'I remember the connection right' to mean 'I use "S" when and only when I really have S.' They then take Wittgenstein's argument to be based on scepticism about memory: how can you be sure that you have remembered aright when next you call a sensation 'S'? In support of this interpretation they may quote Wittgenstein's advice 'Always get rid of the private object in this way: assume that it constantly changes, but that you do not notice the change because your memory constantly deceives you' (PI II, 207).

Critics of Wittgenstein have found the argument, so interpreted, quite unconvincing. Surely, they say, the untrustworthiness of memory presents no more and no less a problem for the user of a private language than for the user of a public one. No, Wittgenstein's defenders have said, for memory-mistakes about public objects may be corrected, memory-mistakes about private sensations cannot; and where correction is impossible, talk of correctness is out of place. At this point critics of Wittgenstein have either denied that truth demands corrigibility, or have sought to show that checking is possible in the private case too.

Both criticism and defence rest on a misunderstanding of the argument. Wittgenstein is not arguing 'When next I call something "S" how will I know it really is S?' He is arguing 'When next I call something "S" how will I know what I mean by "S"?' Even to think *falsely* that something is S I must know the meaning of 'S'; and this is what Wittgenstein argues is impossible in the private language.

> Let us imagine a table (something like a dictionary) that exists only in our imagination. A dictionary can be used to justify the translation of a word X into a word Y. But are we also to call it a justification if such a table is to be looked up only in the imagination? 'Well, yes; then it is a subjective justification.' – But justification consists in appealing to something independent. – 'But surely I can appeal from one memory to another. For example, I don't know if I have remembered the time of departure of a train right and to check it I call to mind how a page of the timetable looked. Isn't it the same here?' – No; for this process has got to produce the right memory. If the mental image of the timetable could not itself be tested for correctness, how could it confirm the correctness of the first memory? (As if someone were to buy several copies of the morning paper to assure himself that what it said was true.)(PII, 265)

This passage has puzzled commentators, but what it means is this. We are supposing that I wish to justify my calling a private sensation 'S' by appealing to a mental table in which memory-samples of private objects of various kinds are listed in correlation with symbols (z 546–8, 552). To make use of such a table one must call up the right memory-sample: e.g. I must make sure to call up the memory-sample that belongs alongside 'S' and not the one which belongs to 'T'. But as this table exists only in the imagination, there can be no real looking up to see which sample goes with 'S'. All there can be is *remembering* which sample goes with 'S', i.e. remembering what 'S' means. But this is precisely what the table was supposed to confirm. In other words, the memory of the meaning of 'S' is being used to confirm itself. Once we realize this, we can see the point of the comparison with the newspaper. Since the process involves making use twice over of a single memory – the memory of which sample corresponds to 'S' – it is fairly compared to purchasing two copies of the same newspaper, and not just, say, to purchasing two different newspapers owned by the same untrustworthy magnate.

'Remembering the connection between sign and sensation', then, does not mean always identifying the sensation correctly, but simply remembering which sensation the sign means. This is, of course, what should have been expected: attaching meaning to a name does not mean acquiring infallibility in its use – knowing what 'woman' means does not guarantee that one will never mistake a woman for a man.

With this established, we may return to the key section 258. Wittgenstein wishes to show that the private ostensive definition 'This is called "S"' cannot confer meaning on 'S'. Suppose that at some time after making the would-be definition, the private-language speaker says of a later sensation 'This is S again.' We may ask him 'What do you mean by "S"?' Three types of answer are open to him: he may say 'I mean *this*'; he may appeal to a private memory-sample of S; he may mention a public correlate of S. All three types of reply are countered by Wittgenstein.

If the private-language speaker says 'By "S" I mean *this*', gesturing, as it were, to his current sensation, then it is clear that 'This is S' is not a genuine proposition capable of being true or false; for what gives it its content is the very same thing as gives it its truth: the significance of the predicate is supposed to be settled by the reference of the subject. 'Whatever is going to seem right to me is right' therefore, and 'That only means that here we can't talk about "right"' (PI I, 258; cf. PI II, 207; WWK 97).

Suppose next that the private-language speaker says 'By "S" I mean the sensation I named "S" in the past.' Since he no longer has the past sensation he must rely on memory: he must call up a memory-sample of S and compare it with his current sensation to see if the two are alike. But of course he must call up the *right* memory. Now is it possible that the wrong memory might come at this call? If not, then 'S' means whatever memory occurs to him in connection with 'S', and again whatever seems right is right. If so, then he does not really know what he means. It is no use his saying 'Well, at least I *believe* that this is the sensation "S" again', for he cannot even believe that without knowing what 'S' means (PI I, 260). This appeal to memory-samples, as we have seen, is considered by Wittgenstein in section 265; and it is this memory-sample which is the private object of which Wittgenstein says 'Assume that it constantly changes, but that you do not notice the change' (PI II, 207; cf. I, 271).

The third possibility is that the private-language speaker correlates his use of 'S' with a public phenomenon.

Let us now imagine a use for the entry of the sign 'S' in my diary. I discover that whenever I have a particular sensation a manometer shows that my blood-pressure rises. So I shall be able to say that my blood-pressure is rising without using any apparatus. This is a useful result. And now it seems quite indifferent whether I have recognized the sensation *right* or not. Let us suppose I regularly identify it wrong, it does not matter in the least. And that alone shows that the hypothesis that I make a mistake is mere show (PI I, 270).

Here 'S' has a genuine use, but not as a part of a private language: it is tantamount to 'sensation which means my blood pressure is rising'. Why does Wittgenstein say no mistake is possible? Cannot I say 'S' and then find my blood pressure is *not* rising? Yes, but that is not what Wittgenstein is rejecting: he is talking about a would-be intermediate step between having the sensation and judging 'Now my blood pressure is rising', a step which would consist in recognizing the sensation as a sensation of a particular kind, and remembering that a sensation of that kind indicated a rise in blood-pressure. Misidentification here would not matter, provided that I both misidentified the kind of sensation *and* misremembered what kind of sensation indicated the blood-pressure rise. It is this, according to Wittgenstein, which shows that the hypothesis of a mistake is mere show. Suppose that I say 'S' and the blood-pressure does not rise: what reasons have I to say that I have misidentified the sensation rather than misremembered which kind of sensation goes with the rise? None at all, unless 'identifying the sensation' means 'identifying it as the blood-pressure-rising sensation'; but if it does then there is no room for the intermediate step, and 'S' is not the name of a private object but a word in a public language.

As we have seen, a crucial part is played in the private-language argument by Wittgenstein's advice 'Always get rid of the idea of the private object in this way: assume that it constantly changes, but that you do not notice the change because your memory constantly deceives you.' This advice has a verificationist ring, and some philosophers have thought that the private-language argument depends, in the last analysis, on verificationist premises. But Wittgenstein's advice is not meant to be followed by the question 'How would you ever find out?' but by the question 'What possible difference would it make?' The private-language argument does indeed depend on premises carried forward from Wittgenstein's earlier philosophy; but they are not peculiar to the verificationist period of the 1930s but date back to the time of the picture theory of the proposition in the 1910s.

As we have seen, Wittgenstein's earliest 'Notes on Logic' stress the bi-polarity of the proposition, and insist that every proposition must be capable of both truth and falsehood (NB 94). For a proposition to be capable of being true it must also be capable of being false (NB 55). Every proposition was only a proposition in virtue of being articulated; a simple, non-

articulated sign was incapable of being either true or false
(NB 8). After their classic exposition in the *Tractatus* these
ideas remained influential in the 1930s (cf. WWK 67, 88, 97).

It is clear that 'This is S' does not satisfy the conditions for
propositionhood laid down in the 1910s. It is not articulate,
since 'this' and 'S' are not given their meaning independently.
It has no true–false poles, since what is supposed to give it its
content is the same as what is supposed to give it its truth. In
an early notebook Wittgenstein wrote 'Proposition and situation are related to one another like the yardstick and the length
to be measured' (NB 32). 'This is S' is related to the sensation
which it purports to identify like a yard-stick which grows or
shrinks to the length of the object to be measured. 'Imagine'
Wittgenstein says 'someone saying "But I know how tall I
am" and laying his hand on top of his head to prove it' (PI I,
279; cf. Z 536). A measure must be independent of what is
measured; as we have seen, there is no way of giving 'S'
genuine independence of the object it purports to name short of
taking it into a public language.

It is time to return from 'This is S' to 'I'm in pain.' It cannot
be said of 'I'm in pain' as it could of 'This is S' that what gives
it its content gives it its truth; for 'I'm in pain' may be a lie,
and therefore meaningful but false. ('This is S', of course, being
in a language which only the speaker could understand, could
not be a lie.) So 'I'm in pain' has true–false poles, and passes
that test for being a proposition. Why then does Wittgenstein
appear to reject the idea that 'I'm in pain' is a declarative sentence, a description of a conscious state? (cf. PI I, 290f, 294; II,
189.)

One might seek to give an account of the essence of description in the following manner: to describe a state of affairs is to
read off certain features from the facts and portray them in
words according to rules (PI I, 292). Such a description of a state
of affairs would be a picture of a fact in the sense of the
Tractatus: to see whether such a picture is true or false I
compare it with what it depicts. 'His eye is black' is a picture in

this sense: it is compared with the real eye to see whether it is correct. Now 'He is in pain' – let us leave aside 'I am in pain' for the moment – is not a picture in this sense. It can be compared with reality, and checked for truth and falsehood, certainly; but what it gets compared with is not his pain, but the criteria of his pain, e.g. what he says and does.

The sense in which an image is an image is determined by the way in which it is compared with reality. This we might call the method of projection. Now think of comparing an image of A's toothache with his toothache. How would you compare them? If you say, you compare them 'indirectly' via his bodily behaviour, I answer that this means you *don't* compare them as you compare the picture of his behaviour with his behaviour. (BB 36)

In the *Investigations* and the *Zettel* Wittgenstein repeats that in the language-game with 'pain' there is no comparing of pain with its picture. We are tempted, he says, to say that it is not merely the picture of pain-behaviour which enters into the game, but also the picture of the pain (PI 1, 300). That is, we feel that in order to use 'He is in pain' we need not only a sample of pain-behaviour as a paradigm for comparison with his behaviour, but also a sample of *pain* for comparison with his pain. This sample, of course, need not, we think, be a real pain, but only an imagined pain, a mental proxy for pain. But surely real pain will be at least as good a sample as shadow-pain (BB 4); so in the *Zettel* Wittgenstein imagines someone saying 'I am not certain whether he is in pain' and pricking himself with a pin while saying it, so as to have the meaning of pain vividly before him so that he knows *what* he is in doubt of about the other man. 'So he has real pain; and now he knows what he is to doubt in someone else's case. He has the object before him and it is *not* some piece of behaviour or the like' (Z 546–8).

Of course this would not guarantee the sense of his statement, if it needed guaranteeing: what he needs is not pain but the *concept* of pain, the mastery of the use of 'pain'. 'It is a misunderstanding' Wittgenstein continues (PI 1, 300) 'to say "the picture of pain enters into the language-game with the word 'pain'.'' The image of pain is not a picture and this image is not replaceable in the language-game by anything we should call a picture.' When I imagine someone in pain, my image is not something which is compared with his pain, but something which is compared with his behaviour; it is not replaceable by a picture of pain, because there is no method of projection to enable pain to be pictured (cf. PI I, 301). If I were to construct a table linking pictures with words, in order to help me learn the meaning of 'pain', the table would not contain pictures of pain, (or even my own pain itself, as a model or paradigm: PI I, 302) linked with 'pain': the pictures would have to be pictures of pain-behaviour (cf. PI I, 265; Z 552).

This is summed up in a cryptic metaphor. 'If water boils in a pot, steam comes out of the pot and also pictured steam comes out of the pictured pot. But what if one insisted on saying that there must also be something boiling in the pictured pot?' (PI I, 297). What Wittgenstein is here denying is not that *sensations* enter into the language-game with 'pain', but that *pictures of sensations* do. In the metaphor, the water is the pain, the steam is the pain-behaviour, the pot is the sufferer's body. In the language-game with pain (the *picture* of the water boiling in the pot) there are pictures only of the sufferer and his behaviour, not of his pain.

It is now time to move back again from 'He is in pain' to 'I am in pain.' We have seen that 'X is in pain' is not a picture of what it says, since when it is assessed for truth–falsity it is compared not with X's pain but with X's behaviour. Considered, then, as an instance of 'X is in pain', 'I am in pain' will get compared not with my pain, but with my behaviour, that is, with the part of my behaviour concerned with the expression of pain, with the *criteria* for pain. But my utterance of 'I am in pain' is itself an expression of pain. Consequently, if it is to be a description of my state, it is a description of a special kind: for it is a description which is to be compared with – *inter alia* – itself; and this is a unique type of comparison.

This insight was expressed by Wittgenstein in ways which *prima facie* conflict with each other. In the lectures recorded by Moore he denied that 'I have toothache' was a value of the propositional function 'X has toothache' (ML 307). In the *Investigations* he denied that when I say with truth 'I am in pain' I am identifying my sensation as pain and then describing it. I do not identify my sensation by criteria, but simply make use of the expression I have learnt. That is not the end of the language-game, but the beginning: we must beware of thinking that the beginning of the language-game is the sensation, which I then go on to describe (PI I, 290).

This does not mean that 'I am in pain' is *not* a description. Wittgenstein goes on 'Perhaps the word "describe" tricks us here': there is a great difference between the language-game of describing a room and the language-game of describing a conscious state. It is *correct* to call 'I am in pain' a description: but the use of 'description' differs from that in 'description of my room'. It differs because my description of my room is not a criterion for what my room is like, whereas my description of my conscious state is a criterion for what it is like. The language-game of describing the room begins with observation of the room (PE 330); the language-game of describing sensations begins with criteria for sensations. Hence 'I am in pain' is not the end of a language-game, but a beginning (cf. PI I, 291, 363).

Just as Wittgenstein thought that 'pain' was in one sense a name and in another not, so he can regard 'I am in pain' as in one sense a description and in another not. He can admit that, when a doctor on a ward-round asks a patient how he feels, it is perfectly natural to call the reply 'I am in pain' a description of the patient's state (cf. PI II, 188). But he will deny that 'I am in pain' is a description of a state if that means that it is something read off from an internal state of affairs. To treat the expression of pain in this way as a description of pain is to make it seem too distant from pain. To adapt a metaphor of Wittgenstein's from another context, it is 'as when travelling in a car and feeling in a hurry I instinctively push against something in front of me as though I could push the car from inside'. Or it is as if 'I constructed a clock with all its wheels etc. and in the end fastened the dial to the pointer and made it go round with it' (BB 71). A description must be independent of what it is to be compared with if it is to be assessed as a correct or incorrect description: just as in order to tell the time the hands of a clock must be unfastened to the dial. 'I'm in pain', since it is an utterance which is a criterion for my conscious state, is not independent of it, and so cannot be a description of it in the same way as 'There is a chair in the corner' may be a description of my room (cf. PE 320).

Clearly this point has nothing to do with verificationism. The trouble with a clock whose hands are attached to the dial is not that we can never know whether it is telling the right time, but that it is not telling the time at all. Moreover the point has nothing to do with the nature of the speech-act which 'I'm in pain' may be used to perform. 'We surely do not always say that someone is *complaining* because he says he is in pain. So the words "I am in pain" may be a cry of complaint, and may be something else' (PI II, 189). They might, for instance, be uttered in order to give information to a doctor. But this would not make them in the full sense a description; for the doctor might acquire the same information from a wordless cry. A cry, which cannot be called a description, for all that may perform the same service as a description of one's inner life (PI II, 189; PE 319).

Just as 'I'm in pain' is only a description in a special sense, so it is only true or false in a special sense (cf. PE 293), for its truth coincides with its truthfulness. One might adapt to the case of the avowal of pain what Wittgenstein says about the confession of a past thought (PI II, 222). The criteria for the truth of the avowal that I am in pain are not the criteria for the true description of a process. The importance of the true avowal does not lie in its being a correct and certain report of a process. It resides rather in the special conclusions which can be drawn from an avowal whose truth is guaranteed by the special criteria of truthfulness. In this case there is no comparison of a proposition to reality (PE 294; cf. 295, 301).

We can now see why Wittgenstein rejected the idea that when I am in pain I know that I am in pain. Throughout his life he thought of knowledge as involving the possession of a true description of a state of affairs. That was why in the *Tractatus* he declared knowledge of tautologies impossible, since tautologies were not pictures of states of affairs (TLP 4.462, 5.51362; cf. 5.542). That is why, since 'I am in pain' is not, when I am in pain, a true description in the normal sense, 'I know that I am in pain' cannot be in order if 'know' is being used in the normal sense. Since the truth of 'I am in pain' coincides with its truthfulness, and there is no such thing as making a mistake here, Wittgenstein does not want to call it an assertion, or the expression of a piece of knowledge.

But Wittgenstein's position has nuances. Altogether in his writings Wittgenstein recognized the following senses or would-be senses of 'I know I'm in pain':

(1) Non-philosophical, empirical use (to rule out unconscious pain, if we have fixed experiential criteria for the case in which a man has pain but does not know it) (BB 55).
(2) Non-philosophical, non-empirical use: e.g. 'I know I'm in pain' as a joke; in these cases 'I'm in pain', with some nuance, is substitutable (PI I, 246).
(3) Correct philosophical use: 'When I'm in pain I know I'm in pain' means: the expression of doubt is senseless (PI I, 246).
(4) Philosophers' nonsense: doubt is both logically possible (to make its expression sensible) and logically impossible (I can't *a priori*, be wrong about pain) (PI II, 221; BB 30–55).

The philosophers' nonsense is once again a sin against the *Tractatus* principle that a proposition must be independent of what it records, as a measure must be independent of what it measures. Against this background, the philosophers' nonsense can be seen as treating expressions of mental states as if they were measurements of mental states (and therefore independent) of an infallible kind (the infallibility being secured at the price of non-independence). From this point of view, the epistemologists' complaint 'If I can't know my own sensations, how can I know anything?' appears like the lament 'If I can't place a winning bet after the race has been won, how can I ever place a winning bet at all?'

CHAPTER II

On Scepticism and Certainty

Since the time of Descartes epistemology, or theory of know-ledge, has been one of the major preoccupations of philosophers: the attempt to explain how it is that we know what we know, and how to answer sceptical doubts about the justification of our beliefs. Descartes begins his *Meditations* with a process of systematic doubt designed to separate out what is solid and what is unreliable in the system of commonsense beliefs with a view to establishing a firm foundation on which to build the edifice of science. First of all he doubts the existence of material things, such as the sun and moon and earth, even his own hands and body, and sensible objects like colours, shapes and sounds. This doubt is argued for in three stages: first, the senses have often deceived him in the past; second, he cannot know that he is not dreaming; third, it may be that he is the plaything of a powerful and malevolent spirit who is deceiving him. He does his best also to doubt the truths of logic and mathematics: men sometimes go wrong in calculations even of the simplest kind; may it not be that God likewise makes him go wrong even when adding two to three? There are two things which Descartes, even at his most sceptical, never doubts: one is his consciousness of his own mental states and processes, the other his knowledge of the language he uses in order to express his scepticism.

Descartes's sceptical arguments, in the First and Third Medita-tion, have made more impression on succeeding philosophers than his replies to those arguments in the Fourth and Sixth Meditations. He offered to prove the trustworthiness of our understanding, and the existence of the external world, on the basis of a demonstration of the existence of a veracious God. Few philosophers have been satisfied by these arguments, and many have felt obliged to offer their own answers to the sceptical doubts. Among these philosophers was G. E. Moore, who in his 'A Defence of Common Sense' and 'Proof of an External World' (1925 and 1939) had claimed to know for certain a number of propositions – such as 'Here is one hand and here is another' and 'The earth existed for a long time before my birth' and 'I have never been far from the earth's surface' – from which it followed that the external world existed.

Wittgenstein being preoccupied with theory of meaning was comparatively uninterested in epistemology for much of his life. But his work on the philosophy of mind and the foundations of mathematics naturally overlapped with areas which were the traditional province of epistemologists. Towards the end of his life, while staying with Norman Malcolm in Ithaca in 1949, he was stimulated by the study of Moore's articles to begin to write on epistemology. His notes, which continued until two days before his death and were of course never polished, were published posthumously in 1969 under the title *On Certainty*. In this work, though Descartes is never mentioned by name, Wittgenstein conducts a three-cornered argument with Moore and the Cartesian sceptic.

Descartes had regarded statements about the external world, including one's own body, as being much more vulnerable to doubt than simple mathematical propositions (which he thought could not be doubted while before the mind, but only in retrospect) and than propositions about one's own mental states, e.g. about sense-data (which he never called in question). Wittgenstein thought that Moore was right against Descartes in claiming that some propositions about the external world (e.g. 'This is a chair') could have the same epistemological status as mathematical propositions (o c 455, 651) and propositions about sense-data. But he thought that Moore was wrong in thinking that these propositions provided a proof of the external world (o c 209, 220), and indeed wrong in thinking that he knew the propositions at all: not because the propositions were false, but because the claim to knowledge of them was senseless (o c 6, etc.). Both Moore and the sceptic, he claimed, misunderstood the nature of doubt, knowledge and certainty in several ways. Because of this, Wittgenstein, while rejecting Moore's argument against the sceptic, was able to present a different refutation of the sceptical position – not so much an argument to show the falsehood of the sceptic's conclusion, as an attempt to bring out the meaninglessness of the sceptic's procedure.

In the course of *On Certainty* Wittgenstein enunciates a number of theses about doubt. (1) Doubt needs grounds. (2) Doubt must amount to something more than the verbal utterance of doubt. (3) Doubt presupposes the mastery of a language-game. (4) Doubt outside a language-game, or about a whole language-game, is impossible. (5) Doubt presupposes certainty.

(1) *Doubt needs grounds.* This is repeated several times by Wittgenstein (OC 323, 458, 519). Descartes would have entirely agreed: that was why he invented the evil genius, to provide a ground for Cartesian doubt. But Descartes insisted, surely rightly, that a ground for doubting need not itself be certain in order to cast doubt. No doubt Wittgenstein would have regarded the hypothesis of the evil genius as too idle and speculative to be a genuine ground. The mere imaginability of not-*p* is no ground for doubting that *p* (OC 4). But if Cartesian doubt is groundless to this extent, is it *eo ipso* impossible, or just unreasonable? Wittgenstein says that there is a difference between the cases where doubt is unreasonable, and where it is logically impossible; but he claims that there is no clear boundary between them (OC 454). The need for grounds does not itself settle whether Cartesian doubt is possible.

(2) *Doubt must amount to something.* If someone doubts the existence of material objects, this doubt does not make any difference in practice (OC 120). Indeed it isn't even clear how we could imagine what difference it should make (OC 247). At most, it seems, it makes a difference in what he says and feels (cf. OC 338f.). 'Suppose a person of normal behaviour

assured us that he only believed . . . he had hands and feet when he didn't actually see them, and so on. Can we show him' asks Wittgenstein 'that it is not so from the things he does (and says)?' (oc 428.) Descartes would agree that his doubt was speculative, not practical – indeed he insisted on this against those who accused him of favouring atheism and immorality by his systematic doubt. But he would say that a merely speculative doubt can be a real doubt.

(3) *Doubt presupposes the mastery of a language-game.* In order to express the doubt that *p*, one must understand what is meant by saying that *p*. Because of this, Wittgenstein argues, Cartesian doubt in a way destroys itself, since it is so radical that it is bound to call in question the meanings of the words used to express it. This line of thought is explored many times in *On Certainty*. 'If you are not certain of any fact, you cannot be certain of the meaning of your words either' (oc 114). 'I don't know if this is a hand' presupposes that I know what the word 'hand' means (oc 306), but is bound to involve a doubt about it too ('If this isn't a hand, I don't know what a hand is') (oc 369, 456). This seems a fair criticism of the Cartesian doubter: if Descartes is really to doubt whatever can be doubted, then he should try to doubt the meanings of the words he uses. For it is, as Wittgenstein points out, an empirical fact that English, or Latin, words have the meanings they have: it is not even a truth of logic or mathematics (oc 306, 486). But if the Cartesian doubt is taken thus far, it refutes itself. If the evil genius is deceiving me totally, then he is deceiving me about the meaning of the word 'deceive'; and so 'The evil genius is deceiving me totally' does not express the total doubt that it was meant to (cf. oc 507).

Wittgenstein claims further that not only does the expression of doubt presuppose that the language-game within which it is expressed is not doubted, but that in particular cases the nature of the language-game itself may exclude a doubt about existence. Someone who asks 'What right have I not to doubt the existence of my hands?' is overlooking the fact that a doubt about existence only works against the background of a language-game, and in this case no appropriate language-game has been set up (OC 24).

(4) *Universal doubt impossible.* Doubts belong within particular games. Wittgenstein invites us to imagine a pupil who will not let his teacher explain anything to him, because he constantly interrupts with doubts about the existence of things, the meaning of words, etc. The teacher's impatience is justified, because the pupil's doubt is hollow: he has not learnt how to ask questions; he has not learnt the game that he is being taught (OC 310–15). Not calling things in doubt is often a precondition of learning certain games (OC 329). The child learns by believing the adult, and doubt comes *after* belief (OC 160). It is inconceivable that a child might learn the meanings of words by hearing them only in expressions of uncertainty. 'A doubt that doubted everything would not be a doubt' (OC 450). Even if it were possible to doubt every single one of the facts presupposed by our language-games, we could not doubt them all (OC 232). For instance, the language-game that operates with people's names can exist if individuals are mistaken about their names – but it presupposes that it is nonsensical to say that the majority of people are mistaken about their names.

(5) *Doubt presupposes certainty.* Doubt is only possible where testing is possible (OC 125), and tests presuppose something that is not doubted and not tested (OC 163, 337). 'Our doubts depend on the fact that some propositions are exempt from doubt, are as it were like the hinges on which those turn' (OC 341). Hence 'The game of doubting itself presupposes certainty' (OC 115).

Wittgenstein therefore rules out various types of doubt. If there are certain propositions about which we cannot doubt, are they also propositions about which we cannot be mistaken? The second does not, of course, follow from the first – it might be possible for me to be mistaken about *p* without being able to entertain the possibility that I am mistaken about *p* – and indeed the whole purpose of Descartes's appeal to the veracity of God was to show that where we could not doubt (where we clearly and distinctly perceived something) we could not be mistaken either.

Wittgenstein, unlike Descartes, makes a sharp distinction between mistake and other forms of false belief. If someone were to imagine that he had been living for a long time somewhere other than where he had in fact been living during that time 'I should not call this a mistake, but a mental disturbance, perhaps a transient one' (oc 71). The difference between the two is perhaps that reasons can be given for a mistake, but only causes for a mental disturbance (oc 75). If Moore were to announce the opposite of his propositions, we should think him demented, not mistaken (155f.), for mistake has a special place in a language-game (oc 196). To doubt *all* of our calculations is a mark of craziness, not error (oc 217). If someone says that he has flown from America to England in the last few days he cannot be making a mistake: only if he is mad can he have got this sort of thing wrong (oc 674-5).

The reason why Wittgenstein makes this distinction is that the procedure of talking someone out of a mad belief – or, for that matter, of a mad doubt – is quite different from that of correcting a mistake.

If someone said to me that he doubted whether he had a body I should take him to be a half-wit. But I shouldn't know what it would mean to try to convince him that he had one. And if I had said something, and that had removed his doubt, I should not know how or why. (oc 257)

I can make a mistake when I am quite sure of something – e.g. of the date of a battle – and can correct this by referring to authority without losing all faith in my judgement. But I cannot be making a mistake in thinking that the earth existed long before I was born, or that twelve times twelve is a hundred and forty-four. For how could we imagine the mistake being corrected, and why should we trust any other calculation (oc 300–304)? It is impossible to imagine a situation in which I would be brought to admit that my present belief that I am living in England was a mistake. If people came into my room and all declared that I am not in England, and offered proofs of it, I could only think that either I or they had gone mad; or I might perhaps be brought to believe that I had been mad up to that moment (o c 420). But I cannot be *forced* to change my opinion. If something happened calculated to make me doubtful of my own name, there would certainly also be something that made the grounds of these doubts themselves seem doubtful, and I could therefore decide to retain my old belief (o c 512–16).

A Cartesian sceptic might be impatient with the distinction drawn between mistake and madness. Surely, he might say, if it is possible that my belief is false, then that is sufficient to make a doubt; it does not matter whether the falsehood is grounded in a rational system of beliefs, or is the result of some pathological condition (o c 74). Does not Descartes himself, briefly, use the possibility of madness as a ground for doubt in the First Meditation before going on to the better-known argument from dreaming?

'. . . these hands, and my whole body – how can their existence be denied? Unless indeed I likened myself to some lunatics, whose brains are so upset by persistent melancholy vapours that they firmly assert they are kings, when really they are miserably poor; or that they are clad in purple, when really they are naked; or that they have a head of pottery, or are pumpkins, or are made of glass; but then they are madmen, and I should appear no less mad if I took them as a precedent for my own case' – A fine argument! As though I were not a man who habitually sleeps at night and has the same impressions (or even wilder ones) in sleep as these men do when awake. (*Philosophical Writings*, ed. Anscombe and Geach, Nelson, 1954, p. 62)

Wittgenstein would presumably reply that the difference between madness and mistake is that whereas mistake involves false judgement, in madness no judgement is made at all, true or false. So coming to believe that one is, or was, mad does not involve the correction of a false judgement. 'I can't be making a mistake – but some day, rightly or wrongly, I may think I realize that I was not competent to judge' (o c 645).

This is spelt out more fully in connection with the sceptical argument about dreaming. The argument 'I may be dreaming', he says, is senseless for this reason: if I am dreaming this remark is being dreamt as well – and indeed it is also being dreamt that these words have any meaning (o c 383). We feel that we could give a sense to the supposition by saying that I might suddenly as it were wake up, and say 'Just think, I've been dreaming that I live in England etc.' But this cannot cast doubt on my present belief, because it is equally imaginable that I might wake up once again and pronounce the first waking-up a dream (o c 642). In the very last entry in the notes, discussing the belief that one has just flown from America, Wittgenstein wrote

but even if in such cases I can't be mistaken, isn't it possible that I am drugged?' If I am and if the drug has taken away my consciousness, then I am not now really talking and thinking. I cannot seriously suppose that I am at this moment dreaming. Someone who, dreaming, says 'I am dreaming', even if he speaks audibly in doing so, is no more right than if he said in his dream 'It is raining', while it was in fact raining. Even if his dream were actually connected with the noise of the rain. (o c 676)

Following Moore's lead, Wittgenstein lists a number of propositions about which he thinks mistake is impossible, and doubt is impossible. 'I have never been on the moon' cannot be doubted (o c 117); its contradictory cannot be seriously considered (o c 226). 'It is certain that no one has ever been on the moon' wrote Wittgenstein rashly. 'Not merely is nothing of the sort ever seriously reported to us by reasonable people, but our whole system of physics forbids us to believe it' (o c 108). Other examples were happier. To doubt that my friend hasn't sawdust in his head would be madness (o c 281). I cannot doubt that I have two hands (o c 125); that I have two hands is an irreversible belief, I am not ready to let anything count as a disproof of the proposition (o c 245). In very special circumstances a doubt about 'This is my hand' might make sense (OC 413). 'I am now living in England' cannot be a mistake (OC 420). Nor can 'The earth has existed during the last hundred years' be spoken of as a mistake without changing the role of 'mistake' and 'truth' in our lives (OC 138).

But, as we saw in the last chapter, to say that something cannot be doubted, or cannot be the subject of a mistake, is not the same as to say that it can be known. Wittgenstein repeats from the *Investigations* that to say one knows one has a pain means nothing (OC 504); and he adds 'I know where I am feeling pain', 'I know that I feel it *here*', is as wrong as 'I know that I am in pain' (OC 41). To say 'I know I'm in pain' is to give a misleading expression to the grammatical truth that there is no such thing as doubting that I am in pain. The grammatical truth could also be expressed 'The expression "I do not know" makes no sense in this case.' And of course it follows from this, Wittgenstein says, that 'I know' makes no sense, either (OC 58).

Now are the Moore-type propositions, such as 'Here is my hand' on all fours with the propositions about one's own experience? Is 'I know that here is my hand' senseless? Once again, as in the last chapter, it takes an effort to achieve consistency between the various things Wittgenstein says here. There seem to be the following main strands in what he says. (1) In 'I know that *p*', where *p* is a Moore-type proposition, the 'I' is superfluous (OC 58, 100, 462, 587, 588), and to this extent at least the expression is misleading (OC 84, 401). (2) 'I know that *p*' where '*p*' is a Moore-type proposition can have an everyday use in sufficiently unusual circumstances (OC 23, 258, 262 347, 349, 387, 412, 433, 526, 596, 622). In such cases its meaning is clear but it does not provide the philosopher with an answer to scepticism (OC 347). (3) Unless it is possible to doubt that *p*, be mistaken in believing that *p*, inform oneself that *p*, one cannot be said to know that *p* (OC 10, 372, 550, 564, 576). Hence, out of a suitable context, to say that I know a Moore-type proposition is not just superfluous but senseless (OC 461,

464, 347–50, 469). (4) None the less 'I know . . .' is sometimes used in ordinary language with Moore-type propositions, either as a misleading expression of a grammatical proposition (OC 58) or as what Wittgenstein technically calls 'an utterance' (OC 510) or as an expression of linguistic capacity (OC 371, 585–6). (5) But in no case does this type of 'I know that p' provide an answer to the sceptic (OC 520, 521). I will develop each of these five points from Wittgenstein's text.

(1) *'I know that* p*' not specially about me.* The propositions that Moore chooses are not cases where he has special knowledge unavailable to the rest of us, or information which he and not others have acquired (OC 462). He chooses cases where we all seem to know the same as he, or, more accurately, if he knows these things, then so do we all (OC 84, 100). Consequently the suggestion which 'I know' makes, that this is a personal statement about the speaker, is misleading (OC 84). One may indeed question whether there is really a difference between what is said by 'I know that that's a . . .' and 'That is a . . .' The fact that in the first sentence a person is mentioned and not in the second does not show that they have different meanings (OC 587). The truth is, Wittgenstein says, that 'I know' has meaning only when it is uttered by a person (there could not, for instance, be an impersonal notice on a cage in a zoo reading 'I know that this is a zebra'). But given that, it is a matter of indifference whether what is uttered is 'I know' or 'that is' (OC 588), unless it is a matter of degree of certainty (OC 485).

(2) *Special circumstances can give 'I know that* p*' a use.* Wittgenstein admits that in unusual circumstances the Moore-type propositions can have a use, but not one which is a help against the sceptic. For instance:

If I don't know whether someone has two hands (say, whether they have been amputated or not) I shall believe his assurance that he has two hands, if he is trustworthy. And if he says he *knows* it, that can only signify to me that he has been able to make sure, and hence that his arms are e.g. not still concealed by coverings and bandages, etc., etc. My believing the trustworthy man stems from my admitting that it is possible for him to make sure. But someone who says that perhaps there are no physical objects makes no such admission (oc 23)

– and hence it is useless for the trustworthy Moore to assure the sceptic that he knows he has two hands. Wittgenstein devises various situations for the use of Moore-type propositions; 'I know that I have always been near the surface of the earth' (to a tribe who think you have come from the moon) (oc 264). 'I know that that's a tree' (worried about one's failing eyesight) (oc 349). He says that he cannot find a situation for 'I know that I am a human being', but thinks that even that might be given a sense (oc 622). 'For each one of these sentences I can imagine circumstances that turn it into a move in one of our language-games, and by that it loses everything that is philosophically astonishing' (oc 622).

(3) *Outside appropriate situations, 'I know that* p' *senseless.* A philosopher may say such things as 'I know that that's a tree' to demonstrate to himself or to someone else that he *knows* something that is not a mathematical or logical truth (oc 350). But without appropriate surroundings such an expression lacks all sense: it is like saying 'Down with him!' out of all context, or thinking that one was sawing because one was making sawing-like movements with one's hand in the air (oc 350). If, while talking to a friend, I suddenly say 'I knew all along that you were so-and-so' that is not just a superfluous, though true, remark: it is more like the words 'Good morning' uttered in the middle of a conversation out of the blue (oc 464). Wittgenstein gives a number of different reasons for this, none of them sufficiently clear to be convincing. One is that the information that if I know that this is a hand is worth imparting, that casts doubt on its truth (oc 461). Another is that the lack of appropriate context means that the sense of the remark is undetermined: 'I know that's a tree' has no focussed meaning, just as

... the words 'I am here' have a meaning only in certain contexts, and not when I say them to someone who is sitting in front of me and sees me clearly – and not because they are superfluous but because their meaning is not determined by the situation, yet stands in need of such determination. (oc 348)

The last clause is to distinguish such a sentence from '$2 \times 2 = 4$' which does not need such determination (oc 10). Wittgenstein knows that sentences such as 'I know that there's a sick man lying here', used in unsuitable situations, seem not to be nonsense but to be matter of course; but he says that that is 'only because one can fairly easily imagine a situation to fit it, and one thinks that the words "I know that . . ." are always in place where there is no doubt, and hence even when the expression of doubt would be unintelligible' (oc 10). This last is his most frequent reason for rejecting Moore's 'I know' – namely, that 'I know that p' makes sense only when 'I do not know', 'I doubt', 'I will check up that . . .' also make sense (oc 574). 'I know' is in place where I can be asked 'How do you know?', and can reply by specifying one of a number of ways of finding out (oc 483–4, 550, 564, 576). 'I know that p' is in place where I can give grounds for p that are surer than p; but I cannot give any surer grounds for the proposition that I have two hands (oc 243, 250).

(4) *Other uses of 'I know'*. 'I know that here is my hand', like 'I know that I'm in pain', may be a misleading expression of the logical, or grammatical, truth that there is no such thing as a doubt in this case (oc 58). Wittgenstein also says 'If I say "Of course I know that that's a towel" I am making an utterance [*Ausserung*]. I have no thought of a verification. For me it is an immediate utterance.' By 'utterance' in his other works Wittgenstein appears to mean a pre-propositional expression of a mental state – e.g. 'I'm in pain' considered as a cry of pain, not a report (oc 510). Again 'I know that that's a hand' can mean: I can play language-games with 'hand' – make statements like 'I have a pain in this hand' or 'This hand is weaker than the other' – language-games in which there is no

doubt as to the existence of the hand (OC 371). But Wittgenstein says that he would prefer to reserve 'I know' for the cases in which it is used in the normal interchange of conversation (OC 1570).

(5) *Moore-propositions and the sceptic.* Surprisingly, there are one or two passages in which Wittgenstein seems to agree that Moore knows Moore-type propositions. For instance 'Moore has every right to say he knows there's a tree there in front of him. Naturally, he may be wrong' (OC 520; cf. also OC 532). But he goes on to say that, whether he is right or wrong in this, it cannot help Moore's case against the sceptic. For if it is the sort of thing of which knowledge can be had, saying 'I know' does not prove that one does know (OC 487–9). On the other hand, if 'I know' is used in a context where it is senseless, then Moore has fallen into the same error as the sceptic who has tried to doubt where doubt is senseless. For the possibility of doubt and the possibility of knowledge go together (OC 10, 450). Either way, it is a mistake to counter the sceptic's assertion that one cannot know something by saying 'I do know it' (OC 521).

Wittgenstein believed that we think we can make sense of Moore's 'I know that here's a hand' because we think of knowledge as a specially infallible psychic or mental state on which one could report. He argued against this many times. 'I know' is unlike 'I believe', 'I surmise', 'I doubt' in that it can be mistaken (OC 21). Unlike 'I'm in pain' it is an utterance subject to doubt (OC 178). One can say 'He believes it, but it isn't so', but not 'He knows it, but it isn't so'; but this does not mean that belief and knowledge are two different mental states: the mental state of conviction may be the same whether it is knowledge or false belief (OC 42, 308). Wittgenstein seems to accuse Moore of subscribing to the following fallacious argument: knowledge is a mental state; I am infallible about my mental states; so if I say truthfully that I know that p, I know that p; but if I know that p, then p; so if I say I know that p, then p (OC 13, 90, 356). In so far as knowledge, as a mental state, differs from belief, it is in that it is a kind of belief which excludes doubt, and willingness for further test (OC 356, 368); but this state of mind of course gives no guarantee of truth (OC 356). It seems to me doubtful whether Moore did accept this fallacious form of argument. Wittgenstein's criticism here would be better directed at Descartes, who did indeed believe that there was a mental state ('clear and distinct perception') which – because of the veracity of the Creator – guaranteed truth.

Though Wittgenstein was unwilling, in general, to agree with Moore that there were certain propositions which he *knew*, which proved the existence of the external world, he thought that Moore was right that there were certain empirical propositions which had a special status. He preferred to describe this status by saying that they are propositions which 'stand fast' for us or 'are solid' (OC 112, 116, 151).

When Moore says he *knows* such and such, he is really enumerating a lot of empirical propositions which we affirm with special testing; propositions, that is, which have a peculiar logical role in the system of our empirical propositions . . . they all have a similar role in the system of our empirical judgements. We don't, for example, arrive at any of them as a result of investigation. (OC 136–8)

They are 'empirical' propositions in a rather special way: they are not the results of inquiry, but the foundations of research: they are as it were fossilized empirical propositions which form channels for the ordinary, fluid propositions (OC 87f., 95–9; cf. 657). They are at the broad borderline between empirical and logical propositions (OC 319f.). 'Propositions of the form of empirical propositions, and not only propositions of logic, form the foundation of all operating with thoughts' (OC 401). They are not, like ordinary empirical propositions, propositions about (parts of) the world: they are ones which make up our world-picture. A world-picture is not learnt by experience. 'I did not get my picture of the world by satisfying myself of its correctness; nor do I have it because I am satisfied of its correctness. No: it is the inherited background against which I distinguish between true and false' (o c 94).

In our world-picture there are included not only propositions which appear to be about simple objects of perception (like 'Here is a hand') but also propositions which look like scientific propositions, e.g. 'There is a brain inside my skull' (o c 4, 118, 207, 281, 284, 327); 'Water boils at 100° centigrade' (o c 555, 558, 567, 599, 618). When someone more primitive is persuaded to accept our world-picture, this is not by our giving him grounds to prove the truth of these propositions; rather, we convert him to a new way of looking at the world, and have to appeal to notions like simplicity and richness of systems (o c 92, 286). The role of such propositions is quite different from that of axioms in a system: it is not as if they were first learnt and conclusions drawn from them. Children do not learn them (o c 476): they as it were swallow them down with what they do learn.

It is quite sure that motor cars don't grow out of the earth. We feel that if someone could believe the contrary he could believe *everything* that we say is untrue, and could question everything that we hold to be sure.

But how does this *one* belief hang together with all the rest? We would like to say that someone who could believe that does not accept our whole system of verification.

The system is something that a human being acquires by means of observation and instruction. I intentionally do not say 'learns'. (o c 279)

When we first begin to believe anything, we believe not a single proposition but a whole system: light dawns gradually over the whole. It is a system in which consequences and premisses give one another mutual support. The system is not a set of axioms, a point of departure, so much as the whole element in which all arguments have their life (o c 105).

The reason for this is that the propositions of this system are the foundations on which the language-games of arguing, testing, etc. are built (o c 403, 446, 524, 558, 617).

If I say '*We assume* that the earth has existed for many years past' or something similar, then of course it sounds strange that we should *assume* such a thing. But in the entire system of our language-games it belongs to the foundations. The assumption, one might say, forms the basis of action, and therefore, naturally, of thought. (OC 411)

Though these propositions give the foundations of the language-games, they do not provide grounds, or premisses, for language-games.

Giving grounds . . . justifying the evidence, comes to an end; but the end is not certain propositions striking us immediately as true, i.e. it is not a kind of *seeing* on our part; it is our acting, which lies at the bottom of the language-game. (OC 204; cf. OC 110, 559)

Descartes, I think, would have been unmoved by the suggestion that some propositions stood fast because they were the foundation of all thought. For the hypothesis of the evil genius was precisely a theological version of the supposition that human nature, with all its language-games of reasoning and testing, was radically defective and misleading. But then Wittgenstein does not think the sceptic can be answered, only silenced.

In describing the foundations of language-games, Wittgenstein found himself, in these last days of his life, driven several times to formulations that resembled the language of his youth. He toyed with the idea of saying that the language-game must show, rather than say, the facts that made it possible (OC 618). And having said 'Any empirical proposition can be transformed into a postulate' he said 'It all sounds too reminiscent of the *Tractatus*!' (OC 321). And finally, a fortnight before his death:

Am I not getting closer and closer to saying that in the end logic cannot be described? You must look at the practice of language, then you will see it. (OC 501)

There is an unmistakable echo of the first entry in his 1914 notebook:

Logic must take care of itself. (NB 2)

CHAPTER 12

The Continuity of
Wittgenstein's Philosophy

We have now traced the evolution of Wittgenstein's thought from his earliest to his latest writings. Because the *Tractatus* and the *Investigations* were the first of his works to be published, and because there are marked differences of style and content between them, there grew up the idea that Wittgenstein had fathered two wholly dissimilar and disconnected philosophies. The posthumous publication of the works of the thirties shows that this view is too simple. There are many connections between the earlier and the later work, and many assumptions common to both. In this final chapter I hope to bring this out.

The contrast commonly drawn between the *Tractatus* and the *Investigations* centres on three principal points. (1) In the *Tractatus* Wittgenstein put forward a metaphysical atomism: the ultimate elements of language are names that designate simple objects; elementary propositions are concatenations of these names, each such proposition being independent of every other such proposition. In the *Investigations* it is argued that the words 'simple' and 'complex' have no absolute meaning, and the search for the ultimate independent elementary propositions is regarded as a delusion. (2) In the *Tractatus* Wittgenstein is interested in the formal structures of symbolic logic as a key to the ideal essence of the proposition and of language; in the *Investigations* he has abandoned the idea that language has an essence and devotes himself to the study of the idioms of ordinary language. (3) Whereas the *Tractatus* held that sentences had meaning or sense because they were pictures, the *Investigations* says that the meaning of a sentence is its use or employment or application; the conception that a significant sentence is a picture is replaced in the later thought by the view that the sense of a sentence is determined by the circumstances in which it is uttered and the language-game to which it belongs.

The first of these contrasts seems to me accurate, the second partly accurate and partly misleading, and the third almost wholly misleading. To justify these judgements I propose to examine the three contrasts in turn.

We have already seen in chapter six how Wittgenstein abandoned, step by step, the atomism of logical atomism. It had been a mistake, he came to think, to treat facts and complexes of objects alike.

A complex is not like a fact. I say, for instance, of a complex that it moves from one place to another, but not of a fact. But that this complex is now there, is a fact . . . To say that a red circle consists of redness and circularity, or is a complex of these component parts, is a misuse of these words, and misleading. (Frege knew this and told me so.) (PG 200)

It is equally misleading to say that the fact that this circle is red is a complex whose component parts are circle and redness. This he wrote in the appendix to the *Bemerkungen* (PB 301) which appears also as the appendix to the *Grammatik* (PG 199); and he repeated the point in the *Blue Book* (BB 31). These remarks appear to be directed against the *Tractatus*, though if they had been written by anyone else one would say they betrayed a misunderstanding of that work. By the time he wrote the *Investigations* Wittgenstein opposed this idea of analysis even as applied to perfectly straightforward spatial complexes. The statement 'My broom is in the corner' is about the complex, my broom, whose component parts are the broomstick and the brush; but because the broom has parts it does not follow that the sentence about it has corresponding parts (PI 1, 60).

The *Philosophical Investigations* contains a long and detailed criticism of the notion of simplicity as used in the *Tractatus* (PII, 39–64).[1] One is inclined to argue that names ought really to

1. This section illustrates that, despite appearances, the *Philosophical Investigations* is constructed on the same lines, and could have been numbered

signify simples, he says, because if a name signifies a complex (as ordinary proper names do) there is the danger that the complex may be broken up; if this happens then the name will have no meaning, and sentences containing them will be nonsense. This argument, he says, is invalid, because it is not true that a word has no meaning if nothing corresponds to it: that is to confuse the meaning of a name with its bearer (PI I, 40–45). He goes on to argue that simplicity itself is not a simple notion, and that absolute simplicity is nonsense: what counts as 'simple' and what counts as 'complex' depends on what language-game one is using (PI I, 47–65). Where analysis is possible, one should not think that the analysed form of a sentence is more fundamental than the unanalysed form (PI I, 60–65).

In the *Tractatus* Wittgenstein had argued that unless there were simple objects, then whether one proposition had a sense would depend on whether another proposition was true (TLP 2.0201–2.0211). That is to say, if every proposition were about a complex, every proposition would depend for its sense on the truth of another proposition stating the existence of that complex, and so on *ad infinitum*. Wittgenstein now argued that the meaning of a sentence containing a name such as 'Moses' did not depend for its meaning either on the existence of Moses (PG 64; PI I, 40), or on the user of the name having a definite description ready to substitute for it (PI I, 79). The substitution of such a description is neither necessary (PI I, 79) nor sufficient (PI I, 87) to remove all doubt about the meaning of the name; the name is used without a fixed meaning, but that does not detract from its usefulness in language. Since it is not analysable into a definite description, the sense of a sentence containing it does not depend on the truth of a proposition saying that the definite description is satisfied, and the regress feared in the *Tractatus* does not start.

---

in the same manner as the *Tractatus*. For instance, if 39 were n., then 40 would be n. I, 41 n. II, 42 n. I2, 43 n. I3, 44 n. 2, 45 n. 21, 46 n. 3, 47 n. 31, 48 n. 32, 49 n. 321, 50 n. 322, 51 n. 323, 52 n. 3231.

The rejection of the atomism of the *Tractatus* leads to a revision of the notion of philosophical analysis. If ordinary language is not analysable into a language containing only names for simples, the task of philosophy in dealing with ordinary language cannot be the one laid down in the *Tractatus*. But it is important not to overstate the contrast between the attitude of the two works to ordinary language.

Both works insist that the sentences of ordinary language are in perfect logical order just as they stand (TLP 5.563; PI I, 98). Both works insist that language is a part of human natural history (TLP 4.001; PI I, 25). Both remark that ordinary language is a deceptive clothing, and that what it conceals are the differences between expressions which look similar (TLP 4.002; PI II, 224). Both use the same examples to illustrate this: the differences between the 'is' in 'The rose is red', 'Two by two is four' 'There is no God' (TLP 3.323; PG 53; PI I, 558). In both the differences which are hidden by the uniform appearance of written and spoken words are revealed by a consideration of their use or application (TLP 3.143, 3.262; PI I, 11).

There is a difference of emphasis, however, in each of these parallels. From the fact that the sentences of ordinary language are in order the *Tractatus* concludes that, appearances notwithstanding, they already have a perfectly definite sense; the *Investigations* concludes that definiteness of sense is not required for logical order (PI I, 99–100). The *Tractatus* in talking of human nature stresses the complication of language, the *Investigations* its commonplaceness. The differences concealed by the disguise of language are in the *Tractatus* especially differences between names, descriptions and propositions (TLP 3.143; 3.261); in the *Investigations* especially different types of names (PI I, 383), different types of descriptions (PI I, 290), different types of verb and proposition (PI 339, 693; Z 123, 472). Above all, in the *Investigations* Wittgenstein had reflected in detail, as he had not in the *Tractatus*, on what was involved in the use or application of a word. In the *Tractatus* the use of a word is its relation to the primitive signs, and through them to the simples which they denote. In the *Investigations* the use of a word is its part in a language-game, in a form of life (cf. TLP 2.0271; PI II, 226).

In his criticism of the *Tractatus* philosophy of logic in PI I, 89–137, Wittgenstein singles out for criticism the misunderstanding of the role of the ideal in language. The *Tractatus* saw the pure unambiguous formulations imagined by the Frege-Russell logic not as an object of comparison with which our language might be contrasted (PI I, 130–31), or as an unreal extrapolation from our particular processes of clarificatory analysis (PI I, 91), but as something which was already present in the proposition. Since they were obviously not present in the proposition on the page, they must be present in the proposition in the thought, a strange intermediary between sentence and fact, hidden and dimly perceived in the medium of the understanding (PI I, 94, 102), a non-spatial, non-temporal phantasm (PI I, 108). The *Investigations* treats it as a mistake to look for something common to all propositions, and a double mistake to look for it in a mental structure. In fact 'proposition', like 'game', is a family-likeness term (PI I, 108), but all the members of the family are spatial and temporal phenomena with physical properties. We are still looking for the essence of language (PI I, 92; PB 85), but the essence is not a mysterious something beneath the surface to be brought to light by analysis but 'something that already lies open to view and becomes surveyable by a rearrangement' (ibid.).

When Wittgenstein wrote the *Tractatus* he thought that notions such as *naming, comparing, thought, rule* did not call for particular philosophical investigation. It was not that they were uncomplicated notions, but that the complications involved belonged to empirical psychology and not to philosophy (TLP 3.263, 4.1121). In the early 1930s, as we have seen, he came to realize that the study of such notions belonged to the study of the nature of symbolism and thus to philosophy. Thus, whereas in the *Tractatus* the notion of reading is briefly introduced as an unexamined comparison for the pictorial nature of the proposition (TLP 4.011), the *Investigations* contains a minute examination of the concept (PI 1, 156ff.). Detailed investigation of these and kindred concepts led him to believe that the datum on which language rests, the framework into which it fits, is given not by a structure of unchanging atoms (PB 72) but by a shifting pattern of forms of life grafted on to a basic common human nature.

Though he did not cease to investigate the essence of language, he came to think that he had been mistaken in looking for the essence as a common structure running through all propositions. General terms such as 'game', 'language', 'proposition' were applied not on the basis of the recognition of common features, but on the basis of family likeness. None the less, the concept of family likeness leaves room for the notion of convergence on, and divergence from, a paradigm, in the way that natural numbers are the paradigm for the family-likeness concept of 'number' (PG 113; PI 1, 67). I believe that the paradigm on which the notion of proposition converges – the paradigm from which divergences are painstakingly noted – is the proposition conceived according to the logical parts of the picture theory.

I have already observed that the picture theory survived the abandonment of the metaphysics of logical atomism. After this abandonment, on 5 January 1930, Wittgenstein could say to Waismann: 'The essential thing in a proposition is that . . . it is a picture' (WWK 90). The development of the notions of language-games and family likenesses necessitated the radical modification, but not the abandonment, of the theory. In the *Grammatik* Wittgenstein observes that the harmony between thought and reality, like everything metaphysical, is to be found in the grammar of language. He goes on:

> Instead of harmony, agreement of thought and reality one could here say: the pictoriality of thought. But is pictoriality an agreement? In the *Tractatus* I said something like: it is an agreement of forms. But that is misleading. [cf. PG 212.] Anything can be a picture of anything else, if we extend the concept of picture sufficiently.

If not, we have to explain what we call a picture of something, and further what we want to call the agreement of the pictoriality, the agreement of form.

For what I said comes just to this: that every projection, no matter what the method of projection, must have something in common with what is projected. But that only means that I am here the extending concept of 'having in common' and making it equivalent to the general concept of projection. I am therefore only drawing attention to a possibility of generalization (which of course can be very important). (PG 163)

He went on, in a passage which he thought worth reproducing in the *Philosophical Investigations* (PI I, 429):

The agreement, the harmony, of thought and reality consists in this: If I say falsely that something is *red*, then, for all that, it isn't red. And when I want to explain the word 'red' to someone, in the sentence 'That is not red', I do it by pointing to something red.

He went on to say in the *Grammatik* that one can say that a sentence must be a picture, if it can show me how to act; but this only means that one can act on a sentence as one can act on a picture. 'To say that a sentence is a picture, stresses certain features in the grammar of the word "sentence"' (PG 163). And he drew attention to the difference between different sorts of picture – historical paintings, genre paintings, etc. (PG 164).

Later in the *Grammatik* he drew attention to different ways in which pictures could be employed; in particular to the difference between a picture's showing what is the case, and showing what is to be the case (PG 212). This too was a point which he took up in the *Investigations*:

Imagine a picture representing a boxer in a particular stance. Now, this picture can be used to tell someone how he should stand, should hold himself; or how he should not hold himself; or how a particular man did stand in such and such a place; and so on. One might (using the language of chemistry) call this picture a proposition-radical. (PI I, p. 11)

He went on, in the *Grammatik*,

We could say that a working-drawing serves as a picture of the object that the workman is to manufacture from it. And one could here call 'method of projection' the manner in which the workman is to convert such a drawing into work. One could then put it in this way: the projection-method is an intermediary between the drawing and the object, it reaches from the drawing to the product. Thus the method of projection gets compared with lines of projection which go from one picture to another. But if the method of projection is a bridge, it is a bridge which is not built until the drawing is employed. (PG 213)

Even with the lines of projection, a picture leaves several modes of employment open, and no 'ethereal' determining of the object is possible. The lines of projection belong to the picture – but not the method of projection (PG 213; cf. TLP 2.1513).

One of the rare remarks in the *Philosophical Investigations* explicitly about the proposition as a picture takes up this point. 'Thinking of a proposition as a word-picture of the facts has something misleading about it: one tends to think only of such pictures as hang on our walls: which seem simply to portray how a thing looks, what it is like. These pictures are as it were idle' (PI I, 291; Z 244).

All these passages seem to suggest that the picture theory needs supplementing, rather than that it is false; that the theory of meaning as use is a complement rather than a rival to the picture theory. They stress the point, so often made since the 1930s, that the signs by themselves are dead and need the use to give them life (PG 132; BB 4; PI I, 430–33).

In the *Blue Book* Wittgenstein says that though the proposition is a picture, it is not a picture by similarity (i.e. a picture whose success depends on its being like what is pictured, like a portrait). We are inclined to conjure up the notion of a shadow of a fact, he says, because the facts which make our thoughts true do not always exist, and so it cannot be the facts which we think, but something shadowy, very like the fact. But if we keep in mind the possibility of a picture which, though correct, has no similarity with its object, the interpolation of a shadow between the sentence and reality loses all point. For now the sentence itself can serve as such a shadow. The sentence itself is just such a picture, which hasn't the slightest similarity with what it represent. If we were doubtful about how the sentence 'King's College is on fire' can be a picture, we need only ask ourselves: How should we explain what the sentence means? Such an explanation might consist of ostensive definitions. (BB 37)

This does not conflict with the *Tractatus*. There too the similarity between the sentence and the fact was a highly abstract one ('same logical multiplicity') quite unlike the mental images which in the *Blue Book* are being contrasted with the words of the sentence.

Earlier I listed eight theses which made up the logical aspect of the picture theory. I will now show how they were later modified.

(1) *A proposition is essentially composite* (TLP 4.032). In 1930 Wittgenstein said that it was more correct to say that the proposition must be a particular case of a general rule for the construction of signs (WWK 107). In the *Investigations* he allows for simple language-games in which the distinction between word and sentence cannot be drawn (PI I, 19). But if anything is to be a genuine subject-predicate proposition, then the subject and the predicate must be genuinely distinct, as we saw two chapters ago in considering the private-language argument.

(2) *Elements of proposition conventionally correlated with elements of reality* (TLP 3.312, 3.342). With the abandonment of the notion of absolute simples, reality does not have 'elements' independent of the existence of a particular language-game. Human convention operates in the setting up of the language-game rather than in the naked linking of words to objects; and the convention must include agreement in judgement as well as in definitions if language is to be a means of communication (PI I, 242). Conventions must be grounded on uniformities of nature (PI I, 240).

(3) *Combined elements yield sense without further convention* (TLP 4.024; 3.318). In the *Investigations* Wittgenstein denied that we always understand a sentence, even if its words are ones we understand, grammatically combined in a correct way (e.g. 'It is five o'clock on the sun' (PI I, 350; BB 48–9)). But there is not here a great difference between the early and the late philosophy. As early as the *Tractatus* there are examples of grammatically correct sentences whose words we understand, which are unintelligible (TLP 4.1274, 5.473, 5.4733, etc.), And as late as the *Blue Book* Wittgenstein admits that we understand the proposition 'I eat a chair' although we weren't specifically taught the meaning of the expression 'eating a chair', and he rejects a certain theory of expectation on the grounds that it would mean that 'expecting that B will come' would not be a value of the function 'expecting that x will come' (BB 21).

(4) *A proposition stands in an internal relation to the possible state of affairs which it presents.* In the 1930s Wittgenstein objected to Pavlovian and behaviourist accounts of mental phenomena on the grounds that they made the relationship between the thought that p, and the state of affairs that p, an external causal one (PB 63–73). In the *Investigations* the relation between the proposition and the state of affairs is made by the language-game.

(5) *This relation can only be shown, not stated informatively.* This thought is developed in the 1930s (WWK 38, 53, 61; PB 84–5). Language-games can indeed be described, but they cannot be informatively described to someone not a participant. The interpretation of rules in the language-game must come to an end, and no rule can be given for the translation from rule into action (PI I, 201ff.).

(6) *A proposition is true or false in virtue of being compared with reality.* This remains true, but what 'being compared with reality' consists in differs from one language-game to another. In particular, in order to be judged true or false, the proposition 'p' need not be compared with the state of affairs that p or that not-p: in some cases this comparison makes no sense. 'He is in

pain', for instance, gets compared not with his pain, or his being in pain, but with his pain-behaviour or lack of it, with the criteria for his pain (PI 1, 50, 300; BB 53).

(7) *A proposition must be independent of the actual state of affairs which makes it true or makes it false.* This is still active, as we saw in the consideration of the private-language argument(cf. PB 78).

(8) *No proposition is* a priori *true.* Wittgenstein continues to insist that if a sentence makes sense, its negation must make sense, consequently any real synthetic *a priori* proposition is impossible. As in the *Tractatus*, so in the *Investigations* he is not consistent about whether analytic propositions, grammatical propositions, are genuine propositions or not; but in both works this seems to be an unimportant matter of terminology (cf. z 442).

The most striking feature of Wittgenstein's work is the permanence of his general conception of philosophy. I have already quoted the introduction to the 1913 'Notes on Logic'.[1]

In philosophy there are no deductions; it is purely descriptive. The word 'philosophy' ought always to designate something over or under, but not beside, the natural sciences. Philosophy gives no picture of reality, and can neither confirm nor confute scientific investigations. It consists of logic and metaphysics, the former its basis. Epistemology is the philosophy of psychology. Distrust of grammar is the first requisite of philosophizing. Philosophy is the doctrine of the logical form of scientific propositions (not primitive propositions only). A correct explanation of the logical propositions must give them a unique position as against all other propositions.

On almost all these points Wittgenstein's mind remained constant.

(1) *Philosophy purely descriptive.* In saying that in philosophy there are no deductions Wittgenstein set himself against the type of philosophy which offers proofs, e.g. of the existence of God or immortality of the soul, or which attempts to explain and predict the course of history. Throughout his life he

1. See p. 3 above.

remained sceptical of and hostile to philosophy of that kind. 'We must do away with all explanation' he wrote 'and description alone must take its place.' The point of the description is the solution of philosophical problems: they are solved not by the amassing of new empirical knowledge, but by the rearrangement of what we already know (PI I, 109). 'Philosophy' he wrote 'simply puts everything before us, and neither explains nor deduces anything' (PI I, 126; cf. PI I, 496)

(2) *Philosophy not a natural science.* This was taken up in the *Tractatus* at 4.III. 'Philosophy is not one of the natural sciences. The word "philosophy" must mean something whose place is above or below the natural sciences, not beside them.' The thought that philosophy is above the sciences (as the queen of the sciences) or below them (as an underlabourer to clear the ground for them) is a thought familiar from other philosophers; but in the *Tractatus* it takes on a new twist. For Wittgenstein has just said (4.II) that the totality of true propositions is the whole of natural science; so that if philosophy is not one of the natural sciences, there are no true philosophical propositions. This contrasts with the traditional conception of philosophy according to which the propositions of philosophy were necessary truths, the most fundamental, perhaps the truest, truths on which all other truths depended and from which they in some way borrowed their truth.

The contrast between philosophy and natural science was often drawn by Wittgenstein in his later writings. In the passage already quoted (PI I, 109) he insists that the philosopher may not advance theories or hypotheses. 'Logic does not treat of language – or of thought – in the sense in which a natural science treats of a natural phenomenon' (PI I, 89, 91). In the *Blue Book* he attacked the preoccupation of philosophers with the method of science, the method of reducing the explanation of natural phenomena to the smallest number of primitive laws (BB 18, 128).

(3) *Philosophy and pictures.* How can we say both that philosophy is purely descriptive, and that it gives no pictures of

reality? The statement about pictures in the 'Notes on Logic' is astonishing, since to a reader of the *Tractatus* it suggests the picture theory of the proposition, which, to judge from the *Notebooks*, appears to have been devised more than a year later. From the context all we can say is that a picture appears to be something which can be in accordance or conflict with scientific investigations. In the *Tractatus*, of course, there is a sharp and precise sense in which philosophical propositions are not pictures of the world, and therefore not really propositions at all. In the *Investigations* Wittgenstein is often concerned to show that philosophy misleads by presenting apparent pictures (pictures in the more or less literal sense in which mental images are pictures) which are not really pictures at all, but misleading illustrations of grammatical turns of speech (PI 422–7).

(4) *Philosophy consists of logic and metaphysics.* In the *Investigations* philosophy is sharply separated off from formal logic; but it is identified with the study of language-games which is also called 'logic', especially in *On Certainty*. Already by the time of the *Tractatus* Wittgenstein reserved the term 'metaphysics' for misleading philosophy: metaphysics is philosophy misinterpreted as natural science (TLP 6.53; 6.111). He continued to hold this: 'The characteristic of a metaphysical question' he wrote in the *Blue Book*, is 'that we express an unclarity about the grammar of words in the form of a scientific question' (BB 35). The right method of philosophy, in both the *Tractatus* and the *Investigations*, consists in putting a stop to metaphysics; in both of the works this is done by showing that the metaphysician has given no meaning to one of his expressions – in the earlier work because he has not correlated it with an element of reality, in the latter because he has not fitted it into a language-game.

(5) *Philosophy is the doctrine of logical form.* The study of logical form is the discernment of what really follows from a proposition from what merely appears to follow from it. This is an abiding concern, but whereas in the earlier period it is done by Russellian analysis, in the later it is done by the study of

language-games. In both early and later systems, there are no primitive propositions enjoying a privileged position as axioms: though *On Certainty*, following Moore, does develop a privileged, though non-axiomatic, position for certain propositions of commonsense experience.

(6) *Logical propositions are unique.* The uniqueness of the propositions of philosophy (for it is these, not the propositions of formal logic that he has in mind in the 'Notes on Logic') is that they cannot be informatively stated. In the *Tractatus* philosophical truths can be only shown, not said; in the *Investigations* the function of philosophy is to assemble reminders of the obvious. 'If one tried to advance theses in philosophy, it would never be possible to discuss them, because everyone would agree to them' (PI I, 128).

The Preface to the *Philosophical Investigations* recognizes 'grave mistakes' in the *Tractatus*; but it does not suggest that the later philosophy is a wholly new one. It is possible that Wittgenstein himself somewhat exaggerated the difference between his earlier and his later philosophy: this would not be surprising since in the decades between them his attention had been concentrated on the problems which divide them. But as we move further in time from the writing of the *Investigations* we can see that the likenesses to the *Tractatus* are as important as the unlikenesses.

Suggestions for Further Reading

Those interested in Wittgenstein's biography should read *Ludwig Wittgenstein: A Memoir* by Norman Malcom with a Biographical Sketch by G. H. von Wright (Oxford University Press, 1958). The most comprehensive book on the *Tractatus* is Max Black's *A Companion to Wittgenstein's Tractatus* (Cambridge University Press, 1964). Two commentaries on the *Tractatus* which are rich in philosophical insights are G. E. M. Anscombe's *An Introduction to Wittgenstein's Tractatus* (Hutchinson, 1959; Harper Torchbook, 1963) and E. Stenius's *Wittgenstein's Tractatus* (Basil Blackwell, 1960). Perhaps the best full-length book on the *Investigations* is E. K. Specht, *The Foundations of Wittgenstein's Late Philosophy* (Manchester University Press, 1967). There is a useful anthology of essays on the *Investigations* edited by George Pitcher in the series *Modern Studies in Philosophy* (Doubleday, 1966, and Macmillan, 1968). A book which stresses the continuity between the early and late philosophy is David Pears's *Wittgenstein* in the *Fontana Modern Masters* series (Fontana/Collins, 1971). There is a full bibliography of books, dissertations and essays on Wittgenstein in K. T. Fann's *Wittgenstein's Conception of Philosophy* (Basil Blackwell, 1969). Readers who intend to make a serious study of Wittgenstein's philosophy should work through the reading and exercises given in *A Wittgenstein Workbook* by Coope, Geach, Potts and White (Blackwell, 1970).

Index

INDEX

236

INDEX